SEX EQUITY
IN EDUCATION

EDUCATIONAL PSYCHOLOGY

Allen J. Edwards, Series Editor
Department of Psychology
Southwest Missouri State University
Springfield, Missouri

In preparation:

Merlin C. Wittrock (eds.). The Brain and Psychology
Marvin J. Fine (ed.). Handbook on Parent Education
James H. McMillan (ed.). The Social Psychology of School Learning

Published

Dale G. Range, James R. Layton, and Darrell L. Roubinek (eds.). Aspects of Early Childhood Education: Theory to Research to Practice

Jean Stockard, Patricia A. Schmuck, Ken Kempner, Peg Williams, Sakre K. Edson, and Mary Ann Smith. Sex Equity in Education

James R. Layton. The Psychology of Learning to Read

Thomas E. Jordan. Development in the Preschool Years: Birth to Age Five

Gary D. Phye and Daniel J. Reschly (eds.). School Psychology: Perspectives and Issues

Norman Steinaker and M. Robert Bell. The Experiential Taxonomy: A New Approach to Teaching and Learning

J. P. Das, John R. Kirby, and Ronald F. Jarman. Simultaneous and Successive Cognitive Processes

Herbert J. Klausmeier and Patricia S. Allen. Cognitive Development of Children and Youth: A Longitudinal Study

The list of titles in this series continues on the last page of this volume

SEX EQUITY IN EDUCATION

Jean Stockard
Patricia A. Schmuck
Ken Kempner
Peg Williams
Sakre K. Edson
Mary Ann Smith

Center for Educational Policy and Management
College of Education
University of Oregon
Eugene, Oregon

1980

ACADEMIC PRESS
A Subsidiary of Harcourt Brace Jovanovich, Publishers

New York   London   Toronto   Sydney   San Francisco

115477

ACADEMIC PRESS, INC.
111 Fifth Avenue, New York, New York 10003

United Kingdom Edition published by
ACADEMIC PRESS, INC. (LONDON) LTD.
24/28 Oval Road, London NW1   7DX

Library of Congress Cataloging in Publication Data

Stockard, Jean.
    Sex equity in education.

    (Educational psychology series)
    Includes bibliographies and index.
    1. Sex discrimination in education——United
States.   2. Sex discrimination——United States.
3. Feminism——United States.   I. Schmuck,
Patricia A. , joint author.   II. Title.
LC212.2.S8   370.19'345   80—10082
ISBN 0—12—671550—5

PRINTED IN THE UNITED STATES OF AMERICA

80 81 82 83   9 8 7 6 5 4 3 2 1

CONTENTS

PREFACE   ix
ACKNOWLEDGMENTS   xi

PART I
SEX INEQUITIES AND WHY THEY EXIST

Chapter 1
Sex Roles in Education   3
Jean Stockard

Chapter 2
Sex Inequities in the Experience of Students   11
Jean Stockard

Sex Differences in Behavior, Learning Problems,
and Attitudes   12
Sex Differences in Intelligence, Test Scores,
and Grades   17
Sex Differences in Achievement   20
Sex Stereotypes in Curriculum Materials   24
Unequal Access to Educational Resources   26
Sex Segregation within Schools   39
References   42

                                                                 v

Chapter 3
Why Sex Inequities Exist for Students   49
Jean Stockard

Theoretical Explanations of Sex-Role Development
and Sex Discrimination   49
Explaining Sex Differences in Academic Achievement   60
Effects of Sex Typing in Curricular Materials   69
Sex Segregation in Education   71
The Possibility of Change   72
References   74

Chapter 4
Differentiation by Sex in Educational Professions   79
Patricia A. Schmuck

Males and Females in the Labor Force
and in Educational Positions   80
Positions in Governing and Regulatory Bodies
in Education   82
Teaching Professionals   84
Administrative Positions   88
Positions in Higher Education   91
Comparisons between the Value of Men's Work
and the Value of Women's Work   92
References   95

Chapter 5
Why Sex Inequities Exist in the Profession of Education   99
Jean Stockard

Analysis of Internal Labor Markets   100
Studies of Organizational Practices   102
Career Patterns in Education   104
Influences on Women's Career Paths   106
References   113

PART II
THE POSSIBILITY OF CHANGE

Chapter 6
A Social–Psychological Analysis of the Context for Change   119
Ken Kempner

Beliefs and Behavior   120
Behavioral Change   125

Internal and External Social Intervention 130
Change through Legislation 132
Changes in the Social System 137
References 140

Chapter 7
Laws Prohibiting Sex Discrimination in the Schools **143**
Peg Williams

Model of the Legal System 143
Development of Law Prohibiting Sex Discrimination 147
Educational Areas Affected by Current Legislation 152
References 163

Chapter 8
Context of Change: The Women's Movement as
a Political Process **165**
Patricia A. Schmuck

Historical View of Feminism and Education 166
Influence of Current Feminist Movement on Education 170
References 181

Chapter 9
Educational Equity: Current and Future Needs **185**
Jean Stockard

Current Attempts at Change 186
Potential Effects of Current Programs 189
References 194

Appendix A
Exercises: Experiential Learning about Sex Roles **195**
Mary Ann Smith and Sakre K. Edson

How to Lead Experiential Learning 197
Exercises for Chapter 1 201
Exercises for Chapter 2 202
Self-Exploration Questionnaire 204
Exercises for Chapter 3 205
Exercises for Chapter 4 206
Career-Choice Worksheet 207
Exercises for Chapter 5 207
Johari Window 209
Exercises for Chapter 6 210
List of Resumes 211
Resume Exercise 213

Exercises for Chapter 7   214
Preemployment Inquiry   215
Double-Standard Quiz: Assessing How we Treat Kids   218
Exercises for Chapter 8   219
General Observation Worksheet   220
Exercises for Chapter 9   220
References   221

Appendix B

Alternatives Available for Changing a Sex Discriminatory Practice   **223**

Peg Williams

INDEX   225

PREFACE

Sex Equity in Education grew out of a course of the same name taught by Jean Stockard, Pat Schmuck, Peg Williams, Sakre Edson, and Mary Ann Smith in 1976. In researching course materials we discovered that there was *no* single work that analyzed comprehensively sex roles and sex inequities in education. Thus, our first reading list included 38 articles from different places, and our classes were organized around integrating the readings and building a conceptual framework to deal with the educational inequities of students and professionals.

It was out of our needs for the course that this book evolved. We attempt here to pull together the mass of literature that we originally used. We also discuss the potential for changing educational inequities. Jean Stockard had primary responsibility for writing Chapters 1, 2, 3, 5, and 9. Patricia Schmuck was primarily responsible for Chapters 4 and 8. Peg Williams wrote Chapter 7 and Appendix B, and Ken Kempner wrote Chapter 6. Mary Ann Smith and Sakre Edson wrote Appendix A. Each author also read and evaluated the work of the others. Thus the book reflects a cooperative effort.

We hope that this book will have wide appeal. For researchers concerned with education and sex roles, it can provide a useful review of the literature and inspire further work needed in this area of study. Since we originally wrote the book for a course, we believe it may also be useful to others in the same way—as a basic text in courses on sex roles in education as well as a secondary text in educational psychology, educational sociology, curriculum courses, and teacher training courses, women's studies, and sex roles. Finally, the women's movement has

ix

taught us that awareness is a basic step in reducing sex inequities; we hope the information provided in this text will help researchers, educators, parents, and students to understand the facts and the complexities of sex inequities in the schools. Information and awareness is one step that must be taken to free all of us from the inhibiting and restricting confines of sex inequalities.

ACKNOWLEDGMENTS

The Women's Educational Equity Act of the Office of Education (WEEA) contributed the funds for this effort. The class and the book were one of the activities of the Sex Equity in Educational Leadership Project (SEEL) at the University of Oregon. We are indebted to the leadership of the Women's Program staff, primarily Joan Duval, Director, and our project officer, Patricia Goins. We are also indebted to Joanne Carlson of the University of Oregon who initially helped to teach us the sense and the nonsense of the labyrinth of federal funding.

We also owe a debt of gratitude to our own SEEL staff members: Spencer Wyant who taught the course in its later stages and to Rita Pougiales, Carole Starling, Janet Hart, and Joan Kalvelage, who offered ideas and assistance. Finally, we owe a great debt of gratitude to Nancy Gubka, who typed the manuscript, checked the references, coordinated the different styles of writing, and offered critical feedback.

The research reported herein was supported in part by funds from the Women's Educational Equity Act, Office of Education, U.S. Department of Health, Education, and Welfare. Opinions expressed in this report do not necessarily represent the policies or positions of the Office of Education, nor should any official endorsement of the report be inferred from the supporting agencies.

We thank the following for permission to quote from their works:

Page 3: Janice Pottker and Andrew Fishel, *Sex Bias in the Schools,* © 1977 by Fairleigh Dickinson Univ. Press, Cranbury, N.J., p. 19.

Pages 11, 49, 99: W. Martin, *The American Sisterhood,* © 1972 by Harper & Row, New York, p. 59.

Page 24: T. N. Saario, C. N. Jacklin, and C. K. Tittle, "Sex Role Stereotyping in the Public Schools," © 1973 by the *Harvard Educational Review,* pp. 394–396.

Page 79: Elizabeth Janeway, *Man's World, Woman's Place,* © 1971 by William Morrow, New York, p. 2.

Page 119: S. R. Schram, *Quotations from Chairman Mao Tse-Tung,* © 1967 by Bantam Books, New York, p. 118.

Page 143: John Rawls, *A Theory of Justice,* © 1971 by Harvard Univ. Press (Belknap Press), Cambridge, Mass., p. 73.

Page 165: Virginia Sapiro, "News from the Front: Inter-Sex and Inter-Generational Conflict over the Status of Women," © 1980 by the *Western Political Quarterly,* p. 1.

Page 185: B. Roszak, *Masculine/feminine,* © 1969 by Harper & Row, New York, pp. 303–304.

SEX EQUITY
IN EDUCATION

PART I

SEX INEQUITIES AND WHY THEY EXIST

Chapter 1

SEX ROLES IN EDUCATION

Jean Stockard

The irony is that children are told that school achievement will bring future life success, which is not true for girls. Having developed the characteristics that are necessary for successful careers in school, once out of schools girls are limited by society's bias from attaining positions for which they are qualified. But most girls never realize to what extent they are restricted and discriminated against because the school has done such an effective job in cooling them out. The schools, acting as agents for the existing social order, contribute to the maintenance of a society where sex rather than ability determines the limits of a person's accomplishments. The perpetration of this system in American schools is clearly not only unjust to girls and women, but it also perpetuates a great loss of American talent [Pottker & Fishel, 1977, p. 19].

Most 6-year-olds in the United States spend almost half their waking hours in school. As children grow older, they spend even more hours in school or participating in activities related to school. Education is second only to the family in its day-to-day impact on young people, and over three million professionals are at work in the elementary, secondary, and higher educational institutions in this country (Grant & Lind, 1977). Yet the school experiences of these males and females—whether boys and girls or women and men—involve subtle as well as apparent sex discrepancies.

Consider the sex differences one might see in a typical school district in the United States. In the elementary school, the principal is probably a man and the first-grade teacher a woman. The teacher usually believes that she treats all students equally and that they have the same educational opportunities; yet there are discrepant outcomes. The children are divided into reading groups based on ability; more girls are in the top group and more boys are in the slowest group. Boys are more frequently called on in classroom discussions and the teacher focuses more attention on the boys than on the girls. Boys are chastised and punished more frequently than girls and are referred more often to counselors for special help. Girls are more likely to have stars placed on their papers saying they have done a good job. When the children go out to the playground during recess they usually go in two lines—one for boys and one for girls. On the playground boys play with boys and girls play with girls. The boys play baseball, soccer, and other team games. The girls jump rope and play hopscotch and other games involving smaller groups. Infrequently, boys and girls play together, sometimes the boys chasing the girls in a spontaneous game of tag and the girls squealing and shouting as they are pursued around the playground. Some of each sex do not play with anyone, remaining outside and watching the different activities.

In the junior high building, the principal again is probably a man. Although there are more men teachers here than at the elementary school, junior high teachers usually teach in special subject areas. Men often teach science, social studies, and math; women more often teach English and foreign languages. Department chairs, regardless of the sex composition of the staff, are more often men. Girls in the junior high still get better grades on the average than boys, although boys are beginning to show more interest and slightly better skills in math and science than the girls. Many courses are required of all students. Where allowed to take elective classes, girls and boys usually do not choose the same ones. Boys more often enroll in shop, mechanics, advanced math, and science classes; girls more often elect courses in home economics, language arts, and foreign languages. The boys still disrupt class more than the girls do and have more referrals because of behavior problems.

At the high school the principal is almost certainly a man and the proportion of men on the teaching staff is higher than in the elementary and junior high schools. As in the junior high, the men and women teach different subject areas and the department chairs are generally men. The salary scales for men and women are equal, but the men may make more money because they more often receive extra duty pay for coaching sports and other extracurricular duties. Although some women coach girls' sports, their pay may be less. Girls' sports are often coached by men, but women generally do not coach boys' sports.

In high school we can see the full effect of adolescence on students' activities and interests. While grade-school boys and girls often studiously avoid each other, high school boys and girls show more interest in each other. The girls still get better grades than the boys, but many of them try not to do "too well" and not to be "excessively brilliant," fearing that this will affect their popularity. With more elective courses available, boys and girls are less often found in the same classes. By now the boys definitely achieve more than girls in math and science courses, and the girls avoid these areas, concentrating more on languages and humanities, where they tend to excel. Extracurricular activities attract both boys and girls, but they are divided by sex. Boys and girls participate in sports after school, but on different teams. Boys are more likely to belong to the chess club and the lettermen's club; girls are more likely to join future homemakers groups, rally clubs, choirs, and dance teams. After graduation, boys and girls from the middle class both tend to go to college, although they usually major in different areas. Boys and girls from the working class more often get jobs and marry soon after graduation. The occupational aspirations of high school boys and girls begin to match the traditional occupational roles for adults of their sex groups. Both social class and sex apparently play a very important role in a student's aspirations at this level.

Just as the assigned roles of educators differ, men and women also do different tasks in the central administration of schools. Principals are usually men, and superintendents and assistant superintendents are almost certainly men. The latter hold the most prestigious and most highly paid posts in the school district and have the greatest number of contacts with community groups and the communications media. Women administrators are often supervisors of curriculum and sometimes of special education. In these positions, they usually supervise other women and give special help to students. Among the nonprofessionals, virtually all members of the clerical and secretarial staff are women; men are usually employed as custodians.

Why do these sex inequities exist? How do they occur? Can the situation be changed? What do our laws say about the situation? Have people tried to change the system? How have these efforts worked? These questions are taken up in the chapters that follow.

Part I of this book reviews the inequities students and professionals in education face because of their sex, and the various reasons for these inequities are examined. In the past, many writers focused on only one aspect of the total situation, for instance, boys' inferior performance in certain academic areas and their behavior problems in schools or girls' narrow range of aspirations for adult life and how their school experiences direct them toward lower-paying occupations in adulthood. Some direct their attention to the absence of men in elementary teaching, while others deplore the lack of women in school administration. In contrast with these earlier works, we try in Chapters 2 through 5 to explore and understand all types of inequities and the differing experiences that students and professionals in education have because of their sex. We show that these inequities cannot be understood in isolation and that all the various problems, including boys' learning problems and girls' underrepresentation in high-paying positions in adulthood, may stem from common sources. By focusing on the problems boys face, we are not ignoring girls' difficulties; and by coping with the inequities girls face we are not slighting boys' special difficulties. The problems are related. Giving women more opportunities in the profession of education does not mean that men will be denied opportunities, but rather that the range of occupational choices for both sexes can be broadened.

Part II of this book reviews the social context for change. In Chapters 6 through 8 we review the social-science literature on change. We discuss legislation regarding sex discrimination in education and procedures that are used to enforce these laws, and then we explore the impact of the contemporary feminist movement on changes in education. Using the analyses of Part I and Part II as a basis, we discuss the possibility of bringing about changes regarding current sex inequities. Because these inequities in education are inextricably linked with those in other institutions, we suggest that in addition to changes in education, effective solutions must also include alterations in social institutions such as the family and the economy.

Some of the works cited in this book come from studies conducted by professional educators. Others are the work of psychologists, sociologists, and sometimes anthropologists and economists. Because we include reports of statistical research studies, it is important to understand the nature of statistical comparisons between the sexes. Any time researchers compare two groups, they contrast central tendencies or averages. Generally there are, however, wide variations among members of any group. Even when we cite evidence that one sex group experiences a condition or has a certain characteristic more often than the other, the two groups will generally show considerable overlap. When statistically significant differences exist between the two groups, the central tendencies or averages of each group are far enough apart so that such large differences would rarely occur by chance. These computations take into account the amount of variation in scores. Sometimes members of one sex will be more like members of the other group than like members of their own. Yet when the average scores of the groups are significantly different statistically, these outlying members are relatively few in number.

Studies of sex differences and discrimination have become more numerous as the feminist movement has grown. The growth of this movement has also forced social scientists to face deficiencies and problems in these studies. Only a few years ago, most social scientists believed that they could conduct their studies free of the influence of personal bias or values. In recent years, however, philosophers of science have pointed out how values and prejudices may enter into all phases of the research process, from the selection of a problem, to the decisions on how to study it, to the analysis of the data.[1] This does not mean that researchers are not adhering to standardized procedures of research or that they are not careful and objective or even that their results are invalid. It simply means that because social scientists study areas of everyday life, about which we all have beliefs and feelings, their attitudes will inevitably influence their work in one way or another.

Feminists have noted that value judgments reflecting a masculine paradigm have often affected studies of sex differences (see Friedan, 1963; Millett, 1970; Weisstein, 1971). This masculine perspective, or masculine bias, is difficult to avoid because all of us, men and women, live in a society where males hold the most valued and well-rewarded positions. Studies of stereotypes or beliefs about differences between the sexes show that people do hold definite views about the nature of men and women (e.g., Broverman, Vogel, Broverman, Clarkson, & Rosenkrantz, 1972). People also hold definite beliefs about what men and women should do. For instance, many people believe that in the society as a whole men should have greater authority than women (e.g., Ferree, 1974). This is reflected in the small number of women who hold high-level administrative positions in government and business and even in the schools. Because social scientists are part of this society, it is inevitable that they will also be influenced by such beliefs about what is or what should be.

The masculine perspective, the cultural belief that males are more important than females, may be reflected in the lack of studies that include women. For instance, a great deal has been written in sociology about what influences the years of education and the social status people attain (e.g., Blau & Duncan, 1967; Hauser, 1972; Duncan, Featherman, & Duncan, 1972; Sewell, Haller, & Ohlendorf, 1970; Spaeth, 1970). However, only a few studies (e.g., Sewell & Shah, 1967, 1968; Alexander & Eckland, 1974; Treiman & Terrell, 1975) have also looked at women's educational attainment.

---

[1]Much of the material on masculine bias that follows is based on insights of Miriam Johnson (see Stockard & Johnson, 1980).

The interpretation of research results may also reflect a masculine bias. For example, in the next chapter we discuss a rather specific sex difference in spatial perception that was once described in terms of field dependence and field independence. It was thought that field independence, the trait men were more likely to possess, was associated with analytic or intellectual ability. This term also implied a link with the psychological characteristics of independence. In actual fact, further research showed that this sex difference is restricted to visual–spatial tasks and is independent of intellectual ability and psychological traits. In this case, the language itself implied an advantage for males in areas actually unrelated to the characteristic studied.

We, the authors of this book, are feminists, and we believe that women should have an equitable share of the opportunities and resources of the society. This does not mean, however, that we have tried to bias or slant the material we are presenting. We have tried to present research evidence and theories of sex roles with a degree of caution. Our intention was not to write a polemic on sex roles in education but to take a judicious and skeptical point of view in evaluating what is known and what is not known about sex inequities in education. Because we recognize that values and attitudes are an important part of learning in the social sciences, we have also included resources to help students and others examine their feelings and beliefs about sex roles and discrimination in education. These are included in Appendix A.

REFERENCES

Alexander, K. L., and Eckland, B. K. (1974). "Sex Differences in the Educational Attainment Process." *American Sociological Review*, 39:668–682.

Blau, P. M., and Duncan, O. D. (1967). *The American Occupational Structure*. Wiley, New York.

Broverman, I. K., Vogel, S. R., Broverman, D. M., Clarkson, F. E., and Rosenkrantz, P. S. (1972). "Sex-Role Stereotypes: A Current Appraisal." *Journal of Social Issues*, 28:59–78.

Duncan, O. D., Featherman, D. I., and Duncan, B. (1972). *Socioeconomic Background and Achievement*. Seminar Press, New York.

Ferree, M. M. (1974). "A Woman for President? Changing Responses: 1958–1972." *Public Opinion Quarterly*, 38:390–399.

Friedan, B. (1963). *The Feminine Mystique*. Dell, New York.

Grant, W. V. and Lind, C. G. (1977). *Digest of Education Statistics*, 1976 ed. Government Printing Office, Washington, D.C.

Hauser, R. M. (1972). "Disaggregating a Social-Psychological Model of Educational Attainment." *Social Science Research*, 1:159–188.

Millett, K. (1970). *Sexual Politics*. Doubleday, New York.

Pottker, J., and Fishel, A. (1977). *Sex Bias in the Schools*. Fairleigh Dickinson Univ. Press, Cranbury, N.J.

Sewell, W. H., Haller, A. O., and Ohlendorf, G. W. (1970). "The Educational and Early Occupational Attainment Process: Replication and Revision." *American Sociological Review*, 35:1014–1027.

Sewell, W. H., and Shah, V. P. (1967). "Socioeconomic Status, Intelligence, and the Attainment of Higher Education." *Sociology of Education*, 40:1–23.

Sewell, W. H., and Shah, V. P. (1968). "Parent's Education and Children's Educational Aspirations and Achievements." *American Sociological Review*, 33:191–209.

Spaeth, J. L. (1970). "Occupational Attainment among Male College Graduates, Part II." *American Journal of Sociology*, 75:632–644.

Stockard, J., and Johnson M. (1980). *Sex Roles: Sex Inequality and Sex Role Development*. Prentice-Hall, Englewood Cliffs, N.J.

Treiman, D., and Terrell, K. (1975). "Sex and the Process of Status Attainment: A Comparison of Working Women and Men." *American Sociological Review*, 40:174–200.

Weisstein, N. (1971). "Psychology Constructs the Female, or the Fantasy Life of the Male Psychologist." In *Roles Women Play* (M. Garskof, ed.). Brooks Cole (Wadsworth), Belmont, Calif.

CHAPTER 2

SEX INEQUITIES IN THE EXPERIENCES OF STUDENTS

Jean Stockard

*In visiting the public school in London . . . , I noticed that the boys were
employed in linear drawing, and instructed upon the blackboard in the
higher branches of arithmetic and mathematics; while the girls, after a
short exercise in the mere elements of arithmetic, were seated during the
bright hours of the morning stitching wristbands. I asked, why there
should be this difference made; why they too should not have the blackboard? The answer was that they would not probably fill any station
in society requiring such knowledge. But the demand for a more extended
education will not cease until girls and boys have equal instruction in all
the departments of useful knowledge [Lucretia Mott, 1849, "Discourse on
Women," in W. Martin, 1972, p. 59]*

Sex inequities that students face in schools involve differences in
achievement patterns and unequal access to resources as well as differences between portrayals of males and females in curricular materials.
Regarding achievement, boys tend to have more behavior and learning
problems in schools than girls do. As children get older, there are areas
in which girls excel and areas in which boys excel, with boys showing
more quantitative skills and girls tending to excel in verbal skills. In
curricular materials sex inequities generally reflect sex stereotypes in the
total society. Textbooks and tests generally depict men and women in
traditional roles and in occupations that are even more sex-segregated
than those they actually fill. In schools, girls often do not have the same
access as boys to courses and extracurricular activities. The discussion in
this chapter is based on research reports of social scientists, such as
those described in Chapter 1. Some of the research may suggest under-

lying reasons for the existence of student inequities, a subject that is treated more fully in Chapter 3. We will see in the following sections that while adult men have more social and occupational advantages and opportunities than adult women, throughout their school years girls receive better grades and display greater compliance with the behavioral codes for what is considered a "good" student. This is especially true in elementary schools. Differences between boys and girls pertaining to academic achievement begin to appear by adolescence, and these persist into adulthood. Sex differences also occur in behavior, learning problems, attitudes, and testing.

SEX DIFFERENCES IN BEHAVIOR, LEARNING PROBLEMS, AND ATTITUDES

Studies in many cultures have found that boys show aggressive behavior toward others more often than girls do, displaying hostility, fighting, and engaging in interactions with the aim of hurting another person, verbally or physically. (For reviews of these studies, see Maccoby & Jacklin, 1974, pp. 227–247; Mischel & Mischel, 1971.) Boys also have physical and medical abnormalities more often than girls do (Barfield, 1976). Not surprisingly, then, studies of students' problems in school consistently report that boys have more difficulties in classroom adjustment and in learning. Bentzen (1966) estimates that learning and behavioral disorders are three to ten times more frequent among boys. She reports the results of a study of over 6000 elementary school children where two-thirds of the students with reading problems and two-thirds with emotional problems were boys. Similarly, Cruickshank (1977) reports finding male–female ratios of learning disabled children as high as 15 to 1 and 25 to 1 in public school systems.

Table 2.1 reports the male–female ratios of all the white children referred over a 10-year period to a special education center in the southern United States. In each of the major categories included in the table, boys far outnumbered girls. For instance, they were referred for low mental ability twice as often (see also Prillaman, 1975), and they were referred for educational retardation three times as often (see also Blom, 1971). Boys were also referred twice as often for the treatment of speech problems, of hearing, visual, and other physical handicaps, and of emotional disturbances (Mumpower, 1970). Boys also "get into trouble" in school more often. For instance, Sexton (1969, p. 7) reports that of 11 sex-segregated secondary schools for "defiant" students in New York in the 1960s, 10 were for boys and only 1 was for girls. While school officials report increasing misbehavior among girls in recent years, they still report that girls behave better than boys.

It is important to note that these studies generally give the ratios of the referrals of males and females for help. Classroom teachers report that boys with learning and emotional problems often show disruptive and obnoxious behavior in the classroom, and it is possible that girls with emotional or learning difficulties are not referred because they are not noticed by teachers and specialists. The actual ratios for learning disorders may be lower than those noted above. The difference in referral patterns may also account for Mumpower's findings (Table 2.1) that more boys than girls were referred for exceptionally high mental ability, although only a small sample was involved. Boys may simply be harder than girls for teachers to ignore, given similar abilities or disabilities.

Student–Teacher Interactions

Observational studies of classroom interactions show that teachers tend to give boys both more negative and more positive feedback about their actions than they give girls. For instance, a study of three sixth-grade classrooms found that boys received significantly more disapproval and blame from teachers than girls did (Meyer & Thompson, 1963). These differences can appear as early as first grade, where Felsenthal found that boys were criticized more often and had their ideas rejected more often (1970, cited in Guttentag & Bray, 1977). A study of 21 classes from fourth to sixth grades supported the finding that boys received more total disapproval than girls and specified the reason for the disapproval. Girls more often received disapproval for "lack of knowledge or skills," while boys were more often reprimanded for violating rules (Spaulding, 1963). These differing reasons for reprimands probably account for Jackson's report that when teachers are criticizing students they more often use a harsh or angry tone of voice for boys and a normal voice for girls (reported in Sears & Feldman, 1966, p. 31). Jackson reports that the sixth-grade boys in his sample received directions from teachers that were designed to manage, control, or prohibit behavior eight times as often as the girls did (Jackson & Lahaderne, 1967). Teachers of preschool children have also been observed to react more loudly and strongly to aggressive behavior when it is displayed by boys (Serbin, O'Leary, Kent, & Tonick, 1973).

Not all boys receive more disapproval from teachers than girls receive (R. Martin, 1972); most of the negative interactions with boys involve those who have behavior problems and those who are also under-

TABLE 2.1
**Sex Differences in Major Areas and Subareas of Exceptionality in a
Special Education Center in the Southern United States**[a]

	Boys (%)	Girls (%)	Total number of students
High mental ability			
Exceptionally able	72.1	27.9	68
Low mental ability			
Slow learner	72.1	27.9	782
Retarded educable	65.3	34.7	730
Retarded trainable	49.2	50.8	195
Retarded custodial	66.7	33.3	30
Total	66.6	33.4	1,737
Educational retardation			
General	76.9	23.1	702
Reading	76.8	23.2	99
Language	87.5	12.5	8
Arithmetic	85.7	14.3	7
Total	77.1	22.9	816
Neurological impairment			
Suspected	71.4	28.6	255
Medically verified	58.8	41.2	131
Total	67.1	32.9	386
Speech			
Articulation	69.9	30.1	539
Nonfluency	81.3	18.7	80
Voice quality	76.3	23.7	38
Articulation, nonfluency	75.8	24.2	33
Articulation, voice quality	61.1	38.9	54
Nonfluency, voice quality	50.0	50.0	6
Articulation, nonfluency, voice	93.7	6.3	16
Delayed speech	66.7	33.3	39
Total	71.2	28.8	805
Hearing			
Nonsignificant loss	75.0	25.0	40
Mild loss	75.9	24.1	112
Moderate loss	72.5	27.5	69
Severe loss	54.7	45.3	53
Deaf	66.7	33.3	6
Deafened	75.0	25.0	4
Suspected hearing loss	72.0	28.0	107
Total	71.1	28.9	391
Vision			
Vision problem	69.1	30.9	475
Partially sighted	58.3	41.7	12
Blind	68.2	31.8	22
Total	68.8	31.2	509

TABLE 2.1 (*cont.*)

	Boys (%)	Girls (%)	Total number of students
Physical status (handicap)			
Mobile	62.8	37.2	247
Immobile, temporary	50.0	50.0	14
Immobile, permanent	55.6	44.4	9
Total	61.9	38.1	270
Physical condition			
Orthopedic	65.6	34.4	32
Heart	50.0	50.0	10
Chronic health problem	87.5	12.5	8
Total	66.0	34.0	50
Emotional disturbance			
Mild	71.4	28.6	668
Moderate	71.2	28.8	139
Severe	53.6	46.4	28
Total	70.8	29.2	835
Grand total	69.6	30.4	5,867

[a] SOURCE: D. L. Mumpower, "Sex Ratios Found in Various Types of Referred Exceptional Children," *Exceptional Children*, 1970, p. 622.

achievers. Girls who are underachievers tend to be quiet or withdrawn rather than disruptive; and because teachers' attention tends to be a response to achievement and behavior, underachieving and withdrawn girls often receive little attention. While boys are criticized and reprimanded more often, Felsenthal (1970) found that questions are directed to them more often and that more of their ideas are accepted by teachers. Although girls volunteer significantly more often than boys, they are called upon less often. Meyer and Thompson (1963) reported a tendency for boys to receive more praise and approval, and this trend was significant in one classroom. Spaulding (1963) found that teachers gave more approval, instruction, and attention by listening to boys. Serbin and his associates (1973) reported that teachers gave preschool boys and girls the same amount of attention when they were near the teacher, but gave more attention to boys when the children were farther away.

Students' Attitudes toward School and Teachers

Besides examining how teachers respond to students, researchers have studied students' perceptions of the behavior of teachers and students' attitudes toward school in general, toward specific subjects, and toward their teachers. Children apparently recognize there are sex differences in the behavior exhibited by students and in the amount of punishment in school, although it is not clear that they perceive sex differences in rewards. Meyer and Thompson (1963, cited in Sears & Feldman, 1966, p. 33) reported that the sixth-grade boys and girls they studied believed that "boys received more disapproval than girls. There were no sex differences in [the students'] beliefs about the teacher's distribution of praise." McNeil found that first graders believed boys had fewer opportunities to respond in reading groups and received negative comments more often regarding their performance (1964).

It is not surprising then that girls more often say they "like" school. Based on her study of children in four schools with a broad range of philosophies, Minuchin (1966, p. 47) reported that "boys were more resistent and negative about school and education, less concerned about achievement. Girls were more concerned with achievement and recognition, more positively identified with school, more apt to find the entire experience of school life comfortable, pleasant and meaningful." These differences continue into adolescence, when boys may show their negative attitudes by dropping out of school or by skipping school more often (Sexton, 1969).

Girls' greater liking of school may be associated with children's classifying school objects as female. Kagan (1964) reports a study in which children in second and third grade were taught three nonsense syllables (dep, rov, and fas) representing the concepts male, female, and farm, and asked to associate one of the syllables with each of 19 pictures. Objects related to school, specifically, blackboard, book, arithmetic page, and school desk, were identified much more often as feminine than as masculine by the second graders. Third-grade boys identified these objects as feminine less often than second-grade boys, but there was no difference in the responses of third- and second-grade girls. Only a map (similar to the kind pilots and navigators would use) and a pencil were labeled masculine by the students.

Perhaps boys like school less than girls do because they tend to see school generally as a feminine area and thus are not interested in it. There is evidence that bears on this thesis. For instance, a study of fifth graders' reading found that with materials rated highly interesting by each student, the boys read as well as the girls; however, on low-interest materials, the boys' scores were significantly lower than the girls (Asher & Markell, 1974). The results of a study by Wood (1974), however, were that boys and girls had approximately equal scores on comprehension and decoding tests with materials of both high and low interest. The effect of interest on achievement may extend beyond curriculum materials to entire subject areas. Some areas in school are considered more masculine than others, and boys choose to pursue these areas and to excel in them. Neale, Gill, and Tismer (1970) found that sixth-grade girls generally reported more favorable attitudes toward school than the boys did; but there were no sex differences in the attitudes of girls and boys toward science and mathematics, the two areas where boys begin to excel at adolescence. Other studies indicate that perceptions of certain academic areas, such as spelling and art, as feminine and others, such as math, as masculine coincide with growing differences in math and science skills (Stein & Smithells, 1969).

While boys may generally dislike school more than girls do, they apparently are *not* more apt to dislike teachers. Indeed, in a study of students' perceptions of comments by teachers, Solomon and Ali (1972) found that boys display positive perceptions more often than girls. These sex differences, occurring from kindergarten through college age, were most pronounced with younger subjects, whose teachers are mostly female. Although Goldberg's (1968) widely quoted results suggested that college students prefer male professors, his research is contradicted by studies that indicate no sex preferences (Ferber & Huber, 1975; Hesselbart, 1977). There is no firm evidence that college students prefer professors of a particular sex.

SEX DIFFERENCES IN INTELLIGENCE, TEST SCORES, AND GRADES

Even though boys are placed in special classes for the retarded and referred for exceptional ability more often than girls are, on the average there is no difference between the scores of the boys and the scores of girls on standardized intelligence tests. This is because these tests are deliberately constructed so as to eliminate sex differences. Items that produce different distributions of responses for each sex are generally discarded. An analysis of the test results from the 2200 children used in the standardization of the 1974 Wechsler Intelligence Scale for Children found that the boys' mean IQ was only about 2.5 points higher than the girls on the verbal scale and about 1.8 points higher on the full scale. Although with a large sample, these differences are statistically significant, the authors concluded that the differences "are not meaningful in a practical sense. For all intents and purposes, the means and standard deviations of IQs of boys and girls may be considered the same on all three WISC-R scales (verbal, performance, and full) [Kaufman & Doppelt, 1976, p. 166]."

There are sex differences, however, in particular types of cognitive abilities, as indicated by the subtests of general intelligence tests; and these differences seem to become larger as children get older (Terman & Tyler, 1954). For instance, girls score higher on tests of word fluency, rote memory, and reasoning while most studies find boys superior in subtests dealing with spatial and quantitative ability (Ausubel, 1968, citing Carlsmith, 1964; Havighurst & Breese, 1947; Hobson, 1947; Lord, 1941). These differences are not generally apparent, however, in the early years of childhood (see Koch, 1954), as we will see in the discussion that follows. Many contradictory findings are reported regarding superiority on subtests of vocabulary development (see Ausubel, 1968, p. 242).

While numerous authors have commented on the supposed greater variability in boys' intelligence scores, this appears to result mainly from the greater representation of males at the two extremes of the continuum; and it is difficult to determine if this difference results naturally or from differences in cultural expectations and observations. Mentally deficient boys may be more apparent to others and may be a greater social nuisance than girls with equally low abilities. Gifted boys may also be noticed more readily, and they may be expected to have greater success in adulthood (see Ausubel, 1968). Terman's longitudinal study of gifted children lends support to this supposition. He found that boys were more likely than girls to retain high status through adulthood (Terman & Oden, 1949). Other studies show that males are more likely to exhibit gains in scores on intelligence tests from adolescence to adulthood (Bradway & Thompson, 1962). Sherman (1977) suggests that most studies in the United States, including Terman's, have been hampered by selection biases. Sherman cites two extensive surveys conducted in Scotland that show that the greater variability in males' scores comes from an overabundance of males with very low test results (Scottish Council for Research in Education, 1933, 1949).

While the measured intelligence of girls does not differ from that of boys, girls generally receive better grades. This is true in the early years of school (Achenbach, 1970), and it continues through junior high, high school (Coleman, 1961; Monday, Hout, and Lutz, 1966–1967), and college (Davis, 1964, p. 40). Table 2.2 compares the average grades of men and women college students. In all the institutions listed, the average grades of women students are higher. Girls appear to receive better grades than boys even when there is no difference in scores on standardized achievement tests. For instance, Carter (1952) compared measures of intelligence, scores on a standardized test of achievement in algebra, and teachers' grades for boys and girls enrolled in ninth-grade

TABLE 2.2
Grade-Point Averages during First Year of College, 1966–1967[a]

Grade-point average	Percentage of students							
	All institutions		2-year colleges		4-year colleges		Universities	
	Men	Women	Men	Women	Men	Women	Men	Women
A − or better	3.9	5.4	2.5	4.3	3.7	5.1	5.7	6.8
B or B+	15.7	23.2	14.1	21.8	14.1	23.6	17.9	23.9
B −	14.0	16.5	22.3	29.3	22.6	32.3	24.9	31.1
C+	22.1	22.0	24.3	22.5	22.2	22.8	20.0	20.3
C	34.3	27.6	37.3	32.5	34.5	26.0	31.4	25.7
D	9.9	5.2	8.5	4.0	10.6	5.3	10.3	6.2

[a]SOURCE: Bayer, A. E., Drew, D. E., Astin, A. W., Boruch, R. F., and Creager, J. A. "The First Year of College: A Follow-up Normative Report." *American Council on Education Research Reports*, 1970, (1), p. 19.

algebra classes. Even though there were no statistically significant differences between the sex groups in intelligence or in achievement, the average grades of the girls were significantly higher than the average grades of the boys. Similarly, McCandless, Roberts, & Starnes (1974) examined the relationship between seventh-grade students' grades and their scores on standardized achievement and intelligence tests while controlling for the impact of both race and social class. They found that "teachers mark boys, regardless of race, more severely than girls of either race, even though   there is neither a statistically nor a practically significant difference in accomplishment as measured by standard achievement tests and no differences in intelligence" within each race and class category (1974, p. 158). Because achievement scores and to a large extent scores on intelligence tests do not adequately account for students' grades, other variables must influence the lower marks that teachers give boys.

Boys are termed underachievers more often than girls because they tend to do less well in school than would be predicted from their scores on standardized intelligence tests. While male academic underachievers first show this pattern in the early grades, female underachievement generally first appears at puberty, when females encounter pressure to avoid being excessively brilliant (Shaw & McKuen, 1960). Girls continue to do better than boys as measured by grades received throughout their years in school. Yet by the end of their high school careers, they are less likely than boys to want to be remembered by others as a "brilliant student." Girls' popularity among boys is a greater guarantee of belonging to the socially elite than academic successes. These constraints show in comparisons of grades at adolescence. Even though the average grades of girls are higher, the variance is smaller, indicating that less capable girl students do better than would be expected and also that the most capable girls tend to hold their achievement down. This pattern appeared more strongly in the middle-class schools in Coleman's sample than in the working-class schools (Coleman, 1961, pp. 252–255).

SEX DIFFERENCES IN ACHIEVEMENT

Table 2.3 summarizes national data on the achievement of males and females in different subject areas. While males do better than the national average in mathematics and science, females do better in verbal areas such as reading and writing. These differences, especially in mathematical areas, become stronger in adulthood.

Verbal Achievement

Females' greater verbal fluency appears at about age 10 or 11 and continues through high school and college. Sex differences do not appear in the results of general knowledge tests that are called verbal tests; but they appear in measures of more specific skills, including spelling and punctuation, and of higher-level skills, such as "comprehension of complex written text, quick understanding of complex logical relations expressed in verbal terms, and in some instances, verbal creativity [Maccoby & Jacklin, 1974, p 84]." Generally these differences first appear before the age of 3, and they reappear and become more pronounced at adolescence. There is some evidence that sex differences in favor of girls between age 3 and adolescence occur more commonly in disadvantaged populations than in advantaged groups. In this country, girls' higher reading scores are usually seen from the first grade on (Bond & Tinker, 1967; Gates, 1961; Herman, 1975). These scores do appear to be related to reading readiness, however, and boys and girls with equal readiness achieve equally well (Balow, 1963).

While it does not appear that having a man for a teacher can improve boys' reading scores in this country (Asher & Gootman, 1973; Brophy & Good, 1973), there is some evidence that the sex of the other students in the class may influence boys' achievement. A pilot program in Fairfax County, Virginia, found that when children in grades 1 to 6 were separated for academic work, boys in the single-sex classes made better academic progress than did boys in mixed classes. In the first year

TABLE 2.3
Achievement in School Subjects[a]

Difference between percentage of correct responses and median percentage of correct responses for all subjects in each age group

	9-year-olds		13-year-olds		17-year-olds[b]		26–35-year olds	
	Males	Females	Males	Females	Males	Females	Males	Females
Science	1.5	−1.6	1.8	−1.7	2.6	−2.6	5.2	−4.7
Writing	−4.0	4.1	−3.4	3.2	−3.4	3.0	−2.3	2.1
Citizenship	0.3	−0.3	−0.1	0.1	0.0	0.0	1.4	−1.3
Reading	−2.4	2.3	−2.5	2.3	−2.0	1.9	0.2	−0.3
Literature	−0.7	0.6	−1.6	1.6	−1.1	1.0	0.0	−0.1
Art	−0.3	0.3	−0.9	0.9	−0.9	0.8	n.d.	n.d.
Social studies	0.4	−0.4	+0.1	−0.1	0.6	−0.6	2.3	−2.2
Mathematics	0.7	−0.7	0.4	−0.4	2.3	−2.2	5.4	−5.0

[a] SOURCE: Adapted from W. V. Grant and C. G. Lind, *Digest of Education Statistics*, 1979, National Center for Education Statistics, Department of Health, Education and Welfare, Washington, D.C., 1979, pp. 27–30.

[b] Of those 17 years of age, only students in school were included in the sample. Data were collected in the following years for those 9, 13, and 17 years old: science in 1976–1977; reading and art in 1974–1975; citizenship and social studies in 1975–1976; literature in 1970–1971; writing in 1969–1970; mathematics in 1972–1973. Data for those 26–35 years old were gathered in the following years: science, writing, and citizenship in 1969–1970; reading and literature in 1970–1971; social studies in 1971–1972; and mathematics in 1972–1973. n.d. indicates no data. Data were gathered by the National Assessment of Educational Progress, 1860 Lincoln Street, Denver, Colorado 80203.

of the study, the girls in mixed classes did somewhat better than the girls in single-sex classes; but the improvement did not extend into the second year of the program (Lyles, 1966).

Boys' lower scores in reading achievement do not appear consistently in other countries. For instance, studies of fourth- and sixth-grade children found that while girls had higher reading scores than boys in a United States sample, boys scored higher than girls in a German sample (Preston, 1962). Similarly, a study of second-, fourth-, and sixth-grade students (all English-speaking) found that while girls had higher scores in reading achievement in the United States and Canada, boys tended to have higher scores in England and Nigeria (Johnson, 1973–1974). More boys than girls were shown to be in remedial reading classes in studies in Germany (Johnson, 1976; Orlow, 1976), Britain (Morris, 1966), and Canada (Hoiland, 1973); but this was not so in Sweden (Malmquist, 1960). In general, the sex differences may be strongest in the United States. Studies in Canada, England, and the central European countries often show nonsignificant and inconsistent differences in overall scores (e.g., Johnson, 1976; Klein, 1968; Konshuh, 1971; Orlow, 1976), although they generally find more boys than girls in remedial classes.

Mathematical Achievement

As with differences in verbal ability, sex differences in quantitative ability appear most strongly after puberty. Girls learn to count sooner than boys do; yet "through the school years there are no consistent sex differences in skill at arithmetical computation [Maccoby, 1966, p. 26]." Differences begin to appear around adolescence and then continue into adulthood; boys begin to score higher on tests of mathematics achievement (Aiken, 1976; Anastasi, 1958; Astin, 1974; Fennema, 1974; Fox, 1975). This occurs even though young women continue to receive better marks than boys throughout high school and college. Boys also begin to show more interest and better performance in science areas at adolescence (Maccoby & Jacklin, 1974). Gifted girls appear to be more interested in mathematics than girls of average ability (Fox, Pasternak, & Peiser, 1976). The sex differential in test scores does not appear related to the number of courses taken, for it appears even among students with the same number of math courses (Maccoby & Jacklin, 1974, pp. 85–91; see also Fox, 1977, p. 1). Many more males enroll in advanced courses in mathematics, however. The biggest drop-off apparently occurs after tenth grade, when students enroll in courses in Euclidean geometry (Fennema, 1977). Fennema (1977, p. 85) suggests, however, that the sex differences in mathematics achievement are not as great today as they were in earlier years (see also Turner, 1971).

There is some evidence that the sex differences in math and science achievement may be related to the ability to understand visual–spatial relationships. Tests of this ability involve tasks such as looking at a picture of a system of gears and telling the particular motion in one part that will produce motion in another part; or looking at a two-dimensional picture of three-dimensional blocks and telling how many surfaces would be visible from a perspective that is different from the one shown in the picture. Sex differences in math scores and in visual–spatial ability appear at about the same time, and they appear to be related, although the extent of correlation may vary from one sociocultural setting to another. (See Sherman, 1977, pp. 140–142, for an excellent discussion of this point). These visual–spatial skills are probably related to tasks specifically required in studying geometry, the point at which many women cease studying mathematics. Furthermore, visual–spatial ability may not be associated with just mathematical achievement. A study of physics scores on achievement tests given to a large sample of high school students showed that "on the portions of the test calling for visual–spatial skills, the male physics students did better; on verbal test items, female physics students obtained higher scores [Maccoby & Jacklin, 1974, pp. 89–91]."

As children get older their definitions of school subject areas as masculine or feminine become clearer. They also develop greater interests in these sex-typed subject areas. These two developments correspond to widening differences between the sexes in achievement scores in mathematics. Hilton and Berglund (1973) found that the changes in students' mathematical achievement from fifth through eleventh grade paralleled changes in interest. Boys became more interested in mathematics and simultaneously saw it as helpful in their future occupational lives and became more proficient than girls, as shown by achievement scores (see also Haven, 1971). Attitudes toward mathematics appear to be related to achievement in that area (Aiken, 1963, 1970a, 1970b, 1976; Aiken & Dreger, 1961; Anttonen, 1969). Callahan and Glennon (1975) give a contradictory view, but their study was based only on elementary school children (see Fennema, 1977, pp. 102–3). Girls' grades in mathematics appear to be more highly predictable from attitudes than boys' grades are (Behr, 1973). Confidence in one's mathematical ability appears to be related to taking advanced courses in math, and girls seem to require more self-confidence than boys (Kaminski, Ross, & Bradfield, 1976).

Although the sex of the teacher does not appear to influence the reading achievement of students in this country, it may influence mathematical achievement. A study of ninth-grade algebra students (Carter, 1952) found that although girls had higher grades than boys in all the classes studied, girls had higher achievement scores in classes taught by women and boys had higher achievement scores in classes taught by men.

Obviously these sex differences in areas of academic achievement affect students' adult lives. The lack or presence of mathematical training appears to be an especially crucial filtering device. For instance, Sells noted that 57% of the boys but only 8% of the girls admitted to the University of California at Berkeley in the fall of 1972 had taken four full years of high school mathematics, a prerequisite for mathematics courses that are required for majoring in science fields that are traditionally male and higher paying (cited in Ernest, 1976). Less drastic but similar differences were found at the campus at Santa Barbara (Ernest, 1976). Depending on their sex, therefore, males and females generally major in different areas at college and are found in different occupations.

SEX STEREOTYPES IN CURRICULUM MATERIALS

Sex stereotypes are reified notions of what men and women are like. Sometimes stereotypes correspond to reality, but more often they are rigid and untrue perceptions. These stereotypes influence curricular and testing materials that are used in the schools, and in recent years, a number of authors have examined these materials.

Textbooks

A number of studies have reviewed the sex stereotyping in children's textbooks. Researchers have examined reading texts (Blom, Waite, & Zimet, 1970; Stefflire, 1969; U'Ren, 1971) and also mathematics, science, and social studies books. One of the most thorough studies was conducted by Jacklin, Heuners, Mischell, & Jacobs (1972, reported in Saario, Jacklin, & Tittle, 1973). They looked at series of elementary textbooks for grades K to 3 published by Ginn, by Harper & Row, by Scott, Foresman, and by Bank Street. Systematically analyzing every third story from the readers for a total of 270 stories, they examined the fictitious experiences of male and female children and adults. Female adults and children were much less often included as characters in the stories and much less often main characters. There were also sex differences in the behaviors of the characters.

> Boys were portrayed as demonstrating significantly higher amounts of aggression, physical exertion, and problem-solving [skills]. Girls were significantly more often displayed as characters enveloped in fantasy, carrying out directive behaviors, and making (positive and negative) self-statements. Adult males were shown in significantly higher proportions of constuctive productive behavior, physically exertive behavior, and problem-solving behavior. Adult females were shown in significantly higher proportions of conformity behavior and verbal behavior other than statements about themselves [Saario et al., 1973, pp. 394–396].

Although there were no sex differences in the kinds of environments in which male and female children were portrayed, there were differences in the environments of adults. Adult females were much more often portrayed in the home, and adult males were more often found outdoors, in business, and at school. In examining the experiences of each type of character, the researchers found that while young females more often experienced positive consequences from a *situation*, young males more often experienced positive consequences from their *own actions*. Adult males were more often the recipients of positive consequences coming from others and were also shown as experiencing significantly more self-delivered negative consequences. Women were shown as experiencing more neutral consequences of actions (Saario *et al.*, 1973, pp. 396–397).

In addition to the examination of reading texts by Jacklin and her associates, researchers have also looked at textbooks for other areas (e.g., Trecker, 1971). Weitzman and Rizzo (1974) examined illustrations in science, math, social studies, reading, and spelling textbooks. In all the texts, white males were overly represented, especially in pictures of adults. Furthermore, while white men were shown in over 150 different occupations, women were portrayed in only 4 occupations. Similar results were found in textbooks used in other countries. A study of books used in primary schools in the Netherlands (Schone, van der Sleen, & Vijherizen, 1975) found "a strongly conventional image of the activities and behavior of men and women." Women were shown in the home, caring for their husbands and children; men were shown in occupations and in their lives outside of the family.

Test Materials

Sex-role stereotyping also appears in testing materials, as was found in a study by the Educational Testing Service. As with textbooks, there was a vast overrepresentation of content related to males. From an examination of eight major achievement tests (California Achievement Test, Iowa Test of Basic Skills, Iowa Test of Educational Development, Metropolitan Achievement Test, Sequential Tests of Educational Progress, SRA Achievement Series, Stanford Early School Achievement Test, and Stanford Achievement Test) this study found that "with one exception, each test battery showed a higher frequency of usage of male nouns and pronouns than female nouns and pronouns" (Tittle, 1973, p. 119). This did not occur through the use of generic pronouns, for example, "he" for all people and "man" for human. Subjects (of sentences) that could just as easily have been female, such as doctor or bus driver, were more often referred to as "he" than as "she."

The range of ratios for one battery was from a low of .86, representing slightly more female references than male, to a high of 14.00, or 14 times as many males as females (Tittle, 1973, p. 119). Such results were also found with most of the subtest batteries. In addition, researchers found stereotypes similar to those found in textbooks. The test items often suggested that young girls did stereotypic female chores, such as cooking, buying ribbons, shopping for vegetables; while young boys hiked, camped, and played. Test items frequently referred to a doctor, a professor, and someone occupying the presidency as "he," while teachers were referred to as females. Similarly, an analysis by Donlon (1971) of the items on the Scholastic Aptitude Test in mathematics (SAT-M) found the content overwhelmingly favoring males, with only two items favoring females (Donlon, 1971, cited in Fox, 1977). Fox (1977) suggests that these sex differences may influence the large sex differences found in the scores on this test.

The examples we have cited involve the use of stereotypic ideas and words in constructing tests. Stereotypes related to the administration of tests can also influence students. For instance, a report prepared by the affirmative action office of a school district in the western United States noted that in one school a test for placement in classes for extreme learning problems was given only to boys. When questioned, school officials replied that there seemed no reason to give the test to girls because boys were the only ones with reading problems. In this case, the stereotype probably reinforced boys' predominance in special classes while denying access to girls. In addition, stereotypic views of occupatons for women may limit the number and variety of tests given to girls and influence the subsequent advice that counselors give girls (See Harway & Astin, 1977; Schlossberg & Pietrofesa, 1973). Some tests of vocational interest, such as the Strong Vocational Interest Inventory, have traditionally had male and female forms that yield scores related to the traditional occupational choces of the sexes. Counselors' perceptions of the sex-typed nature of occupations may also influence the advice they give.

UNEQUAL ACCESS TO EDUCATIONAL RESOURCES

Segregation is the process of separating, setting apart, sorting, or differentiating regarding criteria such as race, age, social class, or sex. An example of segregation by age is the placement of students in same-age classes; a common example of segregation by social class and/or race can be found in most city neighborhoods. Segregation occurs through laws and regulations that differentiate opportunities for access and through tradition and custom. Generally, as the formal laws and regulations that differentiate opportunities are eliminated, tradition and custom become more important means of maintaining patterns of sex segregation.

In 1912 universal compulsory education was mandated in the United States at the federal level, and since then females have had legal equal access to public school education in all of the states. Before that time, schools were the province of local communities and were often formed as segregated institutions, with blacks, native Americans, and women consciously excluded. While some community schools included females, the subjects usually studied by girls were different from those studied by boys. The push for equal educational opportunities for females began in the early nineteenth century. In 1819 Emma Willard addressed the segregated school system of New York, and although the legislature turned a deaf ear to her, she began the Troy female seminary in 1821. Oberlin pioneered coeducation on the college level in 1833, at first limiting women to a shortened curriculum but by 1837 allowing them to take the same courses as men. By the late 1800s the elite sister schools that were associated with the Ivy League opened, and higher education became more available, at least to upper-class women. Mount Holyoke opened in 1857, Vassar in 1865, Smith in 1875. Bryn Mawr opened in 1885 and offered the first graduate programs for women (Merritt, 1976, pp. 354–356).

Table 2.4 summarizes the numerical patterns of the men and women high school graduates in the United States since 1869. It is apparent that over the years more women have consistently graduated from high school. This pattern results from the tendency for boys to drop out of school more readily than girls, largely because they can find jobs that do not require a high school diploma. Madden (1978) notes that these decisions are actually economically rational: girls gain more in economic returns from high school graduation than boys do. It should also be noted that until well into this century only a relatively small pro-

TABLE 2.4
High School Graduates in the United States, 1869–1976[a]

School year	Total number	Males (%)	Females (%)	Number per 100 17-year-olds
1869–1870	16,000	44.2	55.8	2.0
1889–1890	43,731	42.4	57.6	3.5
1909–1910	156,429	40.7	59.3	8.8
1929–1930	666,904	45.0	55.0	29.0
1949–1950	1,199,700	47.6	52.4	59.0
1959–1960	1,864,000	48.2	51.8	65.1
1969–1970	2,896,000	49.5	50.5	75.7
1974–1975	3,140,000	49.1	50.9	74.6
1976–1977	3,154,000	49.1	50.9	75.0

[a] SOURCE: Adapted from W. V. Grant and C. G. Lind, *Digest of Education Statistics*, 1979, National Center for Education Statistics, Department of Health, Education and Welfare, Washington, D.C., 1979, p. 63.

portion of the total population graduated from high school. Now, as job requirements are changing, a much larger percentage are going to college. Tables 2.5 and 2.6 summarize trends in college enrollments and in the educational attainment of males and females over the last century. It is apparent that universities have continually grown in size, as shown by the number of faculty members, number of students enrolled, and number of degrees awarded. Yet the proportion of women teaching, enrolled, or receiving degrees has fluctuated over the years, rising gradually to a peak in the 1920s and 1930s, dropping during the depression and especially the post–World War II years, and rising again to the levels of 50 years ago in the late 1960s and 1970s.

These trends reflect cultural and class-specific definitions of the importance of a college education as well as specific economic conditions and educational policies. For instance, the increasing representation of women in college until the 1930s may reflect the growing assumption among upper-middle-class families that women should also go to college, if only as a means of meeting their future husbands and of being trained in case they *had* to work. The economic problems of the depression influenced a sharp decline in the rate of growth of total college enrollment, and this decline showed most clearly in women's enrollments (see Table 2.6). The numbers of men and of women enrolled in college continued to rise during the depression, but the number of women enrolled rose much more slowly. This trend probably resulted from decisions of families to invest more heavily in their sons' rather than in their daughters' college education.

The even greater difference between the percentage increase in enrollment of males and females in 1949–1950 probably reflects specific national educational policies (see Table 2.6). Campbell (1973, p. 93, citing McGuigan, 1970) notes that colleges in the post–World War II years set quotas limiting the admission of women in order to absorb veterans returning to school on the GI Education Bill. It is important to note, however, that funding for the GI Education Bill may have been prompted not only by humanitarian concerns for the intellectual future of former servicemen, but also by a need to keep returning military men out of the job market and thus keep national unemployment rates down. As a result of this policy of quotas, the proportion of women students enrolled in 1949–1950 was lower than their rate of enrollment in 1879–1880. After World War II, more and more young people entered college. While 14% of the people 18–24 years of age were enrolled in colleges in 1950, 35% of the people in that age bracket were enrolled by 1975. The changes in enrollment after World War II helped alter the social class distribution of college students, as men of lower-middle-

TABLE 2.5

Women on Faculties, Enrolled in Higher Education, and Receiving Degrees in the United States, 1869–1974[a]

| Year | Faculty members[b] | | Resident enrollment[e] | | Degree recipients | | | | | |
| | | | | | Bachelor's and first professional | | Master's except first professional[h] | | Doctoral | |
	Women (%)	(Total number)	Women (%)	(Total number)	Women (%)	(Total number)	Women (%)	(Total number)	Women (%)	(Total number)
1869–1870	11.9[c]	5,553[c]	21.3[c]	52,236[c]	14.7	9,371	0	0	0	1
1889–1890	19.6[c]	15,809[c]	35.9[c]	156,756[c]	17.3	15,539	19.1	1,015	1.3	149
1909–1910	20.1	36,480	39.6[c]	355,213[c]	22.7	37,199	26.4	2,113	9.9	443
1929–1930	27.2	82,386	43.7	1,100,737	40.0	122,484	40.4	14,969	15.4	2,299
1949–1950	24.5	246,722	30.3	2,659,021	23.9	432,058	29.2	58,183	9.6	6,420
1959–1960	22.0	380,554	35.3[f]	3,215,544[f]	35.5	392,440	31.6	74,435	10.5	9,829
1969–1970	25.0[c]	825,000[c]	41.0[g]	7,484,073[g]	41.5	827,234	39.7	208,291	13.3	29,866
1973–1974	27.5[d]	881,655[d]	44.0[g]	8,518,150[g]	42.4	999,592	43.0	277,033	19.1	33,816
1976–1977	32.0[d]	1,073,119[d]	47.2[g]	11,012,137[g]	44.3	983,908	47.1	317,164	24.3	33,232

[a] SOURCE: W. V. Grant and C. G. Lind, *Digest of Education Statistics*, 1979, National Center for Education Statistics, Department of Health, Education and Welfare, Washington, D.C., 1979, p. 100.

[b] Total number of different individuals, male and female (not reduced to full-time equivalents). Beginning 1959–1960, data are for first term of academic year and include Alaska and Hawaii.

[c] Estimated.

[d] Data for fall.

[e] Unless otherwise indicated, includes students enrolled at any time during academic year.

[f] Data for first term of academic year.

[g] Fall enrollment (includes resident and extension students).

[h] Beginning in 1969–1970, includes all master of arts degrees.

TABLE 2.6
Growth in Resident, Degree-Credit, College Enrollment, 1879–1974[a]

| Year | Percent increase in enrollment from last 10-year period | | | Enrollment of women as percentage of total enrollment |
	Total	Men	Women	
1879–1880	121.5	89.4	240.1	32.7
1889–1890	35.3	28.8	48.8	35.9
1899–1900	51.6	51.6	51.6	35.9
1909–1910	49.5	41.0	64.7	39.6
1919–1920	68.3	46.7	101.3	47.3
1929–1930	84.1	96.8	69.9	43.7
1939–1940	35.7	44.1	25.0	40.2
1949–1950	78.0	107.4	34.1	30.3
1959–1960	20.9	12.2	40.9	35.3
1969–1970	132.7	112.5	169.8	41.0
1973–1974[b]	13.8	8.0	22.3	44.0

[a] SOURCE: Adapted from W. V. Grant and C. G. Lind, *Digest of Education Statistics*, 1976, National Center for Education Statistics, Department of Health, Education and Welfare, Washington, D.C., 1977, p. 97.

[b] Computed as increase from 1969–1970 school year.

class and working-class backgrounds were able to obtain an education beyond high school. The rising representation of women in higher education in those years parallels the changes in the late 1800s and early 1900s as a greater proportion of the population accepted the idea that women as well as men should have a college education.

From 1968 to 1978 the proportional representation of women in colleges and universities rose much faster than that of men. This sex difference appeared among students of all ages (Current Population Reports, 1979, p. 2), although the increase was sharpest for women re-entering college at the age of 25 or older (Tittle & Dencker, 1977, p. 532, cited by Gappa & Uehling, 1979, p. 11). This recent increased enrollment of women can be found at the undergraduate level as well as in graduate and professional schools (Gappa & Uehling, 1979, p. 11).

Table 2.7 summarizes the proportions of boys and of girls in various age groups enrolled in school. For whites, blacks, and people of Spanish origin there is a definite trend beginning at about 14 years of age for a greater proportion of boys than girls to be enrolled in school. This is especially apparent for people over 20 years of age. These patterns of enrollment are reflected in educational levels attained. In Table 2.8 we see that although females have a higher probability of graduating from high school, their chances of entering college or receiving a bachelor's or

TABLE 2.7
School Enrollment in the United States, October 1975[a]

	Population group					
	White (%)		Black (%)		Spanish origin (%)	
Years of age[b]	Male	Female	Male	Female	Male	Female
Total 3–34	55.4	50.8	60.5	55.3	58.1	51.7
3–4	30.8	30.7	31.1	37.3	26.7	27.9
5–6	94.4	95.3	94.9	94.0	89.7	94.4
7–9	99.6	99.5	99.4	99.2	99.6	99.5
10–13	99.0	99.6	98.9	99.3	98.8	99.7
14–15	98.5	98.1	97.6	97.2	97.4	93.8
16–17	91.0	87.5	88.2	85.6	88.3	84.0
18–19	49.6	43.5	49.9	44.7	51.9	37.1
20–21	36.3	27.5	28.7	25.8	31.3	24.3
22–24	20.5	12.2	14.7	13.8	15.9	12.5
25–29	13.1	7.0	11.8	7.5	11.9	5.3
30–34	7.5	5.7	8.6	5.9	7.2	4.1

[a] SOURCE: W. V. Grant and C. G. Lind, *Digest of Education Statistics,* 1976, National Center for Education Statistics, Department of Health, Education and Welfare, Washington, D.C., 1977, p. 8.
[b] Includes full- or part-time enrollment in any type of graded public, private and parochial school.

master's degree are slightly less than those for males. The greatest difference comes at the highest level where the probability is four times as great that men will obtain a doctoral degree.

Obviously, the probability that one will enroll in and graduate from college is also strongly influenced by one's social class and racial background. Working-class men and women enter higher educational institutions much less frequently than middle-class men and women.

TABLE 2.8
Expected Levels of Education for 17-Year-Olds, Fall 1973[a]

Expected level	Males	Females
High school graduation in 1974	73	77
Enrollment in college in fall 1974	47	44
Bachelor's degree in 1978	25	24
Master's degree in 1978	8	7
Doctoral in 1982	2	0.5

[a] SOURCE: W. V. Grant and C. G. Lind, *Digest of Education Statistics,* 1976, National Center for Education Statistics, Department of Health, Education and Welfare, Washington, D.C., 1977, p. 13.

Minorities are often underrepresented because of their class background and because for many years formal regulations barred their admittance. To some extent, the patterns of the educational attainment of the sexes in this country differ for different racial groups. On the average, differences between the educational attainment of white men and white women even out, the eventual median number of years being 12.1 for both sexes. Among blacks, however, women have a median level of 10.0 years and men of only 9.4 years. This probably occurs due to racial discrimination in the economy, where, in terms of eventual income, black women are more highly rewarded than black men for higher educational attainment (see Suter & Miller, 1973). Thus, the decisions of black men to go to work rather than to proceed further in their education may be economically rational (Michelson, 1972). With people of Spanish heritage, men have an average attainment of 9.9 years, women of 9.4 years (Grant & Lind, 1977, p. 15), perhaps reflecting the more traditional sex-role patterns in Spanish speaking ethnic groups. This pattern continues when we examine enrollment in institutions of higher education. In the total population, as well as in the subgroups of native Americans, Asian Americans, and Spanish surnamed peoples, more men than women are enrolled in all levels of college work, including undergraduate, professional, and graduate schools. Among blacks, however, more women than men are enrolled at all levels, except in the first year of undergraduate school, in professional schools, and in doctoral (not master's) programs (Grant & Lind, 1977, p. 95, data from the fall of 1974). This pattern reflects sexual segregation in employment patterns among black professionals, with men dominating the traditionally male professions of law and medicine and women in social work and teaching, fields that require master's, but not doctoral degrees (Almquist, 1975, p. 138).

A number of social scientists have examined influences on eventual educational achievement. Most of these studies involved only men, but a few have also involved women. Sewell and Shah (1967) found in their study of high school seniors in Wisconsin that family background status was a strong influence on women's educational attainment while academic ability was a stronger influence on males' educational attainment. Alexander and Eckland (1974) expanded the original model of Sewell and Shah and also found that women's educational attainment was more strongly dependent than men's on social-class origins. After controlling for variables generally found to relate to educational attainment—including academic ability, status background, performance, educational goal orientation, academic self-concept, curriculum enrollment, and the influence of significant others, such as parents, teachers, peers—Alexander and Eckland found that a person's sex continued to have an important effect on educational attainment. In other words, when all these variables were equalized, the expected educational attainment of females was lower than that of males. Treiman and Terrell (1975) found similar results. In general, these studies suggest that compared with men, women cannot trade their educational accomplishments for increased income as often or trade their academic skills for increased educational attainment in the same way. In addition to their findings that one's sex affects educational aspirations and achievement, Marini and Greenberger (1978) report that socioeconomic background and academic ability have a greater effect on the educational ambitions of boys, a result opposite to that of Sewell and Shah (1967) and Alexander and Ecklund (1974).

Although it is believed that all children in the United States have the right to an education, and although since 1912 compulsory education laws have applied to both sexes, separate schools have existed in some cities especially for vocational education, math, and sciences, on the high school level. Many of these schools eventually allowed both sexes to attend, but tradition and custom continue to reinforce patterns of segregation. For instance, relatively few girls aspire to enter male-dominated trades, such as welding, carpentry, and printing, and relatively few specialize in academic areas such as mathematics or science; few boys aspire to traditionally female trades, such as those in clerical fields. Parents probably do not encourage such endeavors either. Moreover, young men in male schools do not think their occupational areas are appropriate for women, sentiments that can be conveyed to young women, however subtly, and discourage their entrance. A number of the traditionally male colleges have changed their formal regulations and now admit women. Preliminary evidence suggests, however, that informal traditions and customs to some extent help perpetuate sex segregation in these schools (see DeFleur, Gillman & Marshak, 1978; DeFleur & Gillman, 1978).

Sex segregation is also maintained through unequal opportunities for access. For instance, since adolescent girls begin to avoid math and science courses and to have lower achievement scores in these areas; they may be less prepared to enter the academic high schools once reserved for men (cf. Ernest, 1976). Girls are also less often exposed to shop and mechanics courses, which would prepare them to enter traditionally male vocational high schools. The difficulties of access becomes even clearer at the college level. Today, laws ban discrimination against women in admission policies and awards policies; but as has been noted, women obtain less education on the average than would be expected given their academic background. Probably because the law bans discrimination now, it is very difficult to get current information. Yet studies show that women are more inclined to drop out of college than are men with the same ability; they tend to be admitted less often when they have the same academic standings as men; they rely more on their parents for financial support; and there is a notable absence of specific policies that support women students, such as provisions for child care.

An experiment that involved sending 240 schools college applications that were identical except for variations in race, sex, and ability level found that when other variables were equal, men were more often accepted than women. The discrepancy was especially sharp with students of lower ability (Walster, Cleary, & Clifford, 1970; see also Astin, Harway, & McNamara, 1976). Tables 2.9, 2.10, and 2.11 show that at least in terms of high school grades and academic standing, among the

TABLE 2.9

High School Academic Rank and Grade Point Average of Freshmen Enrolled in Highly Selective Public and Private Universities, by Sex: Fall, 1978[a]

	Men	*Women*
Public universities		
Class rank		
Top quarter	75.7	84.1
2nd quarter	20.1	13.7
3rd quarter	4.0	2.1
Lowest quarter	.2	.1
Average high school grades		
A's	44.5	58.9
B's	50.9	39.8
C's	4.5	1.4
D's	.0	.0
Private universities		
Class rank		
Top quarter	90.6	93.3
2nd quarter	8.3	6.0
3rd quarter	1.0	.7
Lowest quarter	.1	.1
Average high school grades		
A's	71.3	78.6
B's	27.8	21.2
C's	.9	.3
D's	.0	.0

[a] SOURCE: A. W. Astin, M. R. King, and G. T. Richardson, *The American Freshman: National Norms for Fall, 1978.* Laboratory for Research in Higher Education, Graduate School of Education, University of California at Los Angeles, 1978, pp. 115–116.

TABLE 2.10
**High School Academic Rank and Grade Point Average of Freshmen Enrolled
in Public and Private Universities of Medium Selectivity, by Sex: Fall, 1978**

	Men	*Women*
Public universities		
Class rank		
Top quarter	65.0	70.4
2nd quarter	27.5	22.8
3rd quarter	6.9	6.1
Lowest quarter	.5	.7
Average high school grades		
A's	29.1	38.8
B's	61.4	56.5
C's	9.3	4.6
D's	.1	.1
Private universities		
Class rank		
Top quarter	70.4	75.1
2nd quarter	22.8	20.2
3rd quarter	6.1	4.4
Lowest quarter	.7	.2
Average high school grades		
A's	43.8	54.0
B's	50.2	43.6
C's	6.0	2.4
D's	.1	.0

"SOURCE: A. W. Astin, M. R. King, and G. T. Richardson, *The American Freshman:
National Norms for Fall, 1978*. Laboratory for Research in Higher Education, Graduate
School of Education, University of California at Los Angeles, 1978, pp. 115–116.

less well-qualified candidates in 1978 men were more likely to be admitted to college than women were. (It must be remembered, however, that the fact that girls simply get better grades than boys is likely to inflate these differences. We could find no comparable data on admission rates with the Scholastic Aptitude Test, a measure of achievement without large sex differences on the total scores.) These results appear both in private as well as in state institutions. Table 2.12 shows that even in graduate school, men with low undergraduate grades are admitted more often than women with low grades; on the whole, women are overrepresented in the group that has the highest undergraduate grades. On the other hand, women applicants to graduate schools are not superior to men on scores on the Graduate Record Examinations and, in fact, a greater proportion of women than of men who apply to graduate

TABLE 2.11
High School Academic Performance of Freshmen Entering College in Fall 1978[a]

	Percentage of students			
	B+ average or better		Top quarter of class	
	Men	Women	Men	Women
All institutions	36.6	49.8	41.8	49.3
All 2-year colleges	19.8	35.1	23.1	32.3
2-year public	20.1	35.9	23.3	32.3
2-year private	17.0	29.5	20.9	32.4
All 4-year colleges	39.9	53.9	45.0	53.1
Public	37.6	51.5	42.6	50.1
Private nonsectarian	47.0	60.8	52.4	60.4
Protestant	37.3	54.6	44.1	56.4
Catholic	42.5	54.2	44.9	51.6
All universities	55.3	66.6	63.4	69.9
Public	51.5	64.5	61.0	68.5
Private	67.1	74.6	71.1	75.1

[a] SOURCE: A. W. Astin, M. R. King, and G. T. Richardson, *The American Freshman: National Norms for Fall, 1978*. Laboratory for Research in Higher Education, Graduate School of Education, University of California at Los Angeles, 1978, pp. 19–20.

schools are admitted (Solmon, 1976). Out of the total number of college students women are somewhat more likely than men to obtain their bachelor's degree within 4 years. Yet a nationwide study of students beginning school in 1966 at over 200 institutions found that when

TABLE 2.12
Undergraduate Grade-Point Averages of American Students in Doctoral Programs[a]

Undergraduate grade-point average	Percentage of students		
	Men	Women	All students
A or A+	9.7	13.8	10.7
A −	16.2	23.1	17.9
B+	22.6	29.4	24.2
B	18.0	16.6	17.7
B −	17.1	10.7	15.5
C+	13.4	5.7	11.5
C or below	2.9	0.8	2.4

[a] SOURCE: Creager, J. A., *The American Graduate Student: A Normative Description*. American Council on Education Research Reports, 1971, volume 6, No. 5, p. 45.

matched on measures of ability (high school grades and aptitude tests), women were more likely to drop out of school and fewer women than men of equal ability received their degrees within 4 years after entering school. The results of this study are summarized in Table 2.13. Women are also more likely than men to drop out of graduate school programs (see Patterson & Sells, 1973).

Men and women tend to differ in how they finance their college education. Supporting the findings that social status is a more important determinant of women's than of men's educational attainment, women depend more than men on help from their parents to complete school. Of the women college freshmen in 1971, 61% were mainly supported by their parents or family as compared with only 49% of the men freshmen (Roby, 1973, p. 45). However, by the fall of 1977, perhaps because of the rapidly rising cost of a college education or the different phrasing of the question, men and women were almost equally likely to report support of $500 or more from their families or parents (American Council on Education, 1977, p. 192). Because they have greater earning power, 46% of the men as compared with 30% of the women in 1971 relied mainly "on their own earnings from part-time work, summer jobs or savings" in financing their education (Roby, 1973, p. 45). This difference re-

TABLE 2.13

Class of 1970 College Dropouts 4 Years after Entering College by Sex and Selected Ability Measures[a]

Aptitude test interval[b]	Average grade in high school[c]	Percentage not receiving degree and no longer enrolled	
		Men	Women
Low	C	60	67
Low	B	45	56
Low	A	43	44
Middle	C	57	65
Middle	B	42	51
Middle	A	33	43
High	C	46	57
High	B	33	40
High	A	22	31

[a] SOURCE: M. Patterson and L. Sells, 1973, p. 83. From *Academic Women on the Move*, edited by Alice Rossi and Ann Calderwood, © 1973 by the Russell Sage Foundation, New York.

[b] High includes all students with SAT verbal plus mathematical scores above 1054; middle includes all between 838 and 1054; low includes all below 838.

[c] A includes A+ and A −. B includes B+, B, and B − C includes C+, C, and D.

mained in 1977. When asked about the source of their support for school expenses that totalled more than $500, 7% of the first year men, but only 3% of the women cited full-time employment; 33% of the men, but only 20% of the women cited part-time employment; and 23% of the men, but only 17% of the women, cited savings (American Council on Education, 1977, p. 192). Because other sources of support did not differ markedly, it is conceivable that in 1977 women received more aid in actual dollars (above the $500 asked about in the survey) from their parents than the men did. While it is more difficult to determine the extent of discrimination in the granting of financial aid by institutions, Roby (1975, pp. 174–175) notes that many scholarships specify the sex of the recipients. Married women as well as part-time students (who often are women) are sometimes excluded from competitions. Moreover, if financial aid is awarded to women based on their proportional representation, and because of earlier discrimination in admissions the women are more qualified on the whole than the men, well-deserving women may not be given financial help. Solmon (1976, p. 107) suggests, however, that much of the observed sex discrimination in financial aid in graduate schools may result from the fact that women tend to enroll in fields where less total aid is available.

Today, restrictive campus rules regarding closing hours, dormitory check-in times, and clothing regulations have virtually disappeared from most liberal arts schools, but women may still be receiving career counseling that directs them toward more traditional areas and may still be subtly discouraged in less traditional areas of endeavor. In a comparison of males and females at graduate and professional schools at the University of Chicago, Freeman (1975) found that though women were slightly more committed to their career plans, they consistently reported receiving less support from faculty members, parents, and friends for their efforts. This lack of encouragement for women can be seen in individual interactions as well as in organizational policies. On many campuses only minimal child care facilities are available. "One study of women who planned [for] but were not attending graduate school indicated that the availability of child-care facilities topped the list of the factors they considered most important as a condition [for] graduate study [Roby, 1973, p. 53, citing U.S. Department of Health, Education and Welfare, 1968, p. 9]." In spite of this need, universities have consistently resisted providing support for such facilities (see also Roby, 1975). Freeman (1975, p. 204) contrasts the concern universities showed for young men during the Vietnam War and the providing of letters and jobs to help them retain their draft exempt status with the lack of concern shown for pregnant women who must often leave school, lose a fellowship, and get medical care outside the university facilities.

SEX SEGREGATION WITHIN SCHOOLS

While boys and girls have had equal access to most schools since 1912, it took an additional 60 years for sex segregation to be outlawed through the implementation of the Title IX regulations. Nevertheless, just as formal rules and regulations regarding race have yet to be fully implemented, separate and unequal experiences continue in the extracurricular and curricular areas of schools.

Extracurricular Areas

Though the regulations of Title IX require schools to produce plans to provide equal school allocations for males and females in sports, preliminary evidence indicates that practice times for girls are still scheduled at hours when boys are not using the gym and that coaches of girls' teams are usually paid less—presumably because boys' teams and their public support produce more stress for the coaching staff as well as more gate receipts. Newspapers often headline the results of boys' games and rarely mention female athletes. Although it is less common now, women are still prevented from playing the same games that men play. A few states still restrict women to half-court, six-woman basketball games instead of the faster moving full-court five-person game. The Title IX regulations allow women to play on men's teams when they can match the men in skill and when no women's teams are available. Yet they may be excluded from participating with males in games defined as contact sports—a category that now includes football, soccer, rugby, and even basketball.

Segregating the sexes and limiting females' participation in sports may have implications beyond the equal opportunity for learning sports. While it is impossible to tell without longitudinal research designs what effect these practices may have, some people believe that the experience of participating in team sports may have many indirect benefits. For instance, the opportunity to engage in a cooperative exercise with other players in a competitive setting may provide experience in learning the skills involved in taking on leadership. In addition, the comraderie involved in building up the motivation to win, the celebration of victory, and the consolation of defeat may be related to developing survival skills needed in a complex society. (For an excellent discussion of sex differences in play activities and speculation about their consequences, see Lever, 1978.)

Sex segregation also appears in other extracurricular activities. Males more often belong to chess, science, and lettermen's clubs and females more often belong to dance teams and aspire to be cheerleaders on the rally squad. Even though both sexes play in the band, they generally play different instruments (girls on the flutes, boys on the tubas) and have different responsibilities (drum majors who lead the band and majorettes who twirl batons). Jobs on school newspapers and in student government are typically sex segregated. Boys are more often sports editors, girls are feature reporters. Boys are more often presidents of student bodies, while girls are often secretaries.

Curricular Areas

Sex segregation also persists in academic and vocational areas in the school curriculum. Some of this segregation is directly promoted by official policies. Very little of the $40 million appropriated for research and development in vocational education in 1974 was allocated for projects directly related to the areas in which women work or to their needs (Roby, 1976). Yet women are indeed in the labor force. Almost half of all women 16 years old and older were in the labor force in 1974, and most of them were working because of financial necessity. Generally, their occupations are typically female, and they receive wages far below the average wages that men receive. The discrepancy in wages is not a result of unequal pay for equal work; rather it is because women's jobs differ in kind from those of men that the pay is different.

In the schools, there are sex discrepancies in vocational education programs that train students for jobs. Roby (1976) found that women were mainly trained in the clerical and home economics areas and that men, more evenly distributed in various areas, were most highly concentrated in trades and industry. A large proportion of students in programs related to health, home economics, and office work are female, but very few students in agriculture, in technical education and trades, and in industry are women. Notably enough, these latter occupations demand much higher wages than the areas for which women are trained. Moreover, the sex models that students encounter in such classes closely resemble those in the labor force. Women overwhelmingly teach courses in home economics, health, and office skills, while men tend to teach the trades, industrial and technical education, and agriculture (Roby, 1976).

New laws may prompt change, or at least greater recognition of the problem, and laws now require that all states address the issue of sex stereotyping in the vocational education curriculum. All state departments of education in 1977 were required to hire a vocational opportunities specialist to assure equality of opportunities.

As with the vocational curriculum, sex segregation in the academic curriculum is related to sex segregation in the occupational force. As students enter high school and are allowed more choice over their classes, girls are much less likely to choose math and science courses; and without this preparation they cannot enroll in college programs that lead to the lucrative male-dominated professions associated with science and various research and medical fields.

Table 2.14 gives the percentage of bachelors', masters' and doctors' degrees given to women in various fields in 1975–1976. It is clear that sex segregation persists among college students. For instance, women have over half the bachelor's degrees in education, fine and applied art, foreign languages, health professions, home economics, library science, and psychology. At the doctoral level, the only field in which women receive over half the degrees is home economics—a very traditional field for females; and they are also somewhat over represented (in relation to the total proportion of women receiving doctoral degrees) in most of the fields in which they predominate at the bachelor's level. Very few women receive the highest degrees in business, mathematics, the sciences, dentistry, medicine, or law. Again we note how sex segregation in curriculum areas closely resembles sex segregation in occupations.

The regulations that prevented enrollment in traditionally defined sex-typed classes are now prohibited. Yet unofficial norms, traditions, and customs among teachers and students support the maintenance of sex-segregated classes. Students and teachers understand the male–female differences in expectations for people in the society. They have been exposed to messages in curriculum materials and messages in the public media, which also accept the existence of male roles and female roles, and undoubtedly they have communicated these to each other. This does not mean, however, that change cannot occur. In fact, the sex ratios in first-year enrollments in professional schools in the fall of 1976 showed improvement over the ratios in the graduating classes of the previous year. In contrast to the 4% of all dental school graduates who were women in 1975–1976, 13% of the first-year class were women. Of those in the first-year class in medical school, 24% were women, in contrast with 16% of the graduates the year before; and 28% of the first-year law cohort were female in comparison with 15% of the previous graduating class (Grant & Lind, 1978, p. 89). By the fall of 1979 one

TABLE 2.14
Degrees Awarded to Women in the United States in 1975–1976 by Field of Study

Field of study	Percentage of bachelor of arts degrees	Percentage of master of arts degrees	Percentage of doctoral degrees
Agriculture, national resources	18	14	6
Architecture, environmental design	19	21	16
Biological sciences	34	32	21
Business, management	20	12	5
Communications	41	42	24
Computer, information services	20	14	9
Education	73	64	33
Engineering	3	4	2
Fine and applied arts	61	49	28
Foreign languages	76	67	48
Health professions	79	66	29
Home economics	96	91	71
Law	19	12	4
Letters	56	58	36
Library science	93	78	45
Mathematics	41	34	11
Physical science	19	15	9
Psychology	54	47	32
Public affairs and services	43	45	32
Social sciences	38	32	22
Theology	27	32	4
Interdisciplinary degrees			
Interdisciplinary studies	45	46	32
Area studies	56	45	32
All fields	45	46	23
Professional degrees:			
Dentistry (DDS or DMD)	—	—	4
Medicine (MD)	—	—	16
Law (LLB or JD)	—	—	19

[a]SOURCE: Adapted from W. V. Grant and C. G. Lind, *Digest of Education Statistics*, 1977–78, National Center for Education Statistics, Department of Health, Education and Welfare, Washington, D.C., 1978, pp. 108–113, 116.

state college on the west coast reported that 46% of the students in all levels of its science programs, 47% of those in business, and 36% in the school of veterinary medicine were women (Associated Press, 1979).

REFERENCES

Achenbach, T. M. (1970). "Standardization of a Research Instrument for Identifying Associative Responding in Children." *Developmental Psychology*, 2:283–91.

Aiken, L. R., Jr. (1963). "Personality Correlates of Attitudes toward Mathematics." *The Journal of Educational Research,* 56:476–480.

Aiken, L. R., Jr. (1970a). "Non-intellective Variables and Mathematics Achievement: Directions for Research." *Journal of School Psychology,* 8:28–36.

Aiken, L. R., Jr. (1970b). "Attitudes toward Mathematics." *Review of Educational Research,* 40:551–596.

Aiken, L. R., Jr. (1976). "Update on Attitudes and Other Affective Variables in Learning Mathematics." *Review of Educational Research,* 46:293–311.

Aiken, L. R., Jr., and Dreger, R. M. (1961). "The Effect of Attitudes on Performance in Mathematics." *Journal of Educational Psychology,* 52:19–24.

Alexander, K. L., and Eckland, B. K. (1974). "Sex Differences in the Educational Attainment Process." *American Sociological Review,* 39:668–682.

Almquist, E. M. (1975). "Untangling the Effects of Race and Sex: The Disadvantaged Status of Black Women." *Social Science Quarterly,* 56:129–142.

American Council on Education (1977). *A Fact Book on Higher Education.* American Council on Education, Washington, D. C.

Anastasi, A. (1958). *Differential Psychology: Individual and Group Differences in Behavior.* Macmillan, New York.

Anttonen, R. G. (1969). "A Longitudinal Study in Mathematics Attitude." *Journal of Educational Research,* 62:467–471.

Asher, S. R., and Gottman, J. (1973). "Sex of Teacher and Student Reading Achievement." *Journal of Educational Psychology,* 65:168–171.

Asher, S. R., and Markell, R. (1974). "Sex Differences in Comprehension of High- and Low-Interest Reading Material." *Journal of Educational Psychology,* 66:680–687.

Associated Press (1979). "Women Show Gains." *Eugene Register Guard,* Friday, Sept. 21: 10B.

Astin, H. S. (1974). "Sex Differences in Mathematical and Scientific Precocity." In *Mathematical Talent: Discovery, Description and Development* (J. C. Stanley and D. P. Keating, eds.). The Johns Hopkins University Press, Baltimore. Pp. 70–86.

Astin, H. S., Harway, M., and McNamara, P. (1976). *Sex Discrimination in Education: Access to Postsecondary Education.* Higher Education for Research Institute, Los Angeles.

Ausubel, D. P. (1968). *Educational Psychology: A Cognitive View.* Holt, Rinehart and Winston, New York.

Balow, I. H. (1963). "Sex Differences in First Grade Reading." *Elementary English,* 40:303–320.

Barfield, A. (1976). "Biological Influence on Sex Differences in Behavior." In *Sex Differences: Social and Biological Perspectives* (M. Teitelbaum, ed.). Anchor Books, Garden City, New York.

Bayer, A. E., Drew, D. E., Astin, A. W., Boruch, R. F., and Creager, J. A. (1970). "The First Year of College: A follow-up Normative Report." *ACE Research Reports,* 5(1):1–72.

Behr, A. N. (1973). "Achievement, Aptitude and Attitude in Mathematics." *Two Year College Mathematics Journal,* 4:72–74.

Bentzen, F. (1966). "Sex Ratios in Learning and Behavior Disorders." *The National Elementary Principal,* 46(2):13–17.

Blom, G. E. (1971). "Sex Differences in Reading Disability." In *Reading Forum* (E. Calkins, ed.). National Institute of Neurological Disease and Strokes, Bethesda, Maryland.

Blom, G. E., Waite, R. R., and Zimet, S. (1970). "A Motivational Content Analysis of Children's Primers." In *Basic Studies on Reading* (H. Levin and J. P. Williams, eds.). Basic Books, New York.

Bond, G. L. and Tinker, M. A. (1967). *Reading Difficulties: Their Diagnosis and Correction.* Prentice-Hall (Appleton), Englewood Cliffs, N.J.

Bradway, K. P., and Thompson, C. W. (1962). "Intelligence at Adulthood: A Twenty-Five Year Followup." *Journal of Educational Psychology*, 5:1–14.

Brophy, J. E., and Good, T. (1973). "Feminization of American Elementary Schools." *Phi Delta Kappan*, 54:564–566.

Callahan, L. G., and Glennon, V. J. (1975). *Elementary School Mathematics: A Guide to Current Research*. Association for Supervision and Curriculum Development, Washington, D.C.

Campbell, J. W. (1973). "Women Drop Back In: Educational Innovation in the Sixties." In *Academic Women on the Move* (A. S. Rossi and A. Calderwood, eds.). Russell Sage Foundation, New York, pp. 93–124.

Carlsmith, L. (1964). "Effect of Early Father Absence on Scholastic Aptitude." *Harvard Educational Review*, 34:3–21.

Carter, R. S. (1952). "How Invalid Are Marks Assigned by Teachers?" *Journal of Educational Psychology*, 43:218–228.

Coleman, J. (1961). *The Adolescent Society*. Free Press, New York.

Creager, J. (1971). "The American Graduate Student: A Normative Description." *ACE Research Reports*. American Council on Education, Washington, D.C.

Cruickshank, W. (1977). *Learning Disabilities in Home, School and Community*. Syracuse University Press.

Current Population Reports (1979). "School Enrollment—Social and Economic Characteristics of Students: October 1978 (Advance Report)." *Population Characteristics*, Series P-20, No. 335 (April), U.S. Department of Commerce, Bureau of the Census.

Davis, J. A. (1964). *Great Aspirations: The Graduate School Plans of America's College Seniors*. Aldine, Chicago.

DeFleur, L. B., and Gillman, D. (1978). "Cadet Beliefs, Attitudes and Interactions during the Early Phases of Sex Integration." *Youth and Society*, 10:165–190.

DeFleur, L., Gillman, D., and Marshak, W. (1978). "Sex Integration of the U.S. Air Force Academy: Changing Roles for Women." *Armed Forces and Society*, 4:607–622.

Donlon, T. F. (1971). *Content Factors in Sex Differences on Test Questions*. Paper presented at the June 1971 meeting of the New England Educational Research Organization, Boston.

Ernest, J. (1976). "Mathematics and Sex." *American Mathematical Monthly*, 83:595–614.

Felsenthal, H. (1970). *Sex Differences in Teacher Pupil Interaction in First Grade Reading Instruction*. Paper presented at annual meeting of the American Educational Research Association, New York.

Fennema, E. (1974). "Mathematics Learning and the Sexes: A Review." *Journal for Research in Mathematics Education*, 5:126–139.

Fennema, E. (1977). "Influences of Selected Cognitive, Affective and Educational Variables on Sex-related Differences in Mathematics Learning and Studying." In *Women and Mathematics: Research Perspectives for Change*. National Institute of Education Papers in Education and Work, no. 8. Department of HEW, Washington, D.C., pp. 79–135.

Ferber, M., and Huber, J. (1975). "Sex of Student and Instructor: A Study of Student Bias." *American Journal of Sociology*, 80:949–963.

Fox, L. (1975). "Mathematically Precocious: Male or Female." In *Mathematics Learning: What Research Says about Sex Differences* (E. Fennema, ed.). Ohio State University, pp. 1–12.

Fox, L. (1977). "The Effects of Sex Role Socialization on Mathematics Participation and Achievement". In *Women and Mathematics: Research Perspectives for Change*. National Institute of Education Papers in Education and Work, no. 8. Department of HEW, Washington, D.C., pp. 1–77.

Fox, L., Paternak, S. R., and Peiser, N. L. (1976). *Career Related Interests of Adolescent Boys and Girls.* In *Intellectual Talent: Research and Development* (D. P. Keating, ed.). John Hopkins University Press, Baltimore, Md., pp. 242–261.

Freeman, J. (1975). "How to Discriminate Against Women without Really Trying." In *Women: A Feminist Perspective* (J. Freeman, ed.). Mayfield, Palo Alto, Calif.

Gappa, J. M. and Uehling, B. S. (1979). *Women in Academe: Steps to Greater Equality.* American Association for Higher Education, Washington, D.C.

Gates, A. (1961). "Sex Differences in Reading Ability." *Elementary School Journal*, 61:431–434.

Goldberg, P. (1968). "Are Women Prejudiced against Women?" *Transaction*, 5(April):28–30.

Grant, W. V., and Lind, C. G. (1977). *Digest of Education Statistics*, 1976 ed. National Center for Education Statistics, Department of HEW, Washington, D.C.

Grant, W. V., and Lind, C. G. (1978). *Digest of Education Statistics, 1977–1978* ed. National Center for Education Statistics, Department of HEW, Washington, D.C.

Grant, W. V. and Lind, C. G. (1979). *Digest of Education Statistics, 1979.* National Center for Education Statistics, Department of HEW, Washington, D.C.

Guttentag, M., and Bray, H. (1977). "Teachers as Mediators of Sex-Role Standards." In *Beyond Sex Roles.* (A. G. Sargent, ed.). West, St. Paul, Minn.

Harway, M. and Astin, H. S. (1977). *Sex Discrimination in Career Counseling and Education.* Praeger, New York.

Haven, E. W. (1971). "Factors Associated with the Selection of Advanced Academic Mathematics Courses by Girls in High School." Doctoral dissertation, University of Pennsylvania. *Dissertation Abstracts International*, 32:1747A.

Havighurst, R. J., and Breese, F. H. (1947). "Relation between Ability and Social Status in a Mid-Western Community." *Journal of Educational Psychology*, 38:241–247.

Herman, M. (1975). *Male-Female Achievement in Eight Learning Areas.* Education Commission of the States, Denver, Colo.

Hesselbart, S. (1977). "Sex Role and Occupational Stereotypes: Three Studies of Impression Formation." *Sex Roles*, 3:409–432.

Hilton, T. L., and Berglund, G. (1973). "Sex Differences in Mathematics Achievement—a Longitudinal Study." *Journal of Educational Research*. 67:231–237.

Hobson, J. R. (1947). "Sex Differences in Primary Mental Abilities." *Journal of Educational Research*, 41:126–132.

Hoiland, E. A. (1973). *Interpretation of English Idioms by Indians and Non-Indians.* Unpublished Master's thesis. University of Saskatchewan, Canada.

Jacklin, C., Heuners, M., Mischell, H. M., and Jacobs, C. *As the Twig is Bent: Sex Role Stereotyping in Early Readers.* Unpublished manuscript, Stanford University.

Jackson, P., and Lahaderne, H. M. (1967). "Inequalities of Teacher-Pupil Contacts." *Psychology in the Schools*, 4:204–211.

Johnson, D. D. (1973–1974). "Sex Differences in Reading across Cultures. *Reading Research Quarterly*, 9:67–86.

Johnson, D. D. (1976). "Cross-cultural Perspective on Sex Differences in Reaching." *Reading Teacher*, 24:747–752.

Kagan, J. (1964). "The Child's Sex Role Classification of School Objects." *Child Development.* 35:1051–1056.

Kaminski, D. M., Ross, M., and Bradfield, L. (1976). "Why Females Don't Like Mathematics: The Effect of Parental Expectations." Paper presented at the annual meetings of the American Sociological Association, New York City.

Kaufman, A. A., and Doppelt, J. (1976). "Analysis of WISC-R Standardization Data in Terms of the Stratification Varibles." *Child Development*, 47:165–171.

Klein, H. (1968). "Interest and Comprehension in Sex Typed Materials." Unpublished doctoral dissertation, Syracuse University.

Koch, H. L. (1954). "The Relation of 'Primary Mental Abilities' in Five- and Six-Year-Olds to Sex of Child and Characteristics of Sibling." *Child Development*, 25:209–223.

Konshuh, A. (1971). *The Relationship of Sex Typed Adjective Illustrations to Interest and Comprehension of Fifth Grade Boys and Girls.* Unpublished master's thesis, University of Saskatchewan, Canada.

Lever, J. (1978). "Sex Differences in the Complexity of Children's Play." *American Sociological Review*, 43:471–482.

Lord, F. E. (1941). "A Study of Spatial Orientation of Children." *Journal of Educational Research*, 34:481–505.

Lyles, T. B. (1966). "Grouping by Sex." *National Elementary Principal*, 42:38–41.

Maccoby, E. (1966). *The Development of Sex Differences.* Stanford University Press.

Maccoby, E., and Jacklin, C. (1974). *The Psychology of Sex Differences.* Stanford University Press.

Madden, J. F. (1978). "Economic Rationale for Sex Differences in Education." *Southern Economic Journal*, 44:778–797.

Malmquist, E. (1960). *Factors Related to Reading Disabilities in the First Grade of Elementary School.* Almquist and Wiksell, Stockholm, Sweden.

Marini, M. M. and Greenberger, E. (1978). "Sex Differences in Educational Aspirations and Expectations." *American Educational Research Journal*, 15:67–79.

Martin, R. (1972). "Student Sex and Behavior as Determinants of the Type and Frequency of Teacher-Student Contact." *Journal of School Psychology*, 10:339–344.

Martin, W. (1972). *The American Sisterhood.* Harper & Row, New York.

McCandless, B. R., Roberts, A. and Starnes, T. (1974). "Teachers' Marks, Achievement Test Scores, and Aptitude Relations with Respect to Social Class, Race and Sex." *Journal of Educational Psychology*, 63:153–159.

McGuigan, W. (1970). *A Dangerous Experiment—100 Years of Women at the University of Michigan.* University of Michigan Center for Continuing Education for Women.

McNeil, J. D. (1964). "Programmed Instructions versus Usual Classroom Procedures in Teaching Boys to Read." *American Educational Research Journal*, 1:113–120.

Merritt, K. (1976). "Women and Higher Education: Voices from the Sexual Siberia." In *Beyond Intellectual Sexism: A New Woman, a New Reality* (J. I. Roberts, ed.). McKay, New York.

Meyer, W. J., and Thompson, G. (1963). "Teacher's Interactions with Boys as Contrasted with Girls." In *Psychological Studies of Human Development* (Kuhlena, R. G., and Thompson, G. G., eds.). Prentice-Hall, Englewood Cliffs, N.J.

Michelson, S. (1972). "Rational Income Decisions of Blacks and Everyone Else." In *Schooling in a Corporate Society* (M. Carnoy, ed.). McKay, New York; pp. 100–122.

Minuchin, A. (1966). "Sex Differences in Children: Research Findings in an Educational Context." *The National Elementary Principal*, 46(No. 2):45–48.

Mischel, W., and Mischel, H. (1971). "The Nature and Development of Psychological Sex Differences." In *Psychology and Educational Practice* (Lesser, G. S. ed.). Scott, Foresman, Glenview, Ill.

Monday, L. A., Hout, D. P., and Lutz, S. W. (1966–1967). *College Student Profiles: American College Testing Program.* American College Testing Publications, Iowa City, Iowa.

Morris, J. (1966). *Standard and Progress in Reading.* National Foundation for Educational Research in England and Wales, Upton Park, Great Britain.

Mumpower, D. L. (1970). "Sex Ratios Found in Various Types of Referred Exceptional Children." *Exceptional Children*, 36:621–624.

Neale, D. C., Gill, N., and Tismer, W. (1970). "Relationship between Attitudes toward School Subjects and School Achievement." *Journal of Educational Research*, 63:232–237.

Orlow, M. (1976). "Literacy Training in West Germany and in the United States." *Reading Teacher*, 29:460–467.

Patterson, M., and Sells, L. (1973). "Women Dropouts from Higher Education." In *Academic Women on the Move* (Rossi, A. S. and Calderwood, A. eds.). Russell Sage, New York.

Preston, R. C. (1962). "Reading Achievement of German and American Children." *School and Society*, 90:350–354.

Prillaman, D. (1975). "An Analysis of Placement Factors in Classes for the Educable Mentally Retarded." *Exceptional Children*, 42:107–108.

Roby, P. A. (1973). "Institutional Barriers to Women Students in Higher Education." In *Academic Women on the Move* (Rossi, A. S. and Calderwood, A. eds.). Russell Sage Foundation, New York.

Roby, P. A. (1975). "Structural and Internalized Barriers to Women in Higher Education." In *Women: A Feminist Perspective* (J. Freeman, ed.). Mayfield, Palo Alto, Calif.

Roby, P. A. (1976). "Toward Full Equality: More Job Education for Women." *School Review*, 84:181–211.

Saario, T. N., Jacklin, C. N., and Tittle, C. K. (1973). "Sex Role Stereotyping in the Public Schools." *Harvard Educational Review*, 43:386–416.

Schlossberg, N., and Pietrofesa, J. (1973). "Perspective on Counseling Bias: Implications for Counselor Education." *Counseling Psychologist*, 4:44–54.

Schone, F., vander Sleen, J. and Vijhuizen, J. (1975). "Man and Woman in the Textbooks of a Primary School." *Sociologische Gids*, July/August, 280–296. Reported in *Canadian Newsletter of Research on Women*, 1977, 6(2):43.

Scottish Council for Research in Education (1933). *The Intelligence of Children*. University of London Press.

Scottish Council for Research in Education (1949). *The Trend of Scottish Intelligence*. University of London Press.

Sears, P., and Feldman, D. (1966). "Teacher Interactions with Boys and with Girls." *The National Elementary Principal*, 46(No.2):30–35.

Serbin, L. A., O'Leary, K. D., Kent, R. N., and Tonick, I. J. (1973). "A Comparison of Teacher Response to the Preacademic and Problem Behavior of Boys and Girls." *Child Development*, 44:796–804.

Sewell, W. H., and Shah, V. P. (1967). "Socioeconomic Status, Intelligence and the Attainment of Higher Education." *Sociology of Education*, 40:1–23.

Sexton, P. C. (1969). *The Feminized Male: Classrooms, White Collars and the Decline of Manliness*. Vintage, New York.

Shaw, M., and McKuen, J. (1960). "The Onset of Academic Underachievement in Bright Children." *Journal of Educational Psychology*, 51:103–108.

Sherman, J. (1977). "Effects of Biological Factors on Sex-Related Differences in Mathematics Achievement." In *Women and Mathematics: Research Perspectives for Change*. National Institute of Education Papers in Education and Work, no. 8. Department of HEW, Washington, D.C., pp. 137–206.

Solomon, D., and Ali, F. A. (1972). "Age Trends in the Perception of Verbal Reinforcers." *Developmental Psychology*, 7:238–243.

Solomon, L. C. (1976). *Male and Female Graduate Students: The Question of Equal Opportunity*. Praeger, New York.

Spaulding, R. L. (1963). *Achievement, Creativity and Self-Concept Correlates of Teacher-Pupil*

Transactions in Elementary Schools. Cooperative Research Project, Department of HEW, Washington, D.C.

Stefflire, B. (1969). "Run, Mama, Run: Women Workers in Elementary Readers." *Vocational Guidance Quarterly,* 18:99–102.

Stein, A. H., and Smithells, J. (1969). "Age and Sex Differences in Children's Sex-Role Standards about Achievement." *Developmental Psychology,* 1:252–259.

Suter, L. E., and Miller, H. P. (1973). "Income Differences between Men and Career Women." *American Journal of Sociology,* 78:962–974.

Terman, L. M., and Oden, M. H. (1949). *The Gifted Child Grows Up: 25 Year Follow-up of a Superior Group.* Stanford University Press.

Terman, L. M., and Tyler, L. E. (1954). "Psychological Sex Differences." In *Manual of Child Psychology,* 2nd ed. (L. Carmichael, ed.). Wiley, New York, pp. 1004–1114.

Tittle, C. K. (1973). "Women and Educational Testing." *Phi Delta Kappan,* 54:118–119.

Tittle, C. K. and Denker, E. R. (1977). "Re-Entry Women: A Selective View of the Educational Process, Career Choice and Interest Measurement." *Review of Educational Research* 47:531–84.

Trecker, J. L. (1971). "Women in U.S. History High School Textbooks." *Social Education,* 35:249–260, 338.

Treiman, D. J., and Terrell, K. (1975). "Sex and the Process of Status Attainment: A Comparison of Working Women and Men." *American Sociological Review,* 40:174–200.

Turner, N. O. (1971). "Can the Girls Be Creeping Up on the Boys?" *International Journal of Mathematical Education in Science and Technology,* 2:337–340.

U.S. Department of Health, Education and Welfare (1968). *Women and Graduate Study.* Government Printing Office, Washington, D.C.

U'Ren, M. (1971). "The Image of Women in Textbooks." In *Women in Sexist Society* (V. Gornick and B. Moran, eds.). Basic Books, New York.

Walster, E., Cleary, T. A. and Clifford, M. N. (1976). "The Effect of Race and Sex on College Admission." *Sociology of Education,* 44:237–244.

Weitzman, L., and Rizzo, D. (1974). "Images of Males and Females in Elementary School Books." In *Biased Textbooks,* The National Foundation for the Improvement of Education, Washington, D.C.

Wood, J. W. (1974). *The Effect of Interest upon Reading Performance as Assessed by Informal Reading Inventories.* Unpublished doctoral dissertation, University of Oregon.

Chapter 3

WHY SEX INEQUITIES EXIST FOR STUDENTS

Jean Stockard

The same fearful prediction that women would be turned into men has been made before each successive step of the equal rights movement. It was made before in regard to higher education, in regard to the opening of colleges and of the professions; but hitherto it has proved groundless. In Wyoming and in England, where women have been voting since 1869, they are not perceptibly less womanly than before. Experience is the best of tests; and experience thus far has born out Whittier's prediction, made years ago: "I have no fear that men will be less manly, or women less womanly, when men and women have equal rights before the law [Alice Stone Blackwell, Making Women into Men, *1893 in Martin, 1972, p. 59]."*

In the previous chapter on sex inequities that students face, we noted differences and stereotypes in behavior patterns, achievement, and curricular materials and segregation in school activities. In this chapter various explanations of sex-role development and sex discrimination are reviewed, and then applied to the areas where sexual inequities are found.

THEORETICAL EXPLANATIONS OF SEX-ROLE DEVELOPMENT AND SEX DISCRIMINATION

Scholars in many academic areas such as psychology, sociology, anthropology, and psychoanalysis have explored the nature of sex differences and how they develop. They explain how males and females come to adopt their sex roles, why roles are so often segregated by sex, and why the roles assigned to men are more highly valued than those assigned to women. Although in this discussion we cannot explore all the details of a particular analysis or approach, we will give the broad outlines of an area and present the material that is most pertinent to analyzing sex roles and discrimination in education. (For a more thorough discussion of each of the areas reviewed, see Stockard & Johnson, 1980.) Explanations of the development of sex differences come from biology, academic psychology, and sociology's focus on social roles and social institutions.

Biological Explanations

The most basic differences between males and females are biological. Women bear children and nurse them; men cannot. While the social roles assigned to each sex have differences that are much more varied and elaborate than this, they nevertheless may have some biological basis. Because biological theories have often been used to disparage women and to limit their activities artificially, many feminists have rejected any attempts to use these explanations. Yet if we are to understand sex-role development fully, it is important to assess any possible biological basis of sexual differences. In fact, recent work does suggest that such explanations do not disparage women at all. While biology may influence the ease with which people learn some behaviors, it does not necessarily impose limits or constraints on behaviors beyond those related to reproduction. Humans have highly developed symbolic and social systems that can alter the meaning and nature of biologically based sex differences. For instance, even though men are usually larger and stronger than women, women in some societies carry the heavy burdens. The effect biology has on people is thus greatly influenced by the meaning that a society or group attaches to biological differences.

There is evidence that physiological sex differences help account for the incidences of certain illnesses and diseases. Although more males than females are conceived, more males die so that the sex ratio is nearly equal at the time of birth. Males also succumb to illness and disease more frequently than females throughout life. This appears to occur even in settings where men and women have very similar diets, activities, and levels of stress, such as in religious communities. Some inherited conditions, such as hemophilia and color blindness, appear more often in males because of their chromosomal structure. Males seem to fall prey to certain diseases and afflictions, for example, speech defects, vision and reading problems, mental retardation, and hearing problems, simply because they mature more slowly than females (Barfield, 1976).

Other accidents and illnesses affect men more frequently than women because of their particular roles and activities. For example, men have "old football injuries" simply because men play football more often than women do.

Biology also explains differences in perceptual ability. Visual-spatial ability appears to be a perceptual skill that is not related to analytic and reasoning abilities or intellectual capacity. (As described earlier, tests that measure this ability usually involve looking at a picture of interlocking gears and deciding which one must be moved in order to move a specific part of the total system; or looking at a two-dimensional picture of a three-dimensional figure and telling how many surfaces are actually on the figure.) More males than females tend to have high scores on visual-spatial tests, and these differences appear fairly consistently cross-culturally (see Lambert, 1978, pp. 112–113). Although training will somewhat improve girls' skills in this area (Conner, Schackman & Serbin, 1978), Maccoby and Jacklin (1974) suggest that boys' greater spatial ability may have a biological base.

The actual nature of such a biological influence is not yet known. Some hypotheses suggest genetic origins such that a recessive gene for superior visula-spatial ability lies on the X chromosome. As with conditions such as color blindness and hemophilia, this theory suggests that superior visual-spatial ability would appear more frequently with boys because they have only one X chromosome. Other hypotheses suggest that the difference may be traced to prenatal and/or postnatal differences in hormone levels. A third hypothesis involves female and male differences in the lateralization of the cerebral hemispheres of the brain. No clear evidence supports any one of these theories, and in fact more than one of them may be needed for a complete explanation. In any case, a good deal of research remains to be done. (For more complete explanations of these theoretical pespectives, see Maccoby & Jacklin, 1974; Lambert, 1978.)

While there is evidence that some part of verbal ability is inherited from parents, there is no evidence that this is sex-linked. In other words, both sexes appear to inherit verbal ability from both mothers and fathers (Maccoby & Jacklin, 1974). Some evidence does suggest, however, that a biological basis for sex differences in verbal ability might involve sex differences in the functioning of the brain hemispheres. Again, much research remains to be done for firm conclusions in this area (Goleman, 1978).

Sex differences in behavioral patterns might also be influenced by biology. In all societies that are known to anthropologists, women have the primary responsibility for early child care, probably because women bear and nurse the children. There is evidence, however, that women are more biologically prepared to care for young children than men are. Studies with animals show that young females are more nurturant and responsive to babies than young males are. Males can be taught to nurture, and in fact baby animals can teach or coerce adult males to nurture them; yet the males appear to react less quickly to the demands of the young. Other evidence suggests that hormones are secreted during pregnancy that prompt the nurturant responses of females to the young (see Maccoby & Jacklin, 1974).

A great deal of evidence also suggests that males are more aggressive than females. This, too, may have a biological base. Such differences in aggression appear in all cultures, and they may be seen in children at very early ages and in the nonhuman primates. Studies of nonhuman primates and of humans who have experienced abnormal doses of hormones while in utero suggest that prenatal doses of androgen in males influence the development of the males' potential for aggression (see Maccoby & Jacklin, 1974; Stockard & Johnson, 1980). However, just as males can nurture, females can aggress. It may be that males are more easily stimulated than females to show aggressive actions.

It should be noted, of course, that aggressive actions are rarely sanctioned or welcomed and that they are not always conducive or important for group survival. Certainly, within the classroom, teachers try to control the aggressive actions of all children. Moreover, it is clear that the basis of the social structure of primate groups is not aggression and dominance patterns but the nurturance and affectional bonds between mothers and young and between females (Hinde, 1972; Lancaster, 1976). Biology influences the threshold at which given behaviors may appear, and these thresholds can be altered by social influences. The potential susceptibility of males to illness and disease can be controlled to an extent by modern medicine; and males can learn to be more nurturant, just as they learn to pattern and control their aggressiveness. In fact, most of the sex differences within a society are probably learned.

Psychological Explanations

Boys and girls choose sex-typed toys and activities at very early ages. Observers at nursery schools note that boys play with some toys and girls play with others, although girls play with boys' toys and engage in boys' activities more often than boys play in girls' areas (Conner & Serbin, 1977; Heuser, 1977). While biological influences prompt some behavior, most sex differences probably come through the learning of sex roles. Although there are sometimes wide sex differences in adult social roles, there appear to be relatively few sexual differences in the *personality* characteristics of young children. Those that appear later could well be influenced by sex roles and the behavioral expectations attached to these roles.

From an extensive review of studies of sex differences, Maccoby and Jacklin (1974) concluded that although boys display increased activity in the presence of other boys, there is no general tendency for boys to be more active than girls. Females are certainly not passive, and there is little evidence that they are more "emotional." Both boys and girls respond to social stimuli, and both are sensitive to the needs of others. They show little overall difference in attachment or affiliation behavior, although their specific ways of seeking proximity and attention may differ. A major difference between the sexes is in the amount of aggressive behavior they display. Boys consistently appear to be more aggressive than girls, in both physical and verbal manifestations; they do make more direct attempts to dominate others than girls do. By interpreting categories of traits such as sociability very broadly, Maccoby and Jacklin (1974) have shown that boys and girls share basic human traits and are actually very similar in psychological capacity. This does not deny, of course, that as they grow older boys and girls develop and learn different sexual roles that call on different aspects of these similar psychological capacities.

Three theories from academic psychology have been used to explain how children learn roles (see Maccoby & Jacklin, 1974).[1] While they were not specifically developed to explain sex-role development, these general theories of human development should apply to the learning of sex roles. The three approaches are not contradictory or mutually exclusive, but instead tend to complement each other.

Social Learning

This theory originally grew out of stimulus–response theory, or behaviorism. It is an approach to learning that many people intuitively believe. In contrast to the pure behaviorists, theorists of social learning do not believe that all behaviors must be directly rewarded in order to be learned. Instead, they recognize that cognitive processes do occur and that people can learn from observing what happens to others or remembering past outcomes and extending these to future events. In any case, these theorists posit that behaviors that are reinforced (whether directly or through some cognitive process) tend to occur more often. Social

[1]We are making a distinction between theories from academic psychology and theories from the psychoanalytic school. The latter, which also have a psychological perspective, have been an important influence on some of the social-role theories discussed.

learning theorists also emphasize the importance of social reinforcements, those from other people and those that occur in a social setting;
and such theorists stress the importance of early childhood—a time
when behavior patterns are first learned.

Parental expectations do differ depending on the sex of the child.
Parents expect that boys' behavior will differ from girls' behavior, and
they attribute different characteristics to children (Birns, 1976). Yet most
of the evidence suggests that even though parents expect differences
between boys and girls, they do not necessarily reinforce these differences when they appear. Maccoby and Jacklin (1974) extensively reviewed studies of how parents treat their children and concluded that in
terms of broad areas such as affection, granting of autonomy, and responses to dependency and aggression, parents' treatment of boys is not
different from their treatment of girls. Parents may reinforce more specific behaviors, however. For instance, in an observational study of
2-year-olds, Fagot (1978a) found clear sex differences in toy and play
preferences. Girls preferred dolls and soft objects, and boys preferred
blocks and objects that could be manipulated. She observed that while
parental reinforcement could not explain the first appearance of chil-
drens' preferences, parents did reinforce play choices. They gave more
positive responses to girls for doll play and to boys for block play, and
they gave negative responses to boys' playing with dolls and to girls'
playing with manipulable objects.

Just as boys receive more punishment in school, studies show that
they also receive more punishment from parents. They also seem to
receive more positive rewards and positive feedback from parents,
which also parallels their school experiences (Block, 1973; Maccoby &
Jacklin, 1974; Taylor & Epstein, 1967). It is not clear, however, how adult
behaviors influence the behavior of children. It may be that positive and
negative feedback balances out. These may be devices used by parents
and teachers to help control boys and to guide them to more acceptable
behavior. They do not appear to reinforce boys' aggression directly.

Modeling

Another explanation of how we acquire sex-typed behavior is
modeling theory, usually seen as part of social learning theory. This
involves imitation or identification, that is, behaving like other people
who are taken as models. While modeling, like social learning, holds a
good deal of appeal as an explanation, research support for the idea that
children model parents is equivocal. Studies tend to show that children
are not especially similar to their parents; girls do not seem to resemble
their mothers' feminine characteristics, and boys do not resemble their
fathers' masculine characteristics (Hetherington, 1965). The reason for

this may lie in the difference between children and adults. While asserting that children learn roles by a process of reinforcement and modeling, Scott (1971) suggests that this learning is not primarily the modeling of individual persons. To understand how individuals learn their social roles, Scott suggests that we must understand the sanctions associated with conforming or not conforming to expected roles, including the sex roles of boys and girls.

Cognitive Development

Kohlberg (1966) suggested that sex roles develop because children understand or decide what behaviors are appropriate for their sex rather than because of reinforcement. Through cognitive development, children first categorize themselves as a boy or a girl; then they begin to perceive and understand what attributes belong to males and females and to develop or accept these attributes. Only after basically deciding that one is a male or a female does one begin to model or identify with people of the same sex. In support of this position, many studies show that young children hold much more rigid stereotypes of sex roles than do older children. As children grow older, they develop more complex views of the world around them and of the nature of sex roles. They gradually tend to develop less rigid and more flexible views of possible roles for men and women and boys and girls.

Summary

Three theories from academic psychology attempt to explain how children learn sex roles. Social learning suggests that sex roles develop because others reinforce or encourage their appearance; modeling suggests that children copy people of the same sex; cognitive development suggests that children adopt behaviors that they perceive as appropriate for their sex. While parents may reinforce specific behaviors, there is little evidence that they reinforce large areas of sex-typed behaviors. In fact, observations in schools suggest that teachers reinforce both boys and girls for feminine behavior. Although some studies of the modeling of television characters suggest that modeling does occur (e.g., Atkin, 1975; Freuh & McGhee, 1975), there is little evidence that children's sex-typed behavior occurs as a result of modeling the parent of the same sex. Most evidence appears to support Kohlberg's cognitive developmental view (Maccoby & Jacklin, 1974).

This does not mean, however, that the processes implied by modeling and social learning do not occur. For instance, young children in nursery schools appear to reinforce strongly sex-typed behaviors in each other (Fagot & Patterson, 1969). Moreover, parents and teachers expect different behavior of boys and girls even though they may not directly reinforce it. Children may perceive these expectations, and their perceptions may actually serve as reinforcers (Stockard & Johnson, 1980). Similarly, children may model each other and also images that they see portrayed on television and in picture books, selecting traits they believe really represent masculinity or femininity. Some pretend to be the Six Million Dollar Man or Wonder Woman.

Social Roles

Sociologists have traditionally been concerned more with the learning of roles and role behaviors than with the learning of individual or discrete behaviors, such as aggression or activity level. Two strands of thought may be distinguished. One deals with the learning of sex roles in early life and derives from the basic work of Talcott Parsons.[2] The other is based on symbolic interaction, a perspective developed from work of George Herbert Mead, and can be used to analyze effectively the learning of sex roles throughout the life cycle.

Learning Sex Roles in the Early Years

Parsons asserted that personalities develop through the interaction of roles in social systems. Roles are sets of behavior patterns that define the expected behavior for individuals in a given status or position. A role does not make sense without another complementary role that has related actions or definitions. For instance, the husband's role is complementary to the wife's role; the child's role is complementary to the parent's role. As individuals learn to play their assigned roles, they become part of the social system to which those roles belong (Parsons, 1955, 1970).

Parsons suggested that males and females first develop their different personalities and social roles through their interactions within the family. In all cultures the child has its first contact with at least one nurturing female; the father and/or other males only enter the child's life after this early period. Even though some children grow up without parents in the home, they do not grow up without the cultural definition of what mothers and fathers are supposed to be. It is not the structure of a given family so much as the cultural definitions of family life and roles that influence sex-role development.

In the first stage of development, the infant is in close contact with the mother or mother substitute. This stage is essentially the same for

[2]This trend of thought was also strongly influenced by psychoanalytic theory (see Stockard and Johnson, 1979).

infants of both sexes. By interacting with the mother, children learn what it is to be nurtured and how to nurture. That is, the social roles of a child and a mother are two aspects of the mother–child role; and the child learns both parts.

It is in the second stage of development, when the child extends its world beyond the mother–infant bond, that sex typing begins to take place. Johnson (1963, 1975) clarified the analysis of this stage by noting that the father facilitates the learning of sex roles for both boys and girls. As children get older and realize that they are boys and girls, the boy understands that he cannot be like the mother because he is a male. He must then deny his early identification with the mother and try to develop his masculine identity. Because fathers are rarely around young children as much as mothers and other females are, boys usually have no real person with whom to identify. Their definition of masculinity may be fairly tenuous or unreal—based more on their idealistic conceptions of what masculinity is than on the real characteristics of an individual (see Chodorow, 1974; Stockard & Johnson, 1979). Parsons (1954a,b) has suggested that boys' rejection of their first feminine identity contributes to a common pattern of being a "bad boy." The mother and femininity are identified with goodness and conformity to rules. In rejecting identification with the mother, boys may also reject good, or conforming, behavior. The process of sex-role development is not as difficult for the young girl. Because her first identification is with a person of the same sex, she need not reject it. Girls' definition of their own femininity is not as tenuous or fragile as boys' definition of their masculinity.

This pattern may be involved in the development of many males' motive to dominate women, in sexual segregation, and in the devaluation of women's activities. Males' definition of their masculinity as "not feminine" develops early in life and is deeply felt. Men are compelled to confirm this identity on a behavioral level, and they thus tend to separate their activities from those of women in order to affirm that *what they do* is not feminine. A good deal of evidence shows that boys are much more concerned than girls with preserving sex differentiation in play and in activity choices. To affirm the validity or worth of their self-identity, they devalue what women do. By concretely assuring that women do different things and that these activities are not as valued as their own, males may reaffirm their tenuous masculine identity (Stockard & Johnson, 1979).

Symbolic Interaction

People continue to enter new situations and to develop variations of their sex roles as they grow older. Symbolic interaction suggests that individuals develop views of themselves and their behavior from their interpretation of the expectations of people around them (Blumer, 1969; Mead, 1934).[3] People enter different social systems as they grow older, moving from the mother–child dyad to interactions with other family members, then to interactions with other children and adults in nursery and day care settings, and then to school, dating, marriage, and work. Each of these settings presents specified roles that individuals are expected to fill and role expectations that are communicated by others. For instance, teachers communicate what they expect children to do and tend to reinforce sex-typed behavior in both males and females that is more in line with a feminine than with a masculine role, and students have expectations of each other that tend to reinforce the sex-typed behavior of their peers (Fagot & Patterson, 1969). In both cases, by symbolic interaction, students perceive the expectations of others, evaluating and interpreting these expectations and acting in accordance with their own interpretations.

A number of factors can influence the interpretation that an individual makes. These include the nature of the relationship between the subject and the others, the individual's own past experiences, and self-definition. For instance, a boy's definition of what masculinity is would influence how he responds to the expectations of students and teachers. As people grow older their definitions of themselves and their repertoire of experiences change. For instance, after adolescence, girls and boys may anticipate marriage and parenthood as well as the world of work. As they become more aware of their potential adult roles, their responses to school situations may take on different meanings.

Symbolic interaction can also account for why sex segregation and the devaluation of women's roles persist in the everyday interactions of males and females. For instance, males' expectations that things females do should be different from things males do may be seen in many everyday settings. Children at play, and expecially boys, discourage cross-sex play choices. Students have strong sanctions, including teasing, ridicule, and even exclusion from activities, for peers who violate the norms of sex segregation. Boys deride other boys who participate in seemingly feminine activities, calling them sissies or wimps. Coaches goad their charges on to greater accomplishments by yelling comments such as, "Don't run like a woman" or "If you don't start playing like men, we'll have to change your uniforms to skirts." These comments

[3]In the sense that both views recognize the ability of individuals to interpret and reflect upon the stimuli they encounter, symbolic interaction resembles cognitive development theory.

clearly communicate to others, both males and females, a devaluation of what women are and what women do.

The behavior of women shows that they acknowledge males' evaluations and male's desire to maintain sex segregation in activities and that women realize men have greater power in the society. A number of analyses of individual interaction patterns show that females recognize such power differentials. Women's actions are those that lower-status people display in interactions. They interrupt men less often than men interrupt women, they talk less often and for shorter periods of time (despite stereotypes to the contrary), and they even take up less space in proportion to their bodies (Henley, 1977).

Although women are not as concerned with role segregation, something which men expect, and although they probably do not accept men's devaluation, in general their responses do not directly challenge these expectations and patterns. Individual feminists have tried to do so, but most women will usually confine their activities to spheres generally seen as appropriate for women or, when they do encroach on males' areas, redefine their activities as suitable for the female role (see Stockard & Johnson, 1980). For instance, a young woman who receives better grades than a male friend may excuse her success by saying, "Oh, I was just lucky." She may minimize direct academic competition with young men by avoiding areas in which males excel, majoring in English, French, or education, for example, while male friends major in engineering, chemistry, or economics. Most evidence suggests that men do not differ from women in their overall self-concepts and feelings of self-worth (Maccoby & Jacklin, 1974; Rosenberg & Simmons, 1975). In an attempt to maintain self-worth, women may consciously deny male devaluation or a particular aspect of it as it relates to themselves. If they do counter men's devaluation they usually do so while in the company of other women.

Social Systems

In addition to looking at individual behavior, the adoption of certain roles, sex-typed personality traits, and males' motive to dominate women, we can analyse patterns of sex segregation and devaluation by looking at available roles and opportunities in social institutions. Various patterns in social institutions reinforce each other and reinforce individuals' concepts of sex roles. The most important linkages for our purposes are those between the economy, the family, and education. Education may be seen as a funneling or connecting institution. It continues the process of socialization begun in the family and helps prepare young people to enter the world of work and establish their own families for procreation. The needs of the economy and the family are reflected in the policies of the school; and patterns in academic and vocational education parallel the sex segregation in the adult work force. Differing roles in extracurricular activities reflect the sources of power and authority found in the family and work world.

Educational institutions respond to sex-role socialization in the family. When young people enter school, they have already developed definitions of masculinity and femininity and views of appropriate sex roles. Young children hold especially strong views, and sex roles in students' lives must at least partly reflect this early learning. Thus patterns and values in other institutions are links with, and influences on, patterns in education. The sex inequities in education and those in other social systems promote and perpetuate each other. These concrete examples of segregation and devaluation in social institutions also influence the individual development of males and females; providing definitions of sex roles as young males and females try to decide what they should be or do (cogniive development). Such institutional patterns may also be seen as general expectations of behavior that people interpret (symbolic interaction).

EXPLAINING SEX DIFFERENCES IN ACADEMIC ACHIEVEMENT

Using various theoretical perspectives we can explain the basis and effect of the inequities discussed in Chapter 2. Of course, not all perspectives speak to each problem area, and some have greater explanatory power than others. Chapter 2 reviewed differences in achievement and behavior in school, including differences in behavior problems, learning disabilities, attitudes toward school, feedback from teachers, and patterns of achievement.

Biological Influences

While biological influences probably can never totally explain behaviors and social patterns, they can help explain some sex differences. For instance, while biological factors probably are not directly responsible for the tendency of boys to dislike school, the different feedback received from teachers, or sex differences in grades, such factors may influence the tendency of boys to have more behavior problems, their greater incidence of learning disabilities, and their greater interest in math and science; these factors may also influence girls' greater verbal skills.

Males' aggressiveness may have a biological basis, and it is possible that a great many of their behavior problems in school stem from this aggressiveness. Such problems often involve disruptive behavior, fighting, and inattention; and while other aspects of the social situation may be influences, it is indeed possible that biology gives an extra little push with the result that boys need less stimulus than girls to show disruptive behavior. Because they are subject to detrimental physical conditions more often than girls, boys may more often develop various developmental and learning problems (Cruickshank, 1977, pp. 25–26). In addition, different maturation rates may account for the greater incidence of behavioral and reading problems among boys (cf. Lindgren, 1976, pp. 64–65).

Different achievement patterns may be at least partly attributed to skills that are physiologically influenced. As noted earlier, some evidence does suggest that sex differences in visual-spatial ability may be partially associated with sex differences in math and science achievement. This relation between achievement and a biologically based perceptual skill does not mean, however, that there must necessarily be extensive sex differences in math and science achievement. There are always several ways to solve mathematical problems, and while plane or spatial geometry may require visual-spatial ability, analytic geometry does not. Even famous mathematicians approach problems from very different angles: "Rumor has it that Karl Pearson did everything by algebra and Fisher thought geometrically, and that was the reason why they were not on speaking terms even though they had offices in the same place [Vandenberg, quoted in Maccoby & Jacklin, 1974, p. 91]."

Sex differences in mathematical achievement might be much smaller if teaching methods drew on skills other than visual-spatial skills. Most math teachers are male, and we suspect that because they have more of this ability, they tend to present the material in a way that assumes that others do too. Some support for this supposition comes from Carter's (1952) finding regarding ninth-grade algebra classes: in those taught by women, girls had higher scores in standardized achievement tests, while in those taught by men, boys had higher test scores, even though girls had higher grades in all the classes. The women teachers may have presented the material in a way that was more easily understood by the girls, thus changing the typical pattern of sex differences in mathematical achievement.[4]

[4]In contrast to the situation with mathematics, there appears to be little evidence that having a male teacher improves boys' reading scores, so a parallel explanation for girls' greater verbal achievement probably would not be valid.

Explanations from Academic Psychology

Social learning, modeling, and cognitive development are theories from academic psychology that describe how children learn sex roles. These theories suggest that the lower grades, the behavior and learning problems, the dislike of school, and the achievement patterns of boys stem from the reinforcements they get, the people they model, and their own view of what masculinity means.

A number of authors have speculated that the greater attention, both positive and negative, that boys get in classrooms makes them more exploratory, more autonomous, more independent and even more oriented toward achievement in mathematics (e.g., Guttentag & Bray, 1977; Sears & Feldman, 1966; Serbin, O'Leary, Kent & Tonick, 1966). Actually, as we noted earlier, boys and girls do not differ on these psychological dimensions; and the different attention they receive, at least from parents, does not seem to affect these psychological traits. With respect to mathematics achievement, girls receive better grades in math than boys do, even though boys generally score better on achievement tests. Because grades are the reinforcer most commonly shown to children (they often do not know their scores on achievement tests), we would expect girls to have *higher* achievement scores in mathematics if reinforcement were the key to their success.

We also noted above that parents as well as teachers tend to give boys more positive and more negative attention than they give girls. This may occur because boys demand more attention. Maccoby and Jacklin (1974) suggest that a major component of boys' dependent behavior is attention-getting. Teachers' interactions with children are often simple attempts to control behavior and responses to attention-getting mechanisms. This, of course, influences the negative feedback children receive, but it may also influence the amount of positive feedback. Courses in behavior management are commonly included by teacher-training institutions, and teachers learn that a most effective means of control is to compliment children's good behavior as well as to correct their bad behavior. The kinds of attention boys receive may be more a result of sex differences than a cause.

Reinforcement, or social learning theory, cannot account for sex differences in academic achievement, but modeling theory may be somewhat more successful as an explanation. Teachers are usually women, especially in the elementary schools in this country; and in school, just as at home, young boys do not have ready models. However, having a male teacher does *not* appear to influence young boys' reading achievement in this country; and whether the teacher is male or female, boys tend to have lower scores (Asher & Gootman, 1973; Brophy & Good, 1973). The presence of a model may affect mathematics achievement, however; as we have already noted Carter (1952) found that ninth-grade algebra students showed higher achievement when taught by a teacher of the same sex. Whether this resulted from a modeling effect, from different teaching styles, or from a combination of both variables is open to question.

Of the three approaches from academic psychology, we believe that cognitive development may be the most helpful explanation of sex differences in academic achievement. That is, young children perceive that they are males or females and then adopt the behaviors they believe appropriate for their sex group. It could well be that young boys perceive that boys should behave badly in school and thus act that way. Some support for this comes from Fagot and Patterson's (1969) finding that while teachers tended to reinforce feminine behavior (more rule-abiding and controlled) in both boys and girls, the children themselves reinforce sex-typed behavior. The boys' perception that they should be bad was thus reinforced in their interactions with each other. Cognitive development may also help explain boys' academic difficulties, dislike of school, and specialization in math and science. They may perceive that certain attitudes and certain areas of expertise (or lack of expertise) are appropriate for boys. Girls may choose to excel in verbal areas and to have better overall grades because they see these as more appropriate for females. The choice of areas as appropriate or inappropriate, however, actually involves definitions of the sex appropriateness of social roles.

Social Roles

It is not surprising that analyzing social roles in order to explain sex-role development provides better insights into the nature of sex differences in achievement than those provided by analyzing biological and psychological influences. Boys' behavioral and learning problems in school and sex differences in achievement may be related to definitions of the masculine role, the nature of school, and the role of student. As children develop definitions of appropriate roles, boys tend to define masculinity as not being feminine, a definition that develops early in life and is reinforced by interactions in later years. As noted earlier, both boys and girls tend to define school and school-related objects as feminine (Kagan, 1964), and this is supported by teachers' views (Fagot & Patterson, 1969). In addition, the good student generally displays behaviors that are sex-typed as feminine in this society. Therefore, since boys are avoiding the behaviors and traits they classify as being feminine, it is understandable that they would like school less than girls do and not try especially hard to conform to the role of the good student. Being a good student could mean being feminine and thus not being a proper boy; and boys' greater incidence of misbehavior in schools might thus result from attempts to show other boys, and reassure themselves, that they are really male. This may also help explain boys' lower grades and greater incidence of learning problems, to the extent that these problems involve a failure or refusal to learn. It is important to realize, however, that on the average, boys' achievement scores usually equal those of girls. It is not correct to say that they generally refuse to learn, only that they may not reveal this learning in the ways usually required for grade rewards in the classroom.

Analysis in terms of social roles can also account for boys' tendency to achieve in math and science and girls' tendency to achieve in more verbal areas. In their sample of sixth graders, Neale, Gill, and Tismer (1970) found that despite the fact that girls had generally more favorable attitudes toward school, the girls did not differ from the boys in their attitudes toward science and mathematics. As children get older, their perceptions of certain academic areas as masculine or feminine become more pronounced. A study of second, sixth and twelfth graders in public schools in New York found that the students' perceptions of artistic, social, and reading skills as feminine and of spatial, mechanical and arithmetic skills as masculine became more definite as the students got older (Stein & Smithells, 1969). Hilton and Berglund (1973) found that the changes in students' mathematical achievement from fifth through eleventh grade paralleled changes in interest. The boys became more interested in mathematics at the same time that they saw it as helpful in their future occupational lives and became more proficient than the girls as shown by achievement scores.

Academic achievement is most influenced by the sex-typed definition of a subject area. In a study of second through twelfth graders, Dwyer (1974) found that a child's perception of an area as appropriate for his or her own sex group influenced achievement more than how much he or she liked the subject or even whether the child was male or female. Boys' achievement was influenced by such sex-typing much more than girls', and boys more often labeled an area as appropriate for only one sex group. This suggests that as boys perceive an area as masculine, they are more apt to achieve in it; if they perceive an area as feminine, they are less apt to achieve (see also Dwyer, 1973). Teachers may contribute to this by communicating cultural definitions of subjects as masculine or feminine. However, in terms of grades, teachers probably do not directly reinforce differences in achievement.

Girls' achievement is not correlated with individuals' interest in an area or with the sex-typed definition of an area as much as boys' achievement is because gender identity is not as fragile or tenuous for girls. An area need not be seen as feminine in order for them to achieve in it. Nevertheless, girls begin to show patterns of underachievement in adolescence, and they choose not to excel in the areas that boys have defined as masculine. Anticipation of their adult roles influences the reaction of young women to their male classmates' definitions of masculine role behavior. As girls enter adolescence they begin to see boys not just as classmates, but also as potential dating and marriage partners. Because they do not want to offend young men, it becomes important to them not to enter male spheres of activity.

Coleman (1961) noted that girls in middle-class schools want to be seen as academically brilliant less often than girls in working-class schools. Middle-class boys and girls of the same age tend to date each other, and both boys and girls are expected to achieve academically and enter college. If a young woman were to encroach on the young men's territory by dramatically upstaging a boy academically, she would fear disastrous social results. In contrast, working-class girls often date boys who are older and not in school. Working-class boys are not expected to achieve as much as middle-class boys academically. Coleman found that boys in working-class schools showed more acceptance of brilliant girls than middle-class boys did. At adolescence, young women realize that their future depends, at least to some extent, on gaining approval from men They also perceive the nature of sex segregation and men's greater power in the adult world. Then, especially among the middle class, they choose not to achieve in the more male-typed areas and also try not to surpass young men excessively in academic achievement. Interestingly enough, some studies suggest that an important influence on a girl's achievement is the approval of men who are "significant others" (Matthews & Tiedeman, 1964), which may involve the attitudes of the father (cf. Johnson, 1963, 1975) or of male friends (cf. Horner, 1972).

Achievement Motivation

A number of researchers, mostly academic psychologists, have explored the possibility that women are not psychologically motivated to achieve. Our interpretation of the multitude of results tends toward a view of achievement motivation in terms of social roles.

The classic work in the field was done over 20 years ago by McClelland, Atkinson, Clark, and Lowell (1953). Most of their studies were of men, but a few included women. They tried to measure achievement motivation with a projective test, showing subjects a picture, asking them to tell a story about it, and then counting the number of achievement related themes in the story. Usually, boys were shown pictures of boys, and girls were shown pictures of girls. Sometimes the picture was shown in arousal situations supposedly designed to make the subjects want to achieve even more. The arousal situation usually involved asking subjects to do tasks that they were told measured their leadership potential. Maccoby and Jacklin (1974, p. 138) summarized the results of these early studies. When shown pictures with males, females in high school and college showed a high level of achievement imagery whether or not it was an arousal situation. Males tended to show high levels of achievement imagery only when shown pictures of males under arousal conditions. Because many studies only showed pictures with same-sex figures, it was once thought that women showed less achievement imagery than men. Yet neither sex group showed as much achievement imagery when asked to tell stories about pictures with females.

McClelland's original research prompted many other studies and further conceptual distinctions. Atkinson (1957; see also Atkinson & Feather, 1966; Atkinson & Raynor, 1974) introduced the idea that a person's hope of success and fear of failure both contribute to a motive to achieve. This then inspired research on the expectancies of people for success. Crandall (1969) found that females tend to have lower initial expectancies than males and that relative to their actual ability, males tend to overestimate and females to underestimate the probability of success. There is evidence, however, that girls both expect to and actually do better at tasks defined as feminine and boys likewise with tasks defined as masculine, even when the content of the task remains unchanged (Frieze, 1975).

Veroff (1977) explored the different ways people cognitively define and experience achievement, or successful accomplishments. Essentially he suggests that males tend to emphasize the impact of their achievement, including what it accomplished and how it compared to the work of others, while women emphasize the process of achievement, including whether or not they accomplished a task alone and if they tried as hard as they could. From a study of adult men and women, Veroff et al. (1975) found that women tend to have lower "assertive competence motivation" than men—a measure related to concern with the power and impact of the achievement—but women also have a higher hope of success and a lower fear of failure. Veroff concluded that women may be less likely to structure a situation in terms of achievement, but that once they are in an achievement setting, they are more likely than men to anticipate success. He suggested that these results differed from Crandall's earlier findings that women had lower expectancies because Crandall used real life settings and Veroff used projective measures, thus controlling for the impact of social desirability in subjects' responses. Hoffman (1972) followed the trend of Veroff's work by suggesting that females tend to achieve in order to attain social approval or satisfy needs for affiliation, while males are motivated to strive for excellence in achievement apart from social approval.

Stein and Baily (1975) suggest that these interpretations ignore "cultural definitions of feminine activities and interests." They note that "the primary area of feminine skill, within the traditional bounds of femininity, is social *skill* (1975, p. 152, italics in original) and that for women, social situations are often achievement situations. They suggest that Hoffman, Crandall, and Veroff have mistaken actual achievement through social skills for needs for affiliation. As support for their position, they cite studies showing that women and not men increased achievement imagery and not affiliation imagery with arousal treatments that stressed social acceptability and social skill. This was especially true for women who valued women's traditional roles. Also, females are not more responsive than males to social approval when the task is nonsocial, as Stein and Baily have pointed out (1975, pp. 152–155). They conclude that females "express achievement motivation in activities that are culturally defined as feminine. In effect they resolve the conflict between achievement motivation as usually defined and prescriptions for the feminine role by translating achievement motivation into a feminine context (p. 153)." In other words, they suggest that women may deal with conflicts regarding achievement by staying only within traditional female areas or by redefining an achievement activity as feminine (see also Stockard & Johnson, 1980).

Horner (1968, 1970, 1972) and others have expanded Atkinson's work on expectancies to explore what Horner calls "the motive to avoid success." Horner devised a technique to tap women's conflicts regarding success, hypothesizing that women would want to do well, but not necessarily to upstage men in the process. She asked subjects to write stories about members of their own sex who were described as being successful in traditionally male areas and then used the number of unpleasant themes in these stories as a measure of the subjects' motive to avoid success. While the preliminary studies showed that females indeed showed much more of the motive to avoid success than males did, later studies have not corroborated these findings. Tresemer (1977) reviewed these many studies and concluded that females generally do not show a higher motive to avoid success than males do. He also concluded that there was not enough evidence yet to show any clear link between imagery that indicates a motive to avoid success and actual behavior.

There is evidence, however, that both males and females tend to give more negative responses to projective stimuli regarding women, and fewer negative responses to stimuli regarding men (Alper, 1974; Feather & Raphelson, 1974; Monahan, Kuhn, & Shaver, 1974; Robbins & Robbins, 1973, all cited in Condry & Dyer, 1976). Condry and Dyer (1976) suggest that the negative expectations concerning the consequences of success that Horner and others interpret as a psychological "motive to avoid success" are actually realistic interpretations of the experiences women have in settings that are generally defined as masculine. Both males and females realize that by violating traditional sex-role expectations, females may face negative reactions. In support of this interpretation, detailed analyses of fear-of-success stories showed that males tended to write stories with negative consequences stemming from achievement because they tended to question the value of success itself, while females' stories regarding negative consequences has especially to do with expectations of negative sanctions from other people (Hoffman, 1974; see also Schnitzer, 1977).

In general, then, the results of the many studies of achievement motivation suggest not that males and females differ in their psychological motives to achieve or to avoid success, but that both groups understand that the social-role expectations for males are different from those for females. Both groups generally show higher achievement motivation and lower motivation to avoid success when the stimulus figure is a male rather than a female. If in the stimulus activity involved there is a cultural expectation for females to achieve, both groups would be expected to show higher achievement motivation and lower motivation to avoid success for the female stimulus figure. These studies suggest that different achievement patterns for the two groups result less from differences in psychological traits and motives and more from differences in social roles.

Social Systems

It is doubtful that sex segregated occupations and the differing values placed on work directly influence the tendency of boys to get into trouble in school or their greater incidence of learning problems or their lower grades. These may influence patterns of achievement, however, and the greater rewards to adult males for increased education. As noted earlier, academic areas in which boys and girls specialize as they grow older correspond to the patterns of sex segregation in the occupational force. Some patterns of achievement are influenced by different skill levels and, of course, by interactions among students regarding role definitions; yet certain areas are perceived as masculine or feminine because they are sex-typed in the adult occupational arena. If most physicists were women, we would predict that boys would avoid this field and girls would enter it. In much of Europe, medical fields are stereotyped as female, and women are much more often found preparing in school for occupations in these areas. Interestingly enough, however, medicine is less rewarded monetarily and has less prestige in these countries than in the United States (Galenson, 1973).

EFFECTS OF SEX TYPING IN CURRICULAR MATERIALS

As was pointed out earlier, women are generally underrepresented and misrepresented in school textbooks and testing materials. To the extent that women are typed as nurturant and motherly, biology may be the basis of some stereotypes. Social institutions also have influence, to the extent that stereotypes reflect actual role divisions within social institutions; but how stereotypes influence young people can best be explained from the view of academic psychology and the analysis of social roles.

Stereotypes in communications media should be seen as "symbolic representations of American society . . . not [as] literal portrayals [Tuchman, 1978, p. 8]." In this sense, female roles represent societal expectations of sex segregation and the general cultural devaluation of women and their roles, even though women's actual roles are usually essential to the maintenance of the society, even if they go unrecognized.

Modeling theory is most often used to analyze the impact on children of stereotypes in curricular materials. It is suggested that children will attend to and copy the attitudes of characters in books and other materials. From a cognitive developmental approach, it could be suggested that children use characters in these media to develop their own views of what masculinity and femininity involve. In some support of these theories, studies of television viewers have shown that viewers watch members of their own sex group more closely than they watch members of the other sex (Maccoby & Wilson, 1957; Miller & Reeves, 1976; Sprafkin & Liebert, 1978).

The perspective of symbolic interaction can also be used to analyze the impact of curricular materials. If the materials provide symbolic representations of cultural expectations, they help define what is expected, what "should be done." If only boys are used in math examples, for instance, this might suggest that only boys should do math. If women are only depicted in a few occupations and men are shown in many more, this suggests sex segregation in occupations. An anecdote illustrates this: A sixth-grade girl once was doing her math homework which consisted of ten story problems. Suddenly, she threw her book down in disgust. When asked what was wrong, she reported, "I'm not supposed to be able to do these problems. Of the ten problems, eight of them are about boys and the two girls are stupid!" None of the characters in her math text were people with whom she wanted to identify.

Research evidence, mainly regarding television's effect on violent behavior, does suggest that representations in the media influence people's attitudes and behavior. Apparently both antisocial and prosocial behavior influence children's actions. Television can also influence racial attitudes and cultural views (see Sprafkin & Liebert, 1978, p. 232 for a short summary). Televised portrayals of occupational and play roles may influence children's definitions of the sexual appropriateness of those activities. Less sex-typed portrayals on television bring about a greater willingness to accept these roles as possible in reality (Atkin, 1975). For instance, in a study of the reaction of preschool children to materials concerning careers, one group was given stories with traditional occupational titles, such as fireman and mailman, and one group was given stories with non-sex-typed labels, such as firefighter and mail carrier. After the exposure to the materials, the children were asked to draw pictures. The group exposed to non-sex-typed titles drew more pictures of women in the occupational roles than the other group did (Lord, 1977).

Despite the attention given to the sex typical characters portrayed in the communications media, it is still unclear exactly what it is that children are modeling. In an interesting and unique study that attempted to clarify this, Quattelbaum (1977) explored the characteristics of the television characters that adolescents consciously model. Over half of the students in her sample reported that they modeled and would like to be similar to certain television characters when they grew up. The boys mentioned 13 different characters, with Starsky (of "Starsky and Hutch") receiving the most votes. The girls identified 16 different characters, with Mary Richards (Mary Tyler Moore) being the most popular choice. When asked what they liked most about these characters, subjects generally cited positive and prosocial traits. Boys most often cited the ability to "care for people." Girls cited a character's "independence," "ability to care for people," and the fact that the character had a career. We suspect that young people might also want to emulate characters in stories they read, although we know of no specific studies in this area. Adolescent girls would probably admire Sue Barton, student nurse; Nancy Drew, girl detective; and Jo, from *Little Women*. They are all capable, active and caring women—not unlike the Mary Richards the girls in Quattelbaum's sample wished to model. Similarly, adolescent boys might want to model Joe and Frank Hardy or Tom Sawyer. Yet many male fictional characters also fit the classic "badboy" image—for example, Huck Finn—and this image is closer to the "Starsky and Hutch" portrayals (cf. Fiedler, 1968).

In general, sex stereotypes in curricular materials may be an exaggerated reflection of the sex segregation and differing values placed on men's and women's activities in reality. Although there is probably too little evidence for firm conclusions, media representations may influence young people's perceptions of expected behavior by helping to define appropriate male and female roles. Concerted efforts have been made by concerned feminists, parents, teachers, and publishers to curb the sexual stereotypes in curricular material. Obviously, however, a major step in eliminating the basis for these representational stereotypes in the first place would be to minimize the differences between valuations of males and females that really exist in the society.

SEX SEGREGATION IN EDUCATION

Sex segregation from educational institutions, which occurs mainly on the highest levels of education, and sex segregation within schools in curricular and extracurricular areas are supported by laws, traditional customs, and informal norms. While biological factors may influence patterns in early child care, it is doubtful that they have much impact on the varied and elaborate patterns of sex segregation found in education and in the occupational world. The causes of sex segregation may be better understood by examining factors in social institutions and in sex-role development.

All boys and girls face the limits imposed by classifications of social status, race, and ethnicity; yet, within each grouping by racial, ethnic, and status factors, women hold positions that are different from those held by men. For instance, while upper-middle class boys are becoming doctors and lawyers, their sisters are probably becoming teachers, social workers, wives, and mothers. Similarly, working-class men enter skilled trades while their sisters probably fill clerical and service positions. Since the sex segregation in education reflects that in the occupational world and in the family, women are excluded from certain areas in vocational training. Women enroll in home economics classes, and men in mechanics and shop classes, because students will assume the roles associated with these classes in the family by adulthood. Men often avoid classes in the humanities in favor of those in math and science. This corresponds to sex segregation in the adult occupational world. Because schools are a connecting institution between the family and the adult world, factors in the economy and in the family influence the sex segregation found in education. In turn, factors in the educational sphere reinforce and help perpetuate sex segregation in occupations and in the family. Because women are not trained for male-dominated occupations, the sex segregation in the occupational force persists. Because the jobs for which women are trained do not pay as much as the jobs men can get, men's greater authority in the family is reinforced (see Stockard & Johnson, 1980). Patterns of sex segregation and discrimination in the family, in education, and in the economy are mutually supportive.

Sex discrimination in admissions, scholarship aid, and other school policies, especially apparent in higher education, also reflect the economy and the family. Women and their work are less valued than men; it is often assumed that only men will *need* to work or *need* their education. Women's education may be seen as more expendable when choices must be made; both families and schools then give lower priority to women's needs than they give to men's.

THE POSSIBILITY OF CHANGE

A key to sex differences in school achievement and behavior patterns is boys' definition of the male role as "not feminine." Because children tend to see school and the role of "good student" as feminine, boys try to find ways not to identify themselves with that role. Some aspects of academic achievement are identified by individuals and by the sexual segregation of related occupations as being more masculine than others, and so males do tend to achieve more in those areas. As girls grow older they recognize boys' definitions of these areas as masculine. Although they do not have the same compulsive need as boys to avoid certain areas, their futures often depend on alliances with men and so they tend to avoid achievement that would directly compete with them. This explanation also underlies much of the segregation of the curriculum and perhaps, albeit more indirectly, the segregation and devaluation of women found in curricular materials.

Much evidence indicates that it would be extremely hard to alter boys' definition of masculinity by simply changing the nature of the school. This self-definition develops very early, largely through interactions in the home and with other children. The sex-typed behaviors that young children display are continually reinforced in their interactions with each other. After years of studying interactions of young children,

Fagot (1978b) suggests that there probably is little teachers can do to change children's sex-typed behavior and play patterns unless they are actually to get down on the floor and actively intervene in their play. It is doubtful that many teachers would really want to do this or that school systems would support such intervention. Even if they would, Fagot suggests that based on previous experience with experimental intervention in other areas, it is doubtful that intervention would have any long-lasting effects.

Obviously, many boys do achieve in school. We suspect this occurs because their own definitions of the male role do not exclude academic success. As we saw earlier, this is especially true of middle-class students. We suspect that definitions by fathers and other significant males of how masculinity relates to a student's role and success influence boys' attitudes. Boys who perceive other males' belief that academic success is important more often accept that belief themselves. Yet even within the middle class, sex differences appear in achievement, and these may stem from general cultural definitions of school as feminine. The fact that having a man for a teacher does not increase young boys' reading achievement in this country (Asher & Gootman, 1973; Brophy & Good, 1973) indicates the impact of cultural definitions, even when they are directly countered by the expectations and the model of the teacher.

Although it may be hard to change boys' definitions of the male role by changes within the school, cross-cultural evidence suggests that the patterns of sex differences in achievement found in the United States are not universal. As mentioned in Chapter 2, German fourth- and sixth-grade boys had higher scores on reading achievement tests than girls (Preston, 1962); and among second, fourth and sixth graders in the United States, Canada, England, and Nigeria, all English-speaking, girls had higher scores in the United States and Canada while boys tended to have higher scores in England and Nigeria (Johnson, 1973–1974). Among these countries, men are elementary teachers more often in England, Nigeria, and Germany—the countries where boys excelled. More importantly, however, academic success is not considered "sissyish" in these countries; it is culturally defined as a valued male area of endeavor.

If sex differences in academic achievement are to lessen, it will be necessary to alter the cultural definitions of academic achievement and the male self-definition, which involves a compulsive need to avoid feminine roles. We suggest that the best way to do this is to lessen the sex-typed definition of school and academic achievement in general (cf. Dwyer, 1974). To diminish or eliminate sex-typing in curricular materials, sex segregation, and inequities in access to education, it will probably be necessary to change other social institutions as well. Inequities in education reflect those in the general culture, the economy, and the family; and social roles and cultural definitions of masculinity and femininity must be altered. Specifically, changes must be made in the familial patterns of child rearing that promote men's motive to dominate women and to preserve sex segregation (see Hunt, 1977; Stockard & Johnson, 1979, 1980).

REFERENCES

Alper, T. G. (1974). "Achievement Motivation in College Women: A Now-You-See-It-Now-You-Don't Phenomenon." *American Psychologist*, 29:194–203.

Asher, S. R., and Gootman, J. M. (1973). "Sex of Teacher and Student Reading Achievement." *Journal of Educational Psychology*, 65:168–171.

Atkin, C. K. (1975). *The Effects of Television Advertising on Children: Second Year Experimental Evidence*. Report submitted to the Office of Child Development, Washington, D.C.

Atkinson, J. W. (1957). "Motivational Determinants of Risk-Taking Behavior." *Psychological Review*, 64:359–372.

Atkinson, J. W., and Feather, N. T., eds. (1966). *A Theory of Achievement Motivation*. Wiley, New York.

Atkinson, J. W., and Raynor, J. O., eds. (1974). *Motivation and Achievement*. Winston, Washington, D.C.

Barfield, A. (1976). "Biological Influences on Sex Differences in Behavior." In *Sex Differences: Social and Biological Perspectives* (M. Teitelbaum, ed.). Doubleday (Anchor Books) Garden City, N.Y.

Birns, B. (1976). "The Emergence and Socialization of Sex Differences in the Earliest Years." *Merrill-Palmer Quarterly*, 22:229–254.

Block, J. (1973). "Conceptions of Sex Role: Some Cross-Cultural and Longitudinal Perspectives." *American Psychologist*, 28:512–526.

Blumer, H. (1969). *Symbolic Interactionism: Perspective and Method*. Prentice-Hall, Englewood Cliffs, N.J.

Brophy, J., and Good, T. (1973). "Feminization of American Elementary Schools." *Phi Delta Kappan*, 54:564–566.

Carter, R. S. (1952). "How Invalid are Marks Assigned by Teachers?" *Journal of Educational Psychology*, 43:218–228.

Chodorow, N. (1974). "Family Structure and Feminine Personality." In *Woman, Culture and Society* (M. Rosaldo and L. Lamphere, eds.). Stanford University Press, pp. 43–66.

Coleman, J. S. (1961). *The Adolescent Society*. Free Press, New York.

Condry, J., and Dyer, S. (1976). "Fear of Success: Attribution of Cause to the Victim." *Journal of Social Issues*, 32(No.3):63–83.

Conner, J. M., Schackman, M., and Serbin, L. (1978). "Sex Related Differences in Response to Practice on a Visual-Spatial Test and Generalization to a Related Test." *Child Development*, 49:240–249.

Conner, J. M., and Serbin, L. (1977). "Behaviorally Based Masculine- and Feminine-Activity-Preference Scales for Preschoolers: Correlates with other Classroom Behaviors and Cognitive Tests." *Child Development*, 47:1411–1416.

Crandall, V. C. (1969). "Sex Differences in Expectancy of Intellectual and Academic Reinforcement." In *Achievement Related Motives in Children* (C. P. Smith, ed.). Russell Sage Foundation, New York.

Cruickshank, W. M. (1977). *Learning Disabilities in Home, School and Community.* Syracuse University Press.

Dwyer, C. A. (1973). "Sex Differences in Reading: An Evaluation and a Critique of Current Theories." *Review of Educational Research,* 43:455–467.

Dwyer, C. A. (1974). "Influences of Children's Sex Role Standards on Reading and Arithmetic Achievement." *Journal of Educational Psychology,* 66:811–816.

Epstein, C. F. (1970). "Encountering the Male Establishment: Sex Status Limits on Women's Careers in the Professions," *American Journal of Sociology,* 75:965–982.

Fagot, B. (1978a). "The Influence of Sex of Child on Parental Reactions to Toddler Children." *Child Development,* 49:459–465. vol. 4.

Fagot, B. (1978b). "The Socialization of Sex Differences in Early Childhood." Presentation at annual meeting of Oregon Psychological Association, Eugene, Oregon.

Fagot, B., and Patterson, G. (1969). "An In Vivo Analysis of Reinforcing Contingencies for Sex Role Behaviors in the Preschool Child." *Developmental Psychology,* 1:563–568.

Feather, N. T., and Raphelson, A. C. (1974). "Fear of Success in Australian and American Student-Groups: Motive of Sex-Role Stereotypes?" *Journal of Personality,* 42:190–201.

Fiedler, L. A. (1968). *The Return of the Vanishing American.* Stein and Day, New York.

Frieze, I. H. (1975). "Women's Expectations for and Causal Attributions of Success and Failure." In *Women and Achievement: Social and Motivational Analyses* (M. Mednick et al., eds.). Hemisphere, Washington, D.C., pp. 158–171.

Fruch, T., and McGhee, P. E. (1975). "Traditional Sex Role Development and Amount of Time Spent Watching Television." *Developmental Psychology,* 11:109.

Galenson, M. (1973). *Women and Work: An International Comparison.* Publications Division, New York School of Industrial Labor Relations, Cornell University, New York.

Goleman, D. (1978). "Special Abilities of the Sexes: Do They Begin in the Brain?" *Psychology Today,* 12:48–59, 120.

Guttentag, M., and Bray, H. (1977). "Teachers as Mediators of Sex-Role Standards." In *Beyond Sex Roles* (A. G. Sargent, ed.). West, St. Paul, Minn.

Henley, N. (1977). *Body Politics: Power, Sex and Non-Verbal Communication.* Prentice-Hall, Englewood Cliffs, N.J.

Hetherington, E. M. (1965). "A Developmental Study of the Effects of Sex of the Dominant Parent on Sex Role Preference, Identification and Imitation in Children." *Journal of Personality and Social Psychology,* 2:188–194.

Heuser, L. (1977). *Sex Typing in Daycare: A Preliminary View.* Paper presented at the annual meetings of the Pacific Sociological Association, April, Sacramento, Calif.

Hilton, T. L., and Berglund, G. (1973). "Sex Differences in Mathematics Achievement—A Longitudinal Study." *Journal of Educational Research,* 67:231–237.

Hinde, R. A. (1972). *Social Behavior and Its Development in Subhuman Primates.* State System of Higher Education, Eugene, Oreg.

Hoffman, L. W. (1972). "Early Childhood Experiences and Women's Achievement Motives." *Journal of Social Issues,* 28:129–155.

Hoffman, L. W. (1974). "Fear of Success in Males and Females: 1965 and 1971." *Journal of Consulting and Clinical Psychology,* 42:353–358. (Reprinted in *Women and Achievement,* M. Mednick et al., eds.), (1975) Hemisphere, Washington, D.C., pp. 221–230.)

Horner, M. S. (1968). *Sex Differences in Achievement Motivation and Preference in Competitive and Non-competitive Situations.* Unpublished doctoral dissertation, University of Michigan.

Horner, M. S. (1970). "Femininity and Successful Achievement: A Basic Inconsistency." In *Feminine Personality and Conflict* (J. Bardwick et al., eds.). Brooks-Cole, Belmont, Calif.

Horner, M. S. (1972). "Toward an Understanding of Achievement-Related Conflicts in Women." *Journal of Social Issues*, 28:157–175.

Hunt, J. G. (1977). *Sex Stratification and Male Biography: From Deprivation to Ascendance.* Paper presented at the annual meeting of the American Sociological Association, Chicago.

Johnson, D. D. (1973–1974). "Sex Differences in Reading Across Culture." *Reading Research Quarterly*, 9:67–86.

Johnson, M. M. (1963). "Sex-Role Learning in the Nuclear Family." *Child Development*, 34:319–333.

Johnson, M. M. (1975). "Fathers, Mothers, and Sex-typing." *Sociological Inquiry*, 45:15–26.

Kagan, J. (1964). "The Child's Sex Role Classification of School Objects." *Child Development*, 35:1051–1056.

Kohlberg, L. (1966). "A Cognitive-Developmental Analysis of Children's Sex-Role Concepts and Attitudes." In *The Development of Sex Differences* (E. Maccoby, ed.). Stanford University Press.

Lambert, H. H. (1978). "Biology and Equality: A Perspective on Sex Differences." *Signs*, 4:97–117.

Lancaster, J. B. (1976). "Sex Roles in Primate Societies." In *Sex Differences: Social and Biological Perspectives* (M. Teitelbaum, ed.). Doubleday (Anchor Books,) Garden City, N.Y., pp. 22–61.

Lindgren, H. C. (1976). *Educational Psychology in the Classroom*, 5th ed. Wiley, New York.

Lord, F. E. (1941). "A Study of Spatial Orientation in Children." *Journal of Educational Research*, 34:481–505.

Maccoby, E. E., and Jacklin, C. (1974). *The Psychology of Sex Differences*. Stanford University Press.

Maccoby, E. E., and Wilson, W. C. (1957). "Identification and Observational Learning from Films." *Journal of Abnormal and Social Psychology*, 55:76–87.

Martin, W. (1972). *The American Sisterhood*. Harper & Row, New York.

Matthews, E., and Tiedeman, D. V. (1964). "Attitudes Toward Career and Marriage and the Development of Life Styles in Young Women." *Journal of Counseling Psychology*. 11:375–383.

McClelland, D. C., Atkinson, J. W., Clark, R. A., and Lowell, E. L. (1953). *The Achievement Motive*. Prentice-Hall (Appleton), Englewood Cliffs, N.J.

Mead, G. H. (1934). *Mind, Self and Society*. University of Chicago Press.

Miller, M. M., and Reeves, B. (1976). "Dramatic TV Content and Children's Sex-Role Stereotypes." *Journal of Broadcasting*, 20:35–50.

Monahan, L., Kuhn, D., and Shaver, P. (1974). "Intrapsychic versus Cultural Explanations of the 'Fear of Success' Motive." *Journal of Personality and Social Psychology*, 29:60–64.

Neale, D. C., Gill, N., and Tismer, W. (1970). "Relationship Between Attitudes toward School Subjects and School Achievement." *Journal of Educational Research*, 63:232–237.

Parsons, T. (1954a). "Age and Sex in the Social Structure of the United States." In *Essays in Sociological Theory*, rev. ed. (T. Parsons, ed.). Free Press, New York.

Parsons, T. (1954b). "Certain Primary Sources and Patterns of Aggression in the Social Structure of the Western World." In *Essays in Sociological Theory*, rev. ed. (T. Parsons, ed.). Free Press, New York.

Parsons, T. (1955). *Family, Socialization and Interaction Process*. Free Press, New York.

Parsons, T. (1970). *Social Structure and Personality*. Free Press, New York.

Preston, R. C. (1962). "Reading Achievement of German and American Children." *School and Society*, 90:350–354.

Quattelbaum, C. (1977). *Perceived Television Model Attributes and Consequent Modeling Behavior as Described by the Viewer.*" Unpublished M.A. paper, University of Oregon.

Robbins, L., and Robbins, E. (1973). "Comment on 'Toward an Understanding of Achievement-Related Conflicts in Women' by Matina A. Horner." *Journal of Social Issues*, 29:133–137.

Rosenberg, F. R., and Simmons, R. A. (1975). "Sex Differences in Self-Concept in Adolescence." *Sex Roles*, 1:147–159.

Schnitzer, P. K. (1977). "The Motive to Avoid Success: Explaining the Nature of the Fear." *Psychology of Women Quarterly*, 1:273.

Scott, J. F. (1971). *Internalization of Norms: A Sociological Theory of Moral Commitment.* Prentice-Hall, Englewood Cliffs, N.J.

Sears, P., and Feldman, D. (1966). "Teachers Interactions with Boys and with Girls." *National Elementary Principal*, 46(No.2):30–35.

Serbin, L. A., O'Leary, K. D., Kent, R. N., and Tonick, I. J. (1973). "A Comparison of Teacher Response to the Pre-Academic and Problem Behavior of Boys and Girls." *Child Development*, 44:796–804.

Sprafkin, J., and Liebert, R. (1978). "Sex-Typing and Children's Television Preferences." In *Hearth and Home: Images of Women in the Mass Media* (G. Tuchman et al., eds.). Oxford University Press, New York.

Stein, A., and Bailey, M. (1975). "The Socialization of Achievement Motivation in Females." In *Women and Achievement* (M. Mednick *et al.*, eds). Hemisphere, Washington, D.C.

Stein, A., and Smithells, J. (1969). "Age and Sex Differences in Children's Sex-Role Standards about Achievement." *Developmental Psychology*, 1:252–259.

Stockard, J., and Johnson, M. (1979). "The Social Origins of Male Dominance." *Sex Roles*, 5:199–218.

Stockard, J., and Johnson, M. (1980). *Sex Roles: Sex Inequality and Sex Role Development*, Prentice-Hall, Englewood Cliffs, N.J.

Taylor, S. P., and Epstein, S. (1967). "Aggression as a Function of the Interaction of the Sex of the Aggressor and the Sex of the Victim." *Journal of Personality*, 35:474–496.

Tresemer, D. W. (1977). *Fear of Success.* Plenum, New York.

Tuchman, G. (1978). "The Symbolic Annihilation of Women by the Mass Media." In *Hearth and Home: Images of Women in the Mass Media.* Tuchman, G., Daniels, A. K., and Benet, J., (eds). Oxford University Press, New York.

Veroff, J. (1977). "Process vs. Impact in Men's and Women's Achievement Motivation." *Psychology of Women Quarterly*, 1:283–293.

Veroff, J., McClelland, L., and Ruhlard, D. (1975). "Varieties of Achievement Motivation." In *Women and Achievement* (M. Mednick et al., eds.). Hemisphere, Washington, D.C.

Chapter 4

DIFFERENTIATION BY SEX IN EDUCATIONAL PROFESSIONS

Patricia A. Schmuck

If there's nothing more powerful than an idea whose time has come, there is nothing more ubiquitously pervasive than an idea whose time won't go. The division of the world by sexes, challenged a century ago by the militants of the first wave of Feminism, still endures and, what's more, still prevails, in spite of new attacks on it. "Man's world" and "woman's place" have confronted each other since Scylla first faced Charybdis. . . . Every society has formed a set of conclusions and prescriptions for proper behavior on sex differences. Ours still does, and they are still far-reaching and deeply bound in the sense of identity carried by everyone [Janeway, 1971, p. 2].

In all known cultures an individual's life has been charted to some degree at the momentous union of the ovum and sperm. One becomes a male or a female, and all cultures have designated certain spheres to women and other spheres to men. All cultures do not ascribe the same roles, experiences, tasks, or rewards to each sex in consistently the same manner; yet as Jessie Bernard (1976) points out, the segregation of the sexes is an ancient, if not necessarily honorable, custom. In *Sex and Temperament in Three Primitive Societies* (1935, p. 11) Margaret Mead wrote: "Three primitive societies have grouped their social attitudes toward temperament about the very obvious facts of sex-difference. . . . Our own society makes great use of this plot. It assigns different roles to the two sexes, surrounds them from birth with an expectation of different behavior, plays out the whole drama of courtship, marriage and parenthood in terms of the types of behavior believed to be innate and therefore appropriate for one sex or the other." Social practices and individual behaviors are governed by laws and social access to opportunities. However, perhaps more important are the customs, traditions, folkways, and norms of a society that are deeply ingrained in all aspects of the culture. Margaret Mead vividly described the bridge between social practices and the psychological temperament of men and women in the three primitive societies as well as in our own. Customs and tradition are deeply ingrained in laws, institutional practices, and psyches of individuals. The reason sex segregation exists is because people believe it *ought* to.

MALES AND FEMALES IN THE LABOR FORCE AND IN EDUCATIONAL POSITIONS

The ratio of male to female workers in the civilian labor force has become more equalized during this century (see Table 4.1). Whereas in 1890, there were 17 women to every 83 men, in 1970 there were 38 women to 62 men. Today, women and men are fairly equitably represented in the labor force; of all working, 53% are male and 47% are female. The greatest change occurred between 1940 and 1970. Between 1940 and 1945 the female labor force expanded by 5.5 million, and 38%

TABLE 4.1
Women in Civilian Labor Force, Selected Years, 1890–1970[a]

Year[b]	Number (in thousands)	As percentage of all workers	As percentage of female population
1890	3,704	17.0	18.2
1900	4,999	18.1	20.0
1920	8,229	20.4	22.7
1930	10,396	21.9	23.6
1940	13,783	25.4	28.6
1945	19,290	36.1	38.1
1947	16,664	27.9	30.8
1950	18,389	29.6	33.9
1955	20,548	31.6	35.7
1960	23,240	33.4	37.7
1965	26,200	35.2	39.2
1970	31,520	38.1	43.3

[a] SOURCES: U.S. Department of Labor Women's Bureau, *1969 Handbook on Women Workers*, p. 10; and U.S. Department of Labor, Manpower Administration, *Manpower Report of the President*, April 1971, pp. 203, 205.
[b] Pre-1940 figures include women 14 years of age and over; figures for 1940 and after include women 16 years of age and over.

of all women 16 years of age and over were working. Although the rates for women's participation in the labor force were never as low as the levels before World War II, the absolute number of women workers surpassed its wartime peak. Participation rates did not regain their 1945 levels until 1961 (Blau, 1975).

In large part, women's increased participation in the labor force comes from the increased demand for their services. The long-range rise in the proportion of women working in this country reflects a rapid growth in the occupations defined as appropriate for women (Oppenheimer, 1968). This means that even with women's increasing representation in the labor force extensive segregation remains.

Using indices of occupational segregation based on the concentration of racial or sex types in one occupation, Blau (1975) concluded that occupational segregation is as severe now as it was in 1900 (if not more so). Gross (as cited in Blau, 1975) determined an index of segregation by looking at the number of job changes needed by women or by blacks to match the occupational distribution of white males. According to his measure, segregation by sex has been even more severe than segregation by race. The index of racial segregation was 46.8%, and that of sex segregation was 68.4%. "Those concerned with sexual segregation as a social problem can take small comfort from these figures. They suggest that the movement of women into the labor market has not meant the disappearance of sexual typing in occupations. Rather, the great expansion in female employment has been accomplished through the expansion of occupations that were already heavily female, through the emergence of wholly new occupations (such as that of keypunch operator) which were defined as female from the start, and through females taking over previously male occupations [Gross, 1968, p. 202]."

Minority women face the issues of race and of sex, a dual negative status (Epstein, 1973; Doughty, 1977). Consequently, black women, as compared to white men, black men, and white women, are more likely to be at the bottom of the administrative structure, to be involuntarily unemployed, to be represented in low-paying jobs, and to account for a larger proportion of the poor. While all women are underemployed and unemployed at a greater rate than their same-race male counterparts, it is especially true for black women. In 1974, the involuntary unemployment rate for black women was 11% as compared to 6% for white women (Barrer, 1976). Because minority women are more often married to men with low-paying jobs, they must work outside the home more often than white women. In 1975, 51% of the married black women with children under the age of 6 were in the labor force, compared with 35% of the married white women with children under 6.

Educational occupations are also characterized by sharply defined male roles and female roles. While there is growing equity in the numbers of each sex employed, their professional status is demarcated by sex. For instance, an analysis of the employment of women and men in Oregon public schools (Schmuck, 1976) found that knowing nothing other than an individual's sex, one could predict with fair accuracy the educational position a person held. Of course, classroom teacher was the most likely position for any person because 85% of Oregon's certified personnel were classroom teachers. However, one could correctly predict that women would be teachers in elementary schools and men would be teachers in junior high or high schools. Predictions became even more accurate with men and women who were not classroom teachers: a woman would probably hold a position in special education and second most often, would be a librarian; a man would probably be an administrator, and if not, he would most likely be in charge of adult professionals in a supervisory capacity. Such sex segregation is of course not unique to Oregon.

POSITIONS IN GOVERNING AND REGULATORY BODIES IN EDUCATION

Men are overrepresented in major decision-making positions in education. This may be seen in federal and state agencies, or departments of education, as well as in local school boards.

Federal and State Agencies

Men hold almost all the high-level decision-making positions in both the United States Office of Education (OE) and the National Institute of Education (NIE) (Fishel & Pottker, 1974). As in the field generally, the majority of civil servants in OE and NIE are women (54% for OE, 59% for NIE). Yet the senior-level civil service ratings are held by men. In January 1974, the average civil service grade for women in OE was GS-7, for men it was GS-12. In NIE, women's average grade was GS-8 and men's was GS-12. In both OE and NIE men constitute the majority of employees from GS-13 to GS-18. There have been some increases recently at the higher levels. Women's representation in positions from GS-16 to 18 rose from 5% in 1972 to 12% in 1974 to 15% in 1976. However, that represents a total of only seven women in 47 positions (Steiger & Szanton, 1977).

At the state level, men are much more often found in leadership positions in state departments of education and on state boards of education. Only 20% of the members of state boards were women in 1972, and in that year, less than 2% were women of those in the top state education posts (chief state school officer and deputy and associate and assistant state superintendents). Of the directors of various areas in 1972, only 8% were women, and 30% of them headed typically female areas, such as library services, home economics education, and school lunch programs (Fishel & Pottker, 1974).

School Boards

In 1916, it was proclaimed by E. Cubberly that "those who did *not* make good school board members were inexperienced young men, unsuccessful men, old men who have retired from business, politicians, saloon keepers, uneducated or ignorant men, men in minor business positions, and women... [Callahan, 1967]." Evidently his viewpoint still prevails. Women members are still a minority on school boards, although their participation has shown some recent gains—in 1926 and 1956 approximately 10%, by 1974, 12%, and in 1976, 18–22% of school board members were women.

It should be noted that women's representation on urban school boards has always been greater than the national figures (National School Boards Association (NSBA), 1974, 1976). Representation is important, primarily because school boards are ultimately responsible for the hiring of administrators who decide, implement, and enforce district policy and also hire other personnel. In many small school districts the board itself hires administrators, and in larger districts screening committees and the superintendent usually make recommendations to the board. Although the influence of school boards on district affairs may be declining (see Ziegler & Tucker, 1979), they have some responsibility for sex inequities in schools.

An article in the *American School Board Journal* in 1977 optimistically highlighted women's increased representation on school boards and stated their belief that the "male-female issue" was no longer important (Doran, 1977). We take issue with such optimism. Female representation is far from equal. In addition, as school bureaucracies grow, a major portion of school boards' activities can become superfluous and irrelevant. Zeigler and Tucker note: "Superintendents usually set agendas for board meetings and load them with trivia—nuts and bolts—problems of administration which neither boards nor interest groups can understand.... Immersed in trivial administrative matters rather than major issues of educational policy, boards do not provide a forum for interest arbitration [1979, p. 19]." Even if women become more equally represented, the diminishing power of school boards in establishing school policy may make their actual impact relatively small, especially as compared with the power of superintendents (who are almost always male).

TEACHING PROFESSIONALS

In this country's early years, most teachers were men; but at the time of the Civil War, as in other times of martial conflict, women moved into the previously male roles. This change was not received with open arms. One superintendent said: "No matter how well qualified, a female teacher could not be employed for the same reason she cannot so well manage a vicious horse or other animal, as a man may do [Heath, 1974, p. 18]." Increased urbanization and the needs for an educated populace, however, required an extensive work force; and a pool of literate, English-speaking women, who were cheaper than men, were available for employment. Ideology gradually shifted from reasoning why *not* to employ a woman to reasoning why a woman *should* be employed. Not only were women cheaper, they were "more nurturant and more amenable to bureaucratic rules and supervision," and the bureaucracy of schools was growing in urban centers. (Strober & Tyack, 1977).

Teaching was a useful activity for young unmarried women; it provided a training ground for their natural destiny as wives and mothers. Women first became teachers in urban areas; rural schools often employed primarily men. In 1870 in urban Washington, D.C. 92% of the teaching force were women; in rural Virginia, 65% were still men (Strober & Tyack, 1977). At the turn of the century, the ratio of women to men in Chicago was 25:1. By 1938 females' numerical supremecy was such an established fact that an entire book was devoted to the school ma'am (Donovan, 1938). Women were almost solely in the elementary school, however, and high school teaching and the management of schools were still primarily the province of men. One major exception was Ella Flagg Young, a superintendent of Chicago schools during tumultuous years (1909–1915). Interestingly enough, it was also in those years that women in Chicago began the unionization movement to provide better educational services for children.

The sex composition of the educational work force began changing again in the middle of the twentieth century, and after World War II, men increasingly joined the ranks. Their increased representation was directly linked to benefits provided by the GI Bill since many might not otherwise have received post-secondary education. In general, there was an increased proportion in the labor force who were college graduates and a relative decline of opportunities in traditionally male professions that required a college education (O'Connor, 1977). As men have continued to enter education, their staying power has also increased. In past years, many men used the field of education as a stepping stone to occupations in business or industry while women educators stayed on in the field. Today, however, it is the opposite; the percentage of men who stay in the profession is greater than the percentage of women [National Education Association (NEA), 1973], and we can expect such a phenomenon to remain with the shrinking job market. Men's increase in the educational work force is represented in Table 4.2.

Elementary School

The increase of men in the profession since World War II is most apparent in the elementary schools. While until 1950 men were rarely more than 10% of all elementary school teachers, their representation has risen since that time (see Table 4.3). The greater representation of men in elementary teaching has been promoted by the American Association of Elementary, Kindergarten-Nursery Educators, which unan-

TABLE 4.2

Percentage of Male Teachers, Librarians, and Other Nonsupervisory Instructional Staff in Elementary Schools in the United States, 1869-1870 to 1973-1974[a]

Year	Percentage
1869–1870	38.7
1879 1880	42.8
1889–1890	34.5
1899–1900	29.9
1909–1910	21.1
1919–1920	14.1
1929–1930	16.6
1939–1940	22.2
1949–1950	21.3
1959–1960	29.0[b]
1969–1970	32.4[b]
1973–1974	33.5[b]

[a] SOURCE: W. V. Grant and C. G. Lind, *Digest of Education Statistics, 1979*, National Center for Education Statistics, Department of Health, Education and Welfare, Washington, D.C., 1979, p. 38.
[b] Estimated by the National Center for Education Statistics.

TABLE 4.3

TABLE 4.3
Men Teachers in Public Elementary Schools[a]

Year[b]	Total number of teachers	Percentage of all teachers who were men
1929–1930	640,957	10.5
1939–1940	575,200	11.7
1949–1950	589,578	9.0
1959–1960	833,772	14.1
1969–1970	1,126,467	15.6
1973–1974	1,175,980	16.7

[a] SOURCE: W. V. Grant and C. G. Lind, *Digest of Education Statistics*, 1979, National Center for Education Statistics, Department of Health, Education and Welfare, Washington, D.C., 1979, p. 11.
[b] Figures for the years before 1959–1960 do not include Alaska and Hawaii.

imously accepted the following resolution in 1975 (Ellenburg, 1975). "The association recognizes the fact that 15% of elementary school teachers are male and believes that your children, especially those brought up without a father in the home, need a male image, [and it] strongly urges the recruitment of more male teachers in elementary classrooms [p. 329]."

Long-standing attitudes that faced women who were moving into male roles had to be met head on. By the 1960s women had become so entrenched that there was a belief that they were superior and males were inappropriate for this role. As McLeod (1967) put it: "Among the mass of half-truths, . . . tales, and misunderstandings that have long clouded the public mind, a share relate to elementary education. One of these "interesting ideas" is that children should be taught by women [because] teaching, like housekeeping, is "women's work [p. 301]." Discussions with male elementary school teachers illustrated their attitude about the prevailing idea that taking care of young children was women's work. "There just seems to be this traditional notion that only women are supposed to be with young children in the developmental phase of 2 to 5 years old," one said. "I'm a man who *loves* working with young children. Some people just don't understand that [Sex Equity in Educational Leadership (SEEL), 1977, p. 1]."

The effort to bring more men into elementary teaching has had some success, and there is sufficient reason to expect a continued growth of their numbers. The shortage of teaching jobs, the dwindling economy, and men's growing consciousness in choosing work they like to do all serve as motivators for their working with young children.

Affirmative action guidelines will also help, and this may not lead to beneficial changes in women's positions. As one disgruntled female elementary school teacher put it: "If this affirmative action stuff continues we can expect to see the day when there are no more women in education. Our school district is applauded for its efforts to reduce sex bias in hiring. They are hiring male elementary teachers by the score. Interestingly enough, however, they are not as successful hiring women high school teachers or women administrators [Schmuck, 1978, p. 1]." In the affirmative action plan of one school district, the following objective was stated: "male staffing in the district is considerable [sic] less than the work force percentage for men in Oregon in the categories of certified and classified"; and the solution was to "seek qualified male applicants for primary teaching positions, when primary positions are available [unpublished files of the Sex Equity in Educational Leadership Project, 1979]."

High School

In 1929–1930, 35% of all public high school teachers were men and 65% were women. Table 4.4 shows that by 1973–1974 this had reversed, 54% being men. Men's increased representation is not coincidental. Teaching in secondary school has been awarded with higher status, prestige, and monetary rewards over the years. Although there appears to be an equitable balance between males and females at the secondary level, there is a clear sex demarcation in subjects taught (see Table 4.5). About two-thirds of the teachers of home economics, foreign languages, business education, and English are women. About two-thirds or more of the teachers of agriculture, industrial arts, science, music, and social

TABLE 4.4
Sex Composition of Public High School Teaching Force 1929 to 1974[a]

Year	Number of teachers	Male (%)	Female (%)
1929–1930	213,306	34.9	65.1
1939–1940	300,277	42.2	57.8
1949–1950	324,093	43.8	56.2
1959–1960	521,186	52.8	47.2
1969–1970	896,786	53.5	46.5
1973–1974	979,468	53.6	46.4

[a] SOURCE: Adapted from W. V. Grant and C. G. Lind, *Digest of Education Statistics,* 1979, National Center for Education Statistics, Department of Health, Education and Welfare, Washington, D.C., 1979, p. 11.

TABLE 4.5
Subjects Taught by Male and Female Teachers in Public Secondary
Schools in the United States in 1971[a]

	Male (%)	Female (%)
Home economics	0	100.0
Foreign language	26.5	73.5
Business education	33.3	66.7
English	35.4	64.6
Health and physical education	45.8	54.2
Art	46.1	53.9
Music	70.4	29.6
Social studies	76.8	23.2
Science	85.3	14.7
Industrial arts	95.4	4.6
Agriculture	100.0	0

[a] SOURCE: Adapted from National Education Association, *Status of the American Public School Teacher, 1970–1971*, Research Report 1972-R3, p. 29.

studies are men. This differentiation by subject matter closely parallels that in the occupational world. Men predominate in pretechnical vocational areas, which are the highest paid in the work force.

Within secondary schools, department heads are usually male. A study in Lexington, Massachusetts, found that although the numbers of men and women junior and senior high teachers were approximately equal, only 3 out of 15 academic departments (20%) were headed by women at the junior high level; and only 2 of 11 departments (18%) were headed by women at the senior high level (Lexington, 1975). Comparable findings have been reported in other school districts (NEA, 1970–1971). College prep classes are similar; chemistry, physics, advanced mathematics are predominated by male students and male teachers. Women who intend to go to college are primarily enrolled in the humanities, social studies, or foreign languages, which are more often taught by women.

ADMINISTRATIVE POSITIONS

The most apparent discrepancy between men's roles and women's roles is in managerial positions in public schools. This is reflected in Table 4.6. Although women represented about 63% of the total number of professionals in education in 1972–1973 in the United States over 99% of the superintendents were men, and the percentages of male princi-

TABLE 4.6

Estimated Percentage Distribution of Full-Time Public School Professional Employees in 1972–1973[a]

	Men	*Women*
Total full-time professional employees	37.2	62.8
Superintendents	99.9	0.1
Deputy and associate superintendents	93.8	6.2
Assistant superintendents	94.7	5.3
Other central-office administrators[b]	65.0	35.0
Senior high principals	98.6	1.4
Junior high principals	97.1	2.9
Elementary principals (including teaching)	80.4	19.6
Assistant principals, all levels	87.5	12.5
School librarians	8.2	91.8
Counselors	53.0	47.0
School nurses	1.4	98.6
Other[c]	49.9	50.1

[a] SOURCE: National Education Association Research Division, *26th Biennial Salary and Staff Survey of Public School Professional Personnel, 1972–1973*, Washington, D.C., 1973, pp. 9–10.

[b] Includes central-office administrator for general administration, finance and school plant, pupil personnel services, instruction administration, and special subject areas.

[c] Includes heads of departments, social workers, visiting teachers, psychologists, and psychometrists.

pals were 98% in the high schools, 97% in the junior high schools, and 80% in the elementary schools (NEA, 1973). While the categories in the national statistics for fall 1976 (Foster & Carpenter) are not as discrete as the 1972 data and direct comparisons are not possible, extensive sex segregation is still apparent (see Table 4.7). Although the 1976 statistics do not provide information on staff positions, the 1972 data indicate that women are represented in positions of staff administrators, such as curriculum coordinators, directors, and supervisors, and in special service departments—positions that provide supportive or coordinating services. As shown in Table 4.6, 65% of the central office staff administrators are men, and 35% women.

Why are women so visible in staff positions but virtually invisible in such line positions as those of superintendents or principals in the public schools? Staff positions often do not involve supervision of adult professionals, which is labelled as a man's job. They are service functions intended to provide resources for teachers. Such positions do not necessarily run contrary to the women's role of helper and facilitator. A study analyzing the different staff functions in Oregon public schools found that when counseling and guidance functions (usually involving direct relations with students) are removed from the

TABLE 4.7
Estimated Percentage Distribution of Full-Time Public School
Employees in 1976[a]

	Male	Female
Superintendents and assistants	94.6	5.4
Principals, assistant principals[b]	87.1	12.9
Classroom teachers	34.0	66.0
Other professionals	31.8	68.2
Teacher aides, interns	6.0	94.0
Office personnel	3.3	96.7
Other nonprofessional	50.3	49.7

[a] B. Foster and J. Carpenter, *Statistics of Public Elementary and Secondary Day Schools*, Department of Health, Education and Welfare, Washington, D.C., 1976, p. 20.
[b] This includes elementary and secondary combined.

staff figures, women's representation decreases. Men actually occupy 85% of the staff positions that involve direct supervision of adult professionals (Schmuck, 1975).

It is interesting to note historical trends regarding women's roles in school management. There has been a decline in the percentages and absolute numbers of women's participation in educational governance. This is especially true for the elementary school principal. In 1928, 55% of the elementary principals were women; in fact, in 1926 the United States Bureau of Education (the forerunner to the Office of Education) published an article called, "The Woman Principal: A Fixture in American Schools" (Gribskov, 1978). She was not a fixture. By 1948 the percentage dropped to 41%; in 1958 it was 38%; in 1968 it was only 22%; and in 1973 it was less than 20% (Pottker and Fishel, 1977 p. 290; Kalvelage, 1978). The vanishing woman principal became the issue, and in 1977 the same agency published an article called, "No Room at the Top," describing the obstacles facing women entering administration (Clement, 1977). The decline in the number of female elementary principals parallels the increase of male elementary teachers and the decrease of school districts resulting from consolidation (from over 100,000 districts in 1945 to less than 17,000 today).

This historical decline may also be seen in other administrative posts. For instance, the staff directory for the Los Angeles School District revealed in 1908 that the district had 84 schools and that half of these had women principals. In 1918 the district had 1 woman among its 7 superintendents, 2 women among its 8 intermediate principals (25%), and 3 women among its 15 high school principals (20%). In 1974 only

31% of the district's 591 elementary and secondary principals were women (186 women, 405 men), and only 3 women were principals of the 49 high schools (6%). Women's participation in Los Angeles remained at about the 30% level in 1976–1977; of the 12 area superintendents, 2 were women; 6 women (11.5%) were principals in the 52 high schools, and 156 women (35.6%) were principals in the 437 elementary schools (Barnes, 1976; Los Angeles Unified School District, 1976–1977).

POSITIONS IN HIGHER EDUCATION

Many fewer women are employed in higher education, as compared with the number in the public schools, but their absence from the higher ranks and the patterns of sex segregation are nevertheless apparent. In 1975–1976, of all the instructional faculty in institutions of higher education, 76% were men and 24% were women; and among the highest rank of full professor, less than 10% were women. Of the associate professors, 17% were women, and of the assistant professors only 29% were women. Most of the women who teach at colleges and universities are at the lowest ranks of instructor and lecturer, positions that often do not even lead to tenure. Within each rank, women faculty earn less than men do (Grant & Lind, 1977).

Sex segregation in higher education follows the patterns noted in secondary schools. Women are more often found in education and the humanities; few women are found in the sciences, in most of the professional fields, and in many of the social sciences. Even in specific academic areas we find extensive sex segregation. Women psychologists are overrepresented in developmental and school psychology and underrepresented in industrial, consumer, and psychopharmacology. Women are more often found as cultural anthropologists and linguists, while men are more often physical anthropologists or archaeologists (Patterson, 1973).

Administration also remains male dominated in higher education, where 6.8% of all college presidents are women—132 as compared with 1808 male presidents. Gribskov (1978) reports that there were 55 women among the 652 university and college presidents in 1928, an 8% representation.

In all the various occupational, administrative, and managerial areas of public education and in related agencies there is extensive sex segregation. Even though women are a majority of teachers, they are generally found in the elementary schools. When they are teaching in secondary schools or in higher education, they are generally found teaching in areas stereotyped as appropriately "female"; When women are in administrative positions, they typically have no line authority over other adult professionals.

COMPARISONS BETWEEN THE VALUE OF MEN'S WORK AND THE VALUE OF WOMEN'S WORK

In 1949, Margaret Mead said that men could hunt, cook, weave, dress dolls, and collect hummingbird wings, and if men did it, such work would be valued. If women do it, such work is devalued. There is a definite and clear pattern by which the value associated with work depends on which sex is doing the work. It even becomes more difficult when we ask people to rank the relative importance of different tasks. Is nursing a sick child more or less valuable than performing surgery? Is passing a district school levy more or less important than passing state legislation guaranteeing equalized financial resources for students? It is impossible to talk about the values of work activities without having some concrete indices of how value is defined. For the following discussion, in which we explore the differences between the value of work that tends to be done by women and the value of work that tends to be done by men, value is used in two ways: value as associated with *prestige* and value as associated with *monetary reward*.

Prestige

In two separate studies, Touhey has found a relationship between the sex of the people in a field of work and its social prestige and desirability. Subjects who were led to expect increased proportions of women practitioners in five typically male professions lowered their ratings of occupational prestige and desirability, while subjects who expected unchanging sex ratios in the professions did not (Touhey, 1974a). Similarly, when proportions of men practitioners were increased in five typically female professions, prestige and desirability increased, but among subjects who expected unchanging ratios, there was no increase (Touhey, 1974b). Touhey concludes that his studies lend considerable support to the hypothesis that occupational prestige and desirability may be directly related to the sex ratio of those in the occupational field. If more males were to become kindergarten teachers, one would expect to see a growing social prestige in that area.

Such a phenomenon has probably occurred in the field of education generally. Education has experienced drastic changes in professional status since World War II. The rising respect and security benefits for public school personnel may be associated with the increase of men in the profession. As one woman said: "We have to give men their quarter. It was when men finally came into education—after World War II—that they were militant enough to get pay raises and make it a respectable profession [Schmuck, 1975, p. 90]."

Value as measured by prestige in education shows some interesting contradictions. On the one hand, teachers are the most important people in the schools; they relate on a day-to-day basis with our nation's most valued resource—our children. They are the most influential adults with respect to students' academic and social growth. Yet the implicit and sometimes explicit messages to teachers are that they are the least valued of the educational personnel. It is interesting to note the restraints that are placed upon teachers. In-service training by "experts," bureaucratic requirements, teacher-proof curriculum materials, and supervision by nonteaching superiors all communicate the value that society and the educational bureaucracy holds for teachers.

Monetary Reward

Large aggregate pay differentials exist between men and women in the labor force. The median income for full-time employment in 1974 was $6,772 for women and $11,835 for men (U.S. Department of Commerce, n.d.). Even with education held constant, aggregated pay differentials for men and women remain (see Table 4.8). At each level of educational attainment, women's median income is significantly lower than men's. The peak discrepancies are at less than 8 years of education and at 4 or more years of college education.

In the field of education, similar discrepancies exist. Based on 1972–1973 figures from the NEA, the average (mean) salary for full-time public school teachers was $10,654 for men and $9,787 for women. In part, the higher average salary is a reflection of the greater proportion of men teaching in secondary schools, where extra earnings are available. The average salary of all teachers increased by 64% from 1959 to 1969. Yet in actual dollars, women's salaries went from $4,009 to $6,236, an increase of $2,227, and men's salaries went from $4,566 to $8,692, an increase of $3,106 (U.S. Bureau of the Census, reported in Kane *et al.*, 1976).

Data on the salaries of men and women administrators are sparse and conflicting. Although women principals, as a group, appear to earn more than men principals, as a group, the mean salary of all women administrators is lower than the mean salary of men administrators.

TABLE 4.8
1974 Median Income of Year-Round, Full-Time Civilian Workers 25 Years Old and Over
as of March of the Following Year[a]

| | Median income in current dollars | | Ratio of |
Educational attainment	Women	Men	women to men
Total of all groups	$7,370	$12,786	.58
Elementary school			
Less than 8 years	5,022	7,912	.63
8 years	5,606	9,891	.57
High school			
1 to 3 years	5,919	11,225	.53
4 years	7,150	12,642	.57
College			
1 to 3 years	8,072	13,718	.59
4 years or more	10,357	17,188	.63

[a] SOURCE: M. Barrer, "Journal of Reprints of Documents Affecting Women." *Today Publications and News Service, Inc.*, Vol. 1, no. 1, 1976, p. 205. Adapted from: U.S. Department of Commerce, Bureau of the Census, *Current Population Reports*, Series P-60, no. 99.

Female principals would earn more than their male counterparts because they assume principal positions later in life and are higher on the salary schedule. Yet women administrators as a whole are more often placed in smaller school districts, which tend to have lower salaries than urban school districts (Kane *et al.*, 1976b).

Within each academic rank, male university and college professors are paid more than females. Statistical analyses indicate that even such variables as degrees earned and records of publications cannot totally account for the differences in income or the tendency for women to be at lower academic ranks (Astin & Bayer, 1973; Patterson, 1973). Extensive statistical analyses show that these salary differences in public education also result from discrimination. Anderson and Murphy (1977) estimated that women educators may lose from $600 to $800 a year because of sex discrimination.

Women within the labor force and in the field of education receive less monetary reward than men even when levels of educational attainment and position title are similar (see Anderson & Murphy, 1977). Such pay differentials are sometimes justified on the basis of the worn-out fiction that men are the heads of households and should be expected to earn more. The fact is that work is a financial necessity for significant numbers of women. Of the women in the labor force in March 1971, 23%

were single, and an additional 19% were widowed, divorced, or separated from their husbands. Of the married women who constituted the remaining 58%, 23% had husbands whose incomes were below $5000. Undoubtedly most of these women, and many whose husbands earned more than $5000, were also working for economic reasons.

While our surge of interest in the role of women in education has clearly been sparked by our realization that women school administrators, like the aardvark, were becoming a vanishing species, we must not overlook the fact that women have *never* held parity with men in the management of our public schools. While women's representation as superintendents and principals has indeed decreased throughout the nation over the last few decades, the fact is that women have always been underrepresented in the management of a field they have dominated at the classroom level since compulsory education began. The reasons for this underrepresentation and decline are explored in the following chapter.

REFERENCES

Anderson, J., and Murphy, N. (1977). "An Empirical Approach to Salary Discrimination: With Case Study of Sex Discrimination in Education." *Educational Research Quarterly,* Spring, 2(1):48–57.

Astin, H., and Bayer, A. (1973). "Sex Discrimination in Academe." In *Academic Women on the Move* (A. S. Rossi and A. Calderwood, eds.). Russell Sage Foundation, New York, pp. 333–338.

Barnes, T. (1976). "America's Forgotten Minority: Women School Administrators." *National Association of Secondary School Principals Bulletin,* April, Reston, Va.

Barrer, M. E. (1976). *Journal of Reprints of Documents Affecting Women.* Today Publications and News Service, Washington, D.C.

Bernard, J. (1976). "Historical and Structural Barriers to Occupational Segregation." In *Women and the Work Place* (M. Blaxall and B. Regan, eds.). University of Chicago Press.

Blau, F. (1975). "Women in the Labor Force: An Overview." In *Women: A Feminist Perspective* (J. Freeman, ed.). Mayfield, Palo Alto, Calif.

Callahan, R. (1967). *Education and the Cult of Efficiency.* University of Chicago Press.

Clement, J. (1977). "No Room at the Top." *American Education,* June, pp. 21–24.

College and University Personnel Association (1977). *Women and Minorities in Administration of Higher Education Institutions: Employment Patterns and Salary Comparisons.* Washington, D.C.

Donovan, F. (1938). *The School Ma'am.* Lippincott, Philadelphia.

Doran, B. (1977). "The Feminist Surge Has Hit the School Boards and They May Never Be the Same Again." *American School Board Journal,* April, pp. 25–27.

Doughty, R. N. (1977). *Training and Hiring of Administrators: Considerations for the Black Woman.* Paper presented at the American Educational Research Association, New York, April.

Ellenburg, F. C. (1975). "Elementary Teachers: Male or Female." *Journal of Teacher Education*, Winter, 26(4):329–334.

Epstein, C. (1973). "Positive Effects of the Multiple Negative: Explaining the Success of Black Professional Women." *American Journal of Sociology*, 78:913–918.

Fishel, A., and Pottker, J. (1974). "Women in Educational Governance: A Statistical Portrait." *Educational Researcher*, 3(7):4–7 July/August.

Foster, B., and Carpenter, J. (1976). *Statistics of Public Elementary and Secondary Day Schools.* Department of HEW, Washington, D.C.

Grant, W. V., and Lind, G. (1977). *Digest of Education Statistics, 1976* ed. National Center for Education Department of Statistics, HEW, Washington, D.C.

Gribskov, M. (1978). *Feminism and the Woman School Administrator.* Unpublished paper, Evergreen State College, Olympia, Washington.

Gross, N. (1968). "Plus ca Change . . .? The Sexual Structure of Occupations Over Time." *Social Problems*, 16:198–208.

Heath, K. (1974). "The Female Equation." *American Education*, November, pp. 2–32.

Janeway, E. (1971). *Man's World, Woman's Place.* Dell, New York.

Kalvelage, J. (1978). *The Decline in Female Elementary Principals Since 1928: Riddles and Clues.* Unpublished paper, Center for Educational Policy and Management, University of Oregon.

Kane, R. D., Frazee, P., and Dee, E. (1976). *Sex Discrimination in Education: A Study of Employment Practices Affecting Professional Personnel;* vol. 1. Department of HEW, Washington, D.C., April.

Lexington, Massachusetts, Citizens Advisory Committee (1975). Reported in Kane et al. (1976), *Sex Discrimination . . . Affecting Personnel.*

Los Angeles Unified School District (1976–1977). *Guide to Schools and Offices.*

McLeod, B. (1967). "Don't Call it Women's Work." *Education*, 87(January):301.

Mead, M. (1935). *Sex and Temperament in Three Primitive Societies.* Monitor Book, New American Library, New York.

Mead, M. (1949). *Male and Female.* New American Library, New York.

National Education Association (1970–1971). *Professional Women in Public Schools.* Washington, D.C.

National Education Association Research Division (1973). *26th Biennial Salary and Staff Survey of Public School Professional Personnel, 1972–1973.* Washington, D.C.

National School Boards Association (1974). *Women on School Boards.* Evanston, Ill.

National School Boards Association (1976). *School Board Poll.* Evanston, Ill., Summer.

O'Connor, J. (1977). *Changes in the Sex Composition of High Status Female Occupations: An Analysis of Teaching, 1950–1970.* Unpublished paper, University of Illinois at Urbana-Champaign.

Oppenheimer, V. K. (1968). "The Sex Labeling of Jobs." *Industrial Relations*, 7:219–234.

Patterson, M. (1973). "Sex Specialization in Academe and the Professions." In *Academic Women on the Move* (A. S. Rossi and A. Calderwood, eds.), Russell Sage Foundation, New York, pp. 313–332.

Pottker, J. and Fishel, A. (eds.) (1977). *Sex Bias in the Schools.* London Associated University Presses.

Schmuck, P. A. (1975). *Sex Differentiation in Public School Administration.* National Council of Administrative Women in Education, Arlington, Virginia.

Schmuck, P. A. (1976). "The Spirit of Title IX: Men's Work and Women's Work in Oregon Public Schools." *Oregon School Study Council*, vol. 20, no. 2, October.

Schmuck, P. A. (1978). Personal correspondence and self-evaluation form of one school district in Oregon. Sex Equity in Educational Leadership Project, Eugene, Oreg.

Sex Equity in Educational Leadership (1977). *The SEEL Report.* Center for Educational Policy and Management, Eugene, Oreg.

Steiger, J., and Szanton, E. (1977). *Women's Participation in Management and Policy Development in the Education Division.* National Advisory Council on Women's Educational Programs, Washington, D.C.

Strober, M., and Tyack, D. (1977). *Sexual Assymmetry in Educational Employment: Male Managers and Female Teachers.* Unpublished paper, Stanford University, Palo Alto, Calif.

Touhey, J. C. (1974a). "Effects of Additional Women Professionals on the Rating of Occupational Prestige and Desirability." *Journal of Personality and Social Psychology,* 29:86–89.

Touhey, J. C. (1974b). "Effects of Men on Prestige and Desirability of Occupations Typically Performed by Women." *Journal of Applied Social Psychology,* 4(4):330–335.

U.S. Department of Commerce (n.d.). *Current Population Reports.* Bureau of the Census, Series P-60, vol. 99, Washington, D.C.

U.S. Department of Commerce (1976). *1960 and 1970 Censuses of Population.* Bureau of the Census, Washington, D.C.

U.S. Department of HEW (n.d.). *Elementary and Secondary School Survey 1959–60 through 1973–74.* National Center for Educational Statistics, Washington, D.C.

U.S. Department of Labor (1969). *Handbook on Women Workers.* Women's Bureau, Washington, D.C.

U.S. Department of Labor (1971). *Manpower Report of the President.* Manpower Administration, Washington, D.C., April.

Zeigler, H., and Tucker, H. (1979). *Final Report of the Responsiveness of Public Schools to Their Clientele.* University of Oregon.

Chapter 5

WHY SEX INEQUITIES EXIST IN THE PROFESSION OF EDUCATION

Jean Stockard

*The question of Woman's Rights is a practical one. The notion has pre-
vailed that it was only an ephermeral idea; that it was but women claiming
the right to smoke cigars in the streets, and to frequent bar-rooms.... We
are told woman has all the rights she wants; and even women, ... I am
ashamed to say, tell us so. They mistake the politeness of men for rights—
seats while men stand in this hall tonight, and their adulations; but these
are mere courtesies. We want rights. The flour merchant, the house build-
er, and the postman charge us no less on account of our sex; but when we
endeavor to earn money to pay all these, then, indeed, we find the difference [Lucy Stone, speech before the National Women's Rights Convention, 1855, in Martin, 1972].*

As we saw in Chapter 4, sex inequities in the profession of education include segregation and differing rewards. Educators work largely
on sex typical levels with women teaching in the lower grades and men
in the upper grades and in colleges and universities. In the upper
grades, women generally teach in certain subject areas, and men teach
in others. Men are administrators much more often than women; and
those women who are in administration are usually concentrated in staff
instead of line positions. Not only are the jobs different, but the jobs
men hold tend to be rewarded with higher wages and prestige than the
jobs women hold. The situation for educators parallels other areas of the
labor force.

In the first section of this chapter, we review the general explanations of sex segregation and discrimination that can be applied to

education, focusing on analyses of the internal labor market and on studies that show how interactions within organizations perpetuate sex discrimination. In the second part of the chapter, we analyze sex discrimination in education specifically, looking at the career patterns of educators and at why those of women differ from those of men.

ANALYSIS OF INTERNAL LABOR MARKETS

Economists often study sex discrimination by looking at the total labor market and at the segregation of women into certain occupations and their lower pay. (See Stockard & Johnson, 1980, for a summary of these views.) The analysis of the internal labor market, however, focuses on specific organizations and on the professions in which people work. As with many theories applied to sex discrimination, this approach was first used to explain the discrimination faced by blacks (Doeringer & Piore, 1971).

The analysis of the internal labor market grew out of the general model of *dual labor markets,* where the market of available jobs and workers is divided into primary and secondary labor markets. The primary labor market is well developed. "Entry is restricted to relatively few lower-level jobs; promotion ladders are long; worker stability is encouraged by high wages, opportunities for advancement, good working conditions, and provisions for job security." In the secondary market, however, "characterized by numerous ports of entry, promotion ladders are short or nonexistent [and] worker stability tends to be discouraged by low wages, little opportunity for advancement, poor working conditions, and little provision for job security [Blau & Jusenius, 1976, p. 196]." It is probable that women, like minorities, are more often found in the secondary market.

Although such a dual labor market would help account for the generally lower wages and fewer promotions of women, it is more suited to analyzing the total economy than to exploring the extensive sex segregation and discrimination that exists within specific professions and work organizations (e.g., differentiation by teaching levels and subject areas and men educators earning more than women).

An analysis of the internal labor market examines sex discrimination within an organization or profession without necessarily examining the total economy. Positions that are filled by recruiting new workers are distinguished from those from outside a firm or profession that are filled by promoting or upgrading workers from sources inside the firm or the field. The filling of positions from inside sources is largely influenced by the administrative apparatus within the firm, the forming of an internal labor market, and competition among those already hired or within the enterprise. In filling educational positions, for example, new teachers come from other areas of work, from other school districts, and from colleges or universities. Administrators and supervisors are almost always former teachers who have been promoted.

An individual's advancement opportunities in the internal labor market are generally determined by a worker's original entry-level job [Blau & Jusenius, 1976]. For instance, women are more often elementary rather than secondary school teachers, and while they might become principals of elementary schools, they rarely become principals of secondary schools. We will see in our discussion of career patterns later in this chapter that school superintendents have often been secondary school principals. Thus, because women usually start out as elementary school teachers, they have little hope of following the usual path to the superintendent's chair. Different entry level positions in occupational areas and firms are linked with different career lines, and because women's entry positions differ from those of men, it is entirely possible that women will continue to hold different jobs and receive different wages.

As noted earlier, women are a majority of the professional workers in education, and yet men predominate in the administrative ranks. Such a discrepancy is not unusual in professions with a majority of women. Men are disproportionately found in the more prestigious special areas and administrative ranks of nursing, teaching, social work, and librarianship, especially as more of their numbers enter these professions. Apparently, as the administrative component of a field expands, more men enter the occupation, and they dominate the administrative areas even more than before (Grimm, 1978; Grimm & Stern, 1974). Even when women are hired into starting positions that would lead to the higher posts usually held by men, they rarely are advanced. A study of several large noneducational organizations found that while different companies use different means of preventing women's advancement, the end result is always the same. Whether women were promoted less often than men or were not given similar wage advances or started their careers in job categories that were different from those of men, the end result was that men's jobs were more prestigeful and demanded higher wages (Cassell, Director, & Doctors, 1975; see also Malkiel & Malkiel, 1973). Even women who are hired as secondary school teachers probably do not become principals; they are promoted to positions "more appropriate" for women (and lower paying), such as those of department heads and curriculum coordinators. Studies of organizations help us understand more about such processes.

STUDIES OF ORGANIZATIONAL PRACTICES

Studies of organizational practices help specify how sex discrimination affects patterns of promotion and work experiences. A good deal of evidence indicates that within sexually mixed groups, such as those in many school settings, men speak more often, and their ideas are given greater credence. Lockheed and Hall (1976) suggest that this reflects the greater value given to males in the society at large. Because males have greater prestige and power in social institutions, this status difference will appear in settings where the sexes interact in performing tasks. Kanter (1975, 1976), however, has contended that there are few sex differences in work organizations that cannot be explained by the hierarchies commonly found in these groups. That is, the fact that women are found predominantly in lower-level positions that do not lead to responsibility and power can account for their greater attention to peers in the work situation and their failure to aspire to higher positions. Kanter suggests that women in low-level positions with blocked mobility have the same responses as men. The core of her argument is that characteristics that have been ascribed to sex-role differences, such as women's concern for good peer relationships, are in fact characteristics of all workers in low mobility situations.

Finigan (1978) has pointed out that Kanter's conclusions are based on only a partial review of the relevant literature and on inadequate evidence. The only organizational study she cites that directly attempts to test her hypothesis does not do so. In Penning's (1970) study of workers in positions of low and high mobility (measured by promotion rates), there was no significant difference between the two groups with regard to their concern for good peer relationships; in addition, out of the 14 factors considered, concern for peer relationships was the one that *least* differentiated the two groups.

Reexamination of classic studies of work organizations also suggest that sex differences must be taken into account. Acker and Van Houten (1974) reviewed two classic studies of organizations, the Hawthorne studies (Roethlisberger & Dickson, 1939; Whitehead, 1938) and Crozier's studies (1964) of French bureaucracies, showing how some of their results were influenced by the fact that the workers were women and the managers and researchers were men. The original research reports made little or no mention of this fact. Acker and Van Houten conclude that both organizational variables such as hierarchy of the organization and the sex composition of positions of power must be considered in analyzing organizational phenomena.

Careful contemporary studies show that women who attain prestigeful and typically masculine positions in organizations have very different experiences from those of the men in those positions. For instance, Miller, Labovitz, & Fry (1975) studied the work experiences of men and women in five different professional organizations, including a public school system. In each of the organizations, many more men than women were in positions of authority over others, although each organization did have women in positions of authority. In general, the women had fewer contacts and friendship choices and reported greater isolation from other people, and those in the higher status positions had much more difficulty than men of similar rank. Miller and his associates suggest: "Unlike men, women who improve their positions by increasing their expertise, by moving up occupationally, or by moving into positions of authority may also run the risk of losing friendship and respect, influence, and access to information. They can expect that the strains created by the work might increase and [that] almost none of this will improve over time [Miller et al., 1975, p. 378]."

Hagen and Kahn (1975) provide support for these findings from an experimental study. They assigned men and women to mixed and single-sex groups where women would appear to do either very well or only average in an assigned task. After completing the tasks, the subjects were asked how well they "liked" each participant. The researchers found that the men tended to dislike competent women only when they were in direct competition with them. Women who did well were liked by the men only when seen from a distance. Such studies help explain why women are not often found in the higher-level ranks of organizations and describe what may happen to them when they attain such status. In general, women's underrepresentation in these positions reflects their lower status in the society. Yet when women do gain positions with greater prestige and authority, they are generally not given the advantages that go with the jobs. They may have less access to information and less influence in the group than their male colleagues. Moreover, they may lose social approval and have fewer friends and less respect in the organization than men of similar expertise and position.

Hagen and Kahn's study indicates that if women are to do a good job and also have approval from men, they had best not show their competence directly to the men from whom they want approval. Miller and his associates (1975) suggest that this situation can be at least partly explained by the vested interests men have in retaining their superiority over women. If men were to acknowledge women's expertise, especially in their own areas of competency, it would challenge the overall system that assigns greater value and worth to men's work and activities. Moreover, given that a basic part of men's self-identity involves seeing themselves as "not feminine," if they were to acknowledge women's ability to do the same work as they do, it would directly challenge the fragile and tenuous masculine identity. This analysis is supported by observations of the number of women who have been hired in top positions in corporations and government. In a nationwide search, Lear (1977) was able to find only a few dozen women who held meaningful top executive positions. Most of the women who had been reported to be top executives by the communications media were in essentially ineffectual positions, with no real access to power or authority.

In summary, analysis of the internal labor market suggests that women's advancement opportunities in professions and organizations are different from men's because they enter in different positions. Organizational studies point out that when men and women do work together, men's input in interactions is valued more than women's and that even when women do attain objectively powerful or important positions, they encounter a good deal of opposition and stress and have little real access to authority. In other words, not only do women and men often begin their careers in different positions, they have different experiences after they start. We turn now to a specific analysis of how discrimination against women occurs in education.

CAREER PATTERNS IN EDUCATION

Women arrive at positions in education that are different from those of men because of differing career paths, or patterns of movement from one job to another. First we will briefly review evidence of these differences in the careers of school administrators, and then we will look at specific explanations of why these differences exist.

We noted earlier that men educators become administrators and hold the most powerful and prestigious positions in education much more often than women educators do. This does not happen by chance. Men more often deliberately plan their educational careers to include advancement to higher posts and take courses that prepare them for administration. Increasingly, both women and men may aspire to administration, but men more often seek the highest posts (McMillan, 1975; Mansergh, 1976). A typical pattern for a young man interested in administration is to begin by teaching and then within a few years to move to a supervisory post. For example, he might become head of an academic department or coordinator of athletics. Within a few more years, he might become an assistant principal, and after that, a principal; and if he is in a large district, he might then move to the central administrative office and subsequently try to attain a superintendent's position. Obviously not all men in education move to the highest administrative positions, but they start on this path more frequently than women do, and they more often attain these high posts.

Male administrators are almost always married, and those in high-level supervisory or line positions (secondary school principal, district superintendents, and assistant superintendents) are almost always white (Carlson, 1972; Gross, Mason, & McEachern, 1958). For both men and women, the position of elementary school principal appears to be terminal rather than transitional in professional careers in education (Gaertner, 1978). However, the women are generally older and less often married; they have more training or classroom experience and receive lower salaries (Gross & Trask, 1976). The profile of women high school principals and superintendents is somewhat similar, but women are less frequently found in these positions. The women superintendents, assistant superintendents, and principals in Paddock's (1977) national sample were often not married and earned less than male administrators with similar qualifications. The time interval between their initial decision to become an administrator and the start of their first job was shorter than that of male administrators. This may indicate that unlike men, who begin to plan their administrative careers when they first enter education, women do not begin to plan until presented with the opportunity for such a job. Moreover, most women teachers are in elementary schools, and the positions as principal for which they are eligible do not generally lead to more advanced administrative positions (Gaertner, 1978).

Interestingly enough, while black men are almost never given line administrative posts in education, Paddock (1977) found that 21% of the women secondary principals in her study were minorities. A 1972 study of male principals found that less than 10% of the group were members of minority groups (Mitchell & Hawley, 1972), and none of Carlson's (1972) sample of male superintendents was a member of a minority group.

Observers of school systems around the country suggest that while black men may be given posts such as assistant principal, they are rarely given the top position. In fact, after the integration of southern schools, many black men lost principalships as white men took over the posts (Coursen, 1975). Apparently, black women attain line administrative positions, at least principalships, in education more often than black men. Given that blacks are approximately 12% of the total population of the United States, black women may be somewhat more likely than white women to become principals, although both groups are vastly underrepresented when we realize that women are over one-half of the total population. Hiring black women over either white women or black men may be the least threatening approach to affirmative action for the men who make hiring decisions. Hiring white women would directly challenge the dominance of white men over the women to whom they are closest, those whom they generally marry. Hiring black men would directly challenge the system of white dominance in the world of work. When pressed to hire someone other than a white male, the hiring of a black woman may provide the least direct challenge to a sexist and racist system. (Hiring black women also allows administrators to fill two affirmative action mandates [race and sex] at one time.)

INFLUENCES ON WOMEN'S CAREER PATHS

Women's underrepresentation in school leadership may be seen as a result either of limited opportunities to attain such posts or of aspirations that are different from those of men (cf. Estler, 1975). There is evidence to support both possibilities, and we now analyze each.

Limited Opportunities

Women administrators generally do a good job when they are hired, and there is little evidence that women are not hired because they are not competent. A number of studies have compared the performance of male and female school administrators, and Fishel and Pottker (1975, p. 113) summarized the results: "These behavioral studies clearly indicate that in terms of ability to supervise and administer a school and to maintain good relations with students and parents, the few women who have been able to obtain administrative positions have performed as capably as, if not more capably than, their male counterparts." In addition these studies support the findings of organizational research that women administrators more often encourage cooperative relationships among teachers than men administrators.

A larger proportion of men educators than of women educators hold advanced degrees. Yet because more women are in education, when actual numbers are compared, just as many men as women educators have master's degrees. Estler (1975) notes that within the pool of people to be promoted to administrative posts, the representation of men and women is equal. When the criterion is either the past performance of women or their formal qualifications in terms of years of education, equal numbers of men and women are prepared for administrative posts.

Even though women are qualified to hold administrative positions, they are apparently encouraged less often than men are to aspire to those positions. A number of studies show that women's supervisors do not encourage them to enter administrative posts (Jenkins, 1966; Mansergh, 1976; Matheny, 1973; Taylor, 1971; Warwick, 1967). Married women may be administrators less often than single women at least partly because school officials do not even consider them as possible candidates. It may be assumed that married women must devote many hours to caring for their families, and their advancement may thus not be encouraged.

Women are almost never part of the "old boy's network"—an expression commonly used to refer to the informal web of contacts that practicing administrators use to recommend people for jobs and to promote themselves and their friends. Because very few women are practicing administrators or in a position to hire others, they are not part of this network. Aspiring male candidates often have this support in job hunting, and it probably helps their advancement in school management.

One of the reasons often given for not hiring or encouraging women administrators is that "the public wouldn't stand for it." Actually, the evidence tends to indicate that the general public is fairly supportive of women educators; it is school officials who are reluctant to hire women. When a Gallup poll asked a representative national sample of adults if they would prefer a man or a woman as a school principal, 39% of the respondents said they would prefer a man, but 52% said that it made no difference (Gallup, 1975, p. 235). In a more recent study in the state of Oregon (a fairly traditional state that usually votes for the more conservative Republican presidential candidates), a representative group of adults were asked how they would feel about having a woman elementary principal, high school principal, and school superintendent in their local schools. For the three positions, respectively, 93%, 84% and 86% of the respondents approved of having a woman. This support was generally stronger among people who were younger, had higher incomes and high-status occupations, had children currently attending public schools, were from more urban areas of the state, and had known a woman school administrator in the past (Stockard, Hart, & Schmuck, 1977).

In contrast to the general public, teachers, school administrators, and members of school boards often do not support women in school administration. Both male and female teachers report that they prefer to work with male administrators (Linton, 1974; Matheny, 1973; Neidig, 1973; all cited by Fishel & Pottker, 1975, p. 113); but teachers who have worked with female administrators express more favorable attitudes toward them than those without such experiences (Barter, 1959, Warwick, 1967; all cited by Fishel & Pottker, 1975, p. 113; Grambs, 1976). Those who hire administrators, including superintendents and school board members, are generally opposed to appointing women (Barter, 1959; Cobbley, 1970; LaBarthe, 1973; Longstreth, 1973; Matheny, 1973; Neidig, 1973; Taylor, 1971; Warwick, 1967; all cited by Fishel & Pottker, 1975, pp. 113–114).

A study of educators in Minnesota found that men teachers who had held administrative positions had less favorable opinions about hiring women than men teachers who had never been administrators (Mansergh, 1976). These more negative attitudes may occur because men administrators are threatened most directly by the hiring of a woman administrator (cf. the men in the studies by Johnson, Johnson, & Yeakey, 1978; and Miller et al., 1975). Potential female domination of the top administrative posts in education poses a very real threat to their prestige and status. If they were to share peer roles with women, their social prestige might decline. If the many women who are potential administrators were to enter school management, its image might change—and men who are now administrators may fear this.

Differences in Aspirations

In addition to the limits women face in attaining administrative posts, it must also be recognized that women do not aspire to such positions or enter graduate school programs in educational administration as often as men do, although these differences may be declining somewhat. In the education field, women tend toward the areas of special education, curriculum, and instruction, and men more often major in administration. This is reflected in the concentration of women in staff positions in special education and curriculum coordination and the concentration of men in administrative line positions. Differences exist even in the educational preparation of those who hold line positions: In Paddock's (1977) sample of line administrators, 57% of the women school superintendents had undergraduate degrees in education as compared with 38% for the men in a comparable study.

Most of the women superintendents in Paddock's study served in small elementary districts. The internal labor market analysis would lead us to suggest that women were able to become superintendents because in small elementary districts most if not all teachers are also women. For those who start their careers as elementary teachers, career ladders would lead to positions as elementary principals (women are more commonly found here as compared with other administrative areas), and in an elementary district, perhaps to a position as superintendent. We would expect women to be less commonly found as principals in secondary schools and as superintendents of high school districts (or those with 12 grades) because they less often fill the early positions on career ladders that lead to these posts; but even among elementary school teachers, men are much more likely than women to be considered for advancement.

Women do not prepare for the more male-dominated areas in education, and they may simply not want to enter these areas. The jobs themselves may be undesirable, having been described as "people-killing" and requiring substantial outlays of time and energy that may not be worth the added financial reimbursement. Jackson (1977) has noted the isolation and loneliness of positions at the top of the hierarchy. The nature of the professional hierarchy may not be attractive to women. Research on interaction in small groups suggests that women are more apt to adopt cooperative strategies when these are appropriate; men are more apt to use competitive strategies, whether or not they are appropriate to the situation (Finigan, 1978). Indeed, the evidence shows that women elementary principals use group decision making and encourage cooperative stances among teachers more often than their male counterparts do (Fishel & Pottker, 1975). It may well be that just as women have no strong motive to dominate men (Stockard & Johnson, 1979), they also have less motivation than men to dominate others in general, and this may be the reason they do not aspire to top administrative positions.

Probably the most important reason is that they see this area as related to the male role and they see such jobs as "men's place" in society (cf. Estler, 1975). In Chapter 3, we discussed sex-role development and the pattern of women avoiding achievement in areas that were defined as appropriate for males. Similarly we see that in education women do achieve; but while they are excellent classroom teachers, very good supervisors of special education, and exemplary librarians, they are much less often found either in line administrative posts or teaching subjects such as math or science—positions that men consider appropriately masculine. Just as women students avoid entering academic areas that are defined as masculine, women educators may avoid achieving in occupational areas that are defined as masculine. Organizational studies have demonstrated that when women do show competence in work with men they are often not given positive rewards. As pointed out earlier, Mansergh (1976) found that men's attitudes toward women administrators were less favorable among men who had also been administrators. Thus women in administrative positions may experience greater isolation and loss of friends and respect (cf. Miller et al., 1975). If being a woman administrator is an unpleasant experience or is anticipated as such, women will avoid the area.

Obviously, however, some women hold leadership posts in education. How do they manage to occupy these positions without violating males' expectations of role segregation and thus avoid possibly negative sanctions? The most common solution is to confine work roles to tasks traditionally seen as feminine. This is the route most female educators take when they assume roles in elementary teaching and other typically feminine fields. In Chapter 4 we noted that the staff administrative positions usually held by women do not involve supervising other adult professionals. Women are thus conforming to views of what the female work role should be. In addition, when a woman is in a role that many men also hold, she may redefine her activities as feminine in nature, for instance, defining work as a female elementary principal in a maternal way by seeing herself as motherly and telling others that her job requires such feminine traits. A male elementary principal might emphasize the administrative tasks and the rational and organizational skills that are stereotyped as masculine. Obviously, in spite of such definitions, all elementary principals are doing very similar tasks. Women who enter male areas and do not redefine their activities as feminine in nature may be seen as the hard-boiled executive, or what Kanter (1975) has termed the "iron maiden." This response is probably rather rare because it directly challenges male expectations and can produce negative reactions from co-workers (cf. Epstein, 1970). Most women cannot avoid at least some typically female roles except for women who are very well-to-do and women who do not assume the roles of wife and mother (Stockard & Johnson, 1980).

While many of our examples have referred to professionals in the public schools, our analysis also applies to the representation of women in colleges and universities. Women on university staffs are found in the lower ranks, and sex segregation appears among, and even within, specific academic areas. These specializations are of course presaged by the sex segregation in students' academic preparation. The various formal and informal procedures discussed earlier serve to maintain this segregation. Again, females avoid directly challenging the system of male dominance because they are generally found in areas defined as more appropriate for them.

Career paths usually culminate in more women having the lower-paying jobs in education since administrators usually earn much more than teachers and secondary teachers have more opportunities for extra-duty pay than elementary teachers. The rationale for this hierarchy is rather obscure. One could well argue that teaching very young children is a more responsible and essential task in the society than teaching students at later ages. Elementary teachers first expose children to learning, guiding them in the most important years of their life and setting the tone for their school careers. One could also argue that the actual teaching, the contact with young minds, is more essential to the well-being and continuance of a society than the administrative tasks of coordinating activities and supervising janitorial and clerical work. A male aspirant to a principal's position who already was a teaching principal told us: "I can't wait to get a full-time principal's post. I'll get paid a whole lot more and work a whole lot less. All I'll have to do is count lunch tickets, make sure the buses run on time, take naps in my office, and talk to parents who call on the phone!"

While we may have overstated the case here, we do wish to point out that there is no apparent reason for devaluing the work that women usually do in the schools as compared with that which men generally do. Both are essential. We suspect that administrators are paid more than teachers simply because men usually hold such jobs. In fact, only a few years ago it was a common practice to pay men teachers more than women teachers—just because they were men. Just as men are reluctant to hire women as fellow administrators for fear that this would lower the prestige and exclusiveness of their posts, paying teachers as much as administrators would also directly challenge male superiority.

Potential for Change

Our discussion suggests that if we are to have more sexual equality in education, the discrimination that restricts and limits women's opportunities must end and women must more often aspire to beginning jobs that are now mainly held by men and that lead to the more prestigious administrative positions. Obviously these two changes are related. Women do not enter graduate programs in school administration because they perceive that it will be difficult for them to get jobs in that area; and women do not aspire to teach in fields such as science and many vocational areas because they see these as areas to which it is inappropriate for women to aspire. The fact that women are not found in such areas reinforces the view that they are men's province. Any change

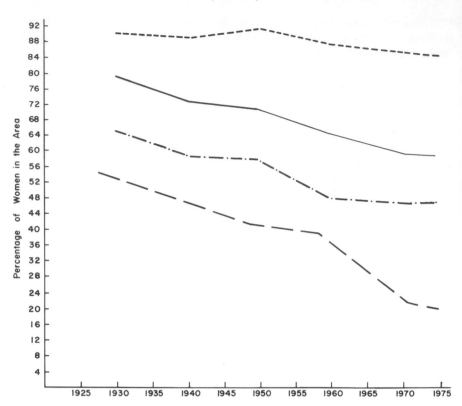

FIGURE 5.1   Percentage of positions held by women educators in subareas of the profes-
sion, 1928-1974. Teaching figures include publicly and privately controlled schools. From
W. V. Grant and C. G. Lind, *Digest of Education Statistics,* National Center for Education
Statistics, Department of Health, Education and Welfare, Washington, D. C., 1970, p. 10; and
J. Pottker and A. Fishel (1977), *Sex Bias in the Schools.* Fairleigh Dickinson Univ. Press,
Cranbury, N.J.,p. 290. All levels of teaching—; elementary teaching---; secondary teaching
(including junior high school)- ·-; elementary principal——.

in these patterns will require breaking into this self-perpetuating cycle
and altering the sex-typed definitions of areas of education.

Moreover, simply dealing with education alone may not be sufficient; the total structure of the occupational world may need to be considered. Figure 5.1 shows the relative proportion of women in the educational profession during the last 40–50 years, which has declined over
time. While this means that the sex ratio has become somewhat more
balanced among elementary teachers and to some extent among secondary teachers, the sex ratio in elementary principalships has become even

less balanced over time.[1] Women seem to be leaving education altogether, probably as a result of an overabundance of college educated men with a lack of other professional areas for them to enter (cf. O'Connor, 1977). When a choice must be made between similarly educated men and women, the men are given professional jobs. In recent years, the typically female professions appear to be more likely than the typically male professions are to have an increased representation of members of the other sex (see Gross, 1968).

The second half of this book examines the basis for social change. By examining theories of social change, legislation regarding sex discrimination, and the impact of the feminist movement on education we can begin to assess what else needs to be done to promote sex equity in education.

REFERENCES

Acker, J., and Van Houten, D. R. (1974). "Differential Recruitment and Control: The Sex Structuring of Organizations." *Administrative Science Quarterly,* 19:152–162.

Barter, A. S. (1959). "The Status of Women in School Administration—Where Will They Go from Here?" *Educational Horizons,* 37:72–75.

Blau, F., and Jusenius, C. L. (1976). "Economists' Approaches to Sex Segregation in the Labor Market: An Appraisal." *Signs,* 1,No.2, pt. 2, pp. 181–200.

Carlson, R. O. (1972). *School Superintendents: Careers and Performance.* Merrill, Columbus, Ohio.

Cassell, F. H., Director, S. M., and Doctors, S. I. (1975). "Discrimination within Internal Labor Markets." *Industrial Relations,* 14:337–344.

Charters, W. W., Jr. (1979). *The Decline of Female Elementary Principals: A Problem in the Data.* Unpublished paper, Center for Educational Policy and Management, University of Oregon.

Cobbley, L. (1970). *A Study of Attitudes and Opportunities for Women in Six Western States to Become Elementary School Principals.* Doctoral dissertation, Brigham Young University; Provo, Utah.

Coursen, D. (1975). *Women and Minorities in Administration.* National Association of Elementary School Principals, Arlington, Va.

Crozier, M. (1964). *The Bureaucratic Phenomenon.* University of Chicago Press, Chicago.

Doeringer, P., and Piore, M. J. (1971). *Internal Labor Markets and Manpower Analysis.* Heath, Lexington, Mass.

[1]The figures for the representation of women in elementary principalships (Pottker & Fishel, 1977) should be interpreted with caution. After examining the original sources of these figures, Charters (1979) concluded that the statistics in Figure 5.1 probably overestimate women's representation in the earlier years. The general trend of a decline in women's representation in elementary principalships is undoubtedly true, but Figure 5.1 may overestimate the degree of that decline from the year 1928 and perhaps from 1948 and 1958.

Epstein, C. F. (1970). "Encountering the Male Establishment: Sex Status Limits on Women's Careers in the Professions." *American Journal of Sociology*, 75:965–982.

Estler, S. (1975). "Women as Leaders in Public Education." *Signs*, 1:363–386.

Finigan, M. (1978). *Sex Differences in Work Organizations: A Critique of the Blocked Mobility Hypothesis*. Paper presented at the annual meeting of the Pacific Sociological Association, Spokane, Washington.

Fishel, A., and Pottker, J. (1974). "Women in Educational Governance: A Statistical Portrait." *Educational Researcher*, 3:4–7.

Fishel, A., and Pottker, J. (1975). "Performances of Women Principals: A Review of Behavioral and Attitudinal Studies." *Journal of the National Association of Women Deans and Counselors*, 38:110–115.

Gaertner, K. N. (1978). *Organizational Careers in Public School Administration*. Paper presented at the annual meetings of the American Sociological Association, San Francisco, Calif.

Gallup, G. H. (1975). "Seventh Annual Gallup Poll of Public Attitudes Toward Education." *Phi Delta Kappa*, 57:227–241.

Grambs, J. D. (1976). "Women and Administration: Confrontation or Accomodation?" *Theory into Practice*, 15:293–300.

Grant, W. V., and Lind, C. G. (1977). *Digest of Education Statistics*, 1976 ed. National Center for Education Statistics, Department of HEW, Washington, D.C.

Grimm, J. W. and Stern, R. (1974). "Sex Roles and Internal Labor Market Structures: The 'Female' Semi-Professions." *Social Problems*, 21:690–705.

Grimm, J. W. (1978). "Women in Female-Dominated Professions." In *Women Working* (Stromberg, A., and Harkess, S. eds.). Mayfield, Palo Alto, Calif.

Gross, N. (1968). "Plus ca change . . . ? The Sexual Structure of Occupations over Time." *Social Problems*, 16:198–208.

Gross, N., Mason, W. S., and McEachern, A. W. (1958). *Explorations in Role Analysis: Studies of the School Superintendency Role*. Wiley, New York.

Gross, N., and Trask, A. E. (1976). *The Sex Factor and the Management of Schools*. Wiley, New York.

Hagen, R. and Kahn, A. (1975). "Discrimination against Competent Women." *Journal of Applied Social Psychology*, 5:362–376.

Jackson, P. W. (1977). "Lonely at the Top: Observations on the Genesis of Administrative Isolation." *School Review*, 85:425–432.

Jenkins, W. J. (1966). *A Study of the Attitudes of Elementary School Teachers in Selected Schools in Montgomery County, Pennsylvania, toward the Women Elementary School Principal*. Doctoral dissertation, Temple University, Pa.

Johnson, G. S., Johnson, H. S., and Yeakey, C. C. (1978). *A Study of the Attitudes of Male Graduate Students toward Professional Women*. Paper presented at the annual meetings of the American Educational Research Association, Toronto, Canada.

Kanter, R. M. (1975). "Women and the Structure of Organizations: Explorations in Theory and Behavior." In *Another Voice* (M. Millman and R. M. Kanter, eds.). Garden City, N.Y.

Kanter, R. M. (1976). "The Impact of Hierarchical Structures on the Work Behavior of Women and Men." *Social Problems*, 23:415–441.

LaBarthe, E. R. (1973). *A Study of the Motivation of Women in Administrative and Supervisory Positions in Selected Unified School Districts in Southern California*. Doctoral dissertation, University of Southern California, Los Angeles.

Lear, F. (1977). "The Real Story about Working Women." *The Washington Post*, Washington, D.C., April 16.

Linton, D. L. (1974). *Teachers' Perceptions of Women as Principals in an Elementary School District.* Doctoral dissertation, United States International University, San Diego, Calif.

Lockheed, M., and Hall, K. P. (1976). "Conceptualizing Sex as a Status Characteristic: Applications to Leadership Training Strategies." *Journal of Social Issues,* 32(No.3):111–123.

Longstreth, C. H. (1973). *An Analysis of the Perceptions of the Leadership Behavior of Male and Female Secondary School Principals in Florida.* Doctoral dissertation, University of Miami.

Malkiel, B. G., and Malkiel, J. A. (1973). "Male-Female Pay Differentials in Professional Employment." *American Economic Review,* 63:693–705.

Mansergh, G. (1976). "Attitudes of Teachers toward Women School Administrators and the Aspirations of Teachers for Administrative Positions in the State of Minnesota." *Catalyst for Change,* 5(Spring): 4–7.

Martin, W. (1972). *The American Sisterhood.* Harper & Row, New York.

Matheny, P. P. (1973). *A Study of the Attitudes of Selected Male and Female Teachers, Administrators and Board of Education Presidents toward Women in Educational Administrative Positions.* Doctoral dissertation, Northwestern University, Evanston, Ill.

McMillan, M. R. (1975). "Leadership Aspirations of Prospective Teachers: A Comparison of Men and Women." *Journal of Teacher Education,* 26:323–325.

Miller, J., Labovitz, S., and Fry, L. (1975). "Inequities in the Organizational Experiences of Women and Men." *Social Forces,* 54:365–381.

Mitchell, D., and Hawley, A. (1972). *Leadership in Public Education: A Look at the Overlooked.* Academy for Educational Development, Washington, D.C.

Neidig, M. B. (1973). *Women Applicants for Administrative Positions: Attitudes Held by Administrators and School Boards.* Doctoral dissertation, University of Iowa.

O'Connor, J. (1977). *Changes in the Sex Composition of High Status Female Occupations: An Analysis of Teaching: 1950–70.* Unpublished paper, University of Illinois at Urbana-Champaign.

Paddock, S. (1977). *Women's Careers in Administration.* Doctoral dissertation, University of Oregon.

Penning, J. M. (1970). "Work-Value Systems of White-Collar Workers." *Administrative Science Quarterly,* 15:397–405.

Pottker, J., and Fishel, A. eds. (1977). *Sex Bias in the Schools.* Fairleigh Dickinson Univ. Press, Cranbury, N.J.

Roethlisberger, F. J. and Dickson, W. J. (1939). *Management and the Worker.* Harvard University Press, Cambridge, Mass.

Stockard, J., and Johnson, M. (1979). "The Social Origins of Male Dominance." *Sex Roles,* 5:199–218.

Stockard, J., and Johnson, M. (1980). *Sex Roles: Sex Inequality and Sex Role Development.* Prentice-Hall, Englewood Cliffs, N.J.

Stockard, J., Hart, J., and Schmuck P. (1977). *Public Prejudice against Women Administrators: Fact or Fiction?* Unpublished paper, Center for Educational Policy and Management, University of Oregon.

Taylor, S. (1971). *The Attitudes of Superintendents and Board of Education Members in Connecticut toward the Employment and Effectiveness of Women as Public School Administrators.* Doctoral dissertation, University of Connecticut.

Warwick, E. B. (1967). *Attitudes towards Women in Administrative Positions as Related to Curricular Implementation and Change.* Doctoral dissertation, University of Wisconsin.

Whitehead, T. N. (1938). *The Industrial Worker, Vol. 1.* Oxford University Press, London.

PART II

THE POSSIBILITY OF CHANGE

Chapter 6

A SOCIAL–PSYCHOLOGICAL ANALYSIS
OF THE CONTEXT FOR CHANGE

Ken Kempner

Whoever wants to know a thing has no way of doing so except by coming into contact with it. . . . If you want knowledge, you must take part in the practice of changing reality [*Mao Tse-Tung, in Schram, 1967, p. 118*].

How can our knowledge about our society and its members assist in the development of effective social change? In this book we have looked at what social inequities exist in education, but we have not yet explored how these inequities may be altered. This chapter investigates changing the sexist nature of our educational system through methods of social intervention. These methods are based on knowledge gained through research in social psychology. We look first at why individuals behave as they do. We then discuss social intervention and the use of legislation as a means of change. Finally, we take a hopeful look at the creation of a structure that could help assure a more humane social system.

By understanding why people behave as they do, we can better select specific strategies to erase the inequities that exist in our social system. Because an individual's behavior is formed by the interaction of beliefs, attitudes, values, and societal norms, it is to this interaction that we must look to predict and change behavior. When societal norms and individual beliefs create behavior that is counterproductive to the maintenance of a just society, people who wish to correct this inequity must choose some form of social intervention. Understanding the causes of behavior may give us a better chance of success, but it does not mean that effecting social changes will be easy. It may appear to be simple to change behavior, but anyone who has attempted to change the behavior of a stubborn child or adult realizes the arduous nature of this task. This chore becomes awesome when we think of changing an entire society of stubborn children and adults.

BELIEFS AND BEHAVIOR

At the basis of behavior that maintains social inequities are the beliefs of individuals and groups. Beliefs of this kind are derived from stereotypes formed by individuals and are expressed in people's attitudes and social norms. Stereotypes, beliefs, attitudes, and norms, which interact to produce individual and group behavior, must be the the focus of social interventions that attempt to alter social inequities.

Stereotypes

Allport (1958) described a stereotype as "an exaggerated belief associated with a category." Stereotypes are formed by each of us to cope with the complex environment in which we live. Our world is greatly simplified when we organize people and events into categories. For example, instead of relearning the purpose of doors each time we encounter them, we can assume from our category for doors that they all will lead somewhere. The formation of stereotypes is not inherently damaging to the social order unless a categorization leads to unjust attributions and behaviors. When such an unjust attribution is made, it is called a prejudice. As we have seen earlier in this book, unjust stereotypes of women are harmful both to women and to the society; we believe, therefore, that the prejudice derived from these stereotypes should be mitigated. Individuals who wish to alter such harmful stereotypes cannot hope to overcome them until they understand what it is within an individual's belief structure that causes these unjust categorizations.

Belief Structure

The structure of an individual's beliefs is much like a brick wall: the strongest beliefs are found at the top (see Figure 6.1). Three general belief levels were identified by Bem (1970): zero order, first order, and higher order. According to Bem, the strongest beliefs (those at the base of the brick wall) are the ones essential to an individual's being. These beliefs are developed from early socialization and direct sensory experiences. Belief in our sensory experience is "the most important primitive belief of all [Bem, 1970, p. 5]." People trust their own experiences first and then rely on secondhand experience from valued individuals.

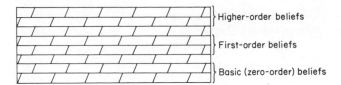

Higher-order beliefs

First-order beliefs

Basic (zero-order) beliefs

FIGURE 6.1   The brick wall structure of beliefs.

The second level of beliefs is rooted less within an individual's sensory experience and derives from ideological justifications. Beliefs at this level are often based on assumed truths, with little conscious rationale. The third level, higher-order beliefs are the least rooted in sensory experience and are formed predominantly on the basis of conscious thought. Level of belief varies inversely with the cognitive origins of the belief; therefore, the more deeply rooted the belief, the less responsibility conscious thought has in its formation.

Beliefs in sex-roles are an excellent example of the stratified beliefs individuals hold. For many men and women, it is a basic belief that the roles women occupy are subservient to men. On the basis of all they have experienced and learned, these individuals believe it is inappropriate for women to hold positions of authority. For other people in the society, however, beliefs in sex-roles are not basic, and with new information or experience, these individuals could approve of women in authority positions. Just as the top rows of a brick wall are more easily changed than the bottom rows, an individual's higher-order beliefs are more changeable than basic beliefs. Basic zero-order beliefs form the foundation of the structure and can be changed only when the entire structure is dismantled and rebuilt. For example, an individual's basic belief in a supreme being or in sex-roles may be virtually unchangeable; but a higher-order belief in the safety of nuclear energy can be changed more readily with appropriate new information. The process of altering an individual's higher-order belief about governmental price controls or reduced speed limits, therefore, requires an approach different from the intervention needed to change basic or first-order beliefs about the role of women in society. To understand how to change beliefs that lead to prejudice and discrimination, we must first understand the effects of attitudes, values, and norms on an individual's behavior.

Attitudes and Values

Individual's belief structures are evidenced in the attitudes they express, and conversely, attitudes provide judgments derived from the beliefs an individual holds. Individuals have positive attitudes toward people with the same beliefs as their own. Intuitively we understand that conservatives prefer conservatives and radicals prefer radicals.

Attitudes, which provide judgments of specific phenomena, are different from *values*, which refer to an "abstract concept of the environment" (Triandis, 1972). Some individuals have a positive *attitude* toward holding a high political office, for example, because they place a high *value* on power. Such an attitude is derived from each individual's belief structure, and subsequently, the value of power is developed. Individuals who believe women are inferior to men have a negative *attitude* toward working with women because they place a negative *value* on the roles or contributions of women in society.

In determining the best way to effect social change, it is important to understand that the formation of values may not be as consistent as the previous examples imply. For example, individuals may value equality, but demand segregation in education. Individuals who value equality but favor segregation resolve this conflict by unconsciously placing priorities on their values; they place a higher priority on segregation than on equality. Equality remains an expressed value, but it may be reserved only for men. In the belief structure of such individuals the belief in segregation of the sexes is more basic than the belief in equality, which is regarded only as an abstract concept.

Logical conflicts may arise from priorities of values, as was documented in a 1969 survey in Detroit (Schuman, 1972). In one section of the survey respondents were asked to answer three questions about a hypothetical situation in which a "good Negro engineer" was applying for a job as an engineering executive. The applicant was told that for him the job offer could only be as a "regular engineer" because the possible friction of a black "at the top could ruin the organization." One question was general in nature and asked if respondents would favor hiring the black as the engineering executive; 85% of the sample said yes and supported nondiscrimination. On another question which raised the problem of the potential economic instability that would be caused by hiring the black, the percentage supporting the black as an executive was reduced to 61%. A third question asked the respondents if they would hire the black over the wishes of the employee majority, and only 50% favored hiring the black against the wishes of the majority. Although 85% of the respondents expressed the value of nondiscrimination, this value was superceded by the higher-priority values of economic stability and democratic decision making. The respondents favored equality only if nondiscrimination did not conflict with a higher-priority value. For the respondents in this study, equality had a limited meaning.

Often in the general society, as in the Schuman study, the value of equal job opportunity is espoused so long as it does not conflict with a higher-priority value, such as money. The agents of social change must realize that these value priorities exist, and they can (*a*) hope that social and economic conditions will remain favorable for equal job opportunity or (*b*) attempt to devise methods that will keep equal opportunity a top-value priority regardless of social or economic conditions. Later in this chapter we look at how to keep nondiscrimination a high-priority value. First, however, to gain a more complete understanding of why individuals behave as they do, we must look at the effect of social norms on behavior.

Norms

Attitudes and values are most often associated with individual psychological perceptions, while norms specify behaviors that are appropriate for members of a culture (Triandis, 1972). Norms are maintained over time because they are transmitted between and within groups, often accompanied by appropriate rationalizations for behavior and ideologies. An example of a norm in our American society is the typical manner (a stereotype) in which men greet one another—with a handshake. Although this is the norm for American males, it is not the norm for Japanese men, who bow, or for western European and South American men, who embrace one another. The rationale for such norms, however, is often weak. This fact would be apparent if one were to query an American male about the justification for greeting with a handshake instead of a bow or a kiss. Few males could provide a logical rationale for their behavior other than by saying: "It is the custom." Since not questioning norms is also a norm, such investigative action would be regarded as suspect behavior.

Social norms can have an important influence on discriminatory behavior and prejudiced attitudes. Pettigrew (1959) found that the prejudice of southern American whites toward blacks was due primarily to whites' conforming to the historic social norms of discrimination against blacks. Pettigrew found southerners not overly prejudiced against Jews and attributed the southerner's prejudice toward blacks to the prevailing social norm—treatment of blacks as property. As with the lack of a conscious rationale for shaking hands among men, southern whites were found to be equally unconscious of a rationale other than custom for discrimination against blacks. In both instances, an historic norm for which there is little conscious rationale influences behavior.

Although handshaking is a norm which causes no particular damage to the social structure, the unconscious norm of discrimination is extremely damaging to blacks and to society. To alter such an inequitable situation, norms must be changed along with attitudes and values.

Unfortunately, norms are extremely resistant to change since they are based on the collective belief structures of group members, often at an unconscious level. A change in norms is analogous to dismantling the belief structure of each group member, brick by brick. It is most difficult to change norms when we attempt to change a basic belief such as the appropriate role of women in American society.

Norms are so resistant to change that they were found to remain, even though they were totally invalid, through successive generations of an experiment by Jacobs and Campbell (1961). This experiment was described as "an effort to demonstrate a perpetuation of 'cultural' characteristics that transcend the replacement of individual persons [p. 649]." In the experiment, confederates established an arbitrary "cultural norm," which was transmitted to new members of the group as the confederates and old members were replaced one by one. Jacobs and Campbell found that "significant remnants of the culture persisted for four or five generations beyond the last confederate [p. 657]." The substitution of new individuals into the experiment was not sufficient to change the norms because the new individuals adopted the prevailing norms to gain acceptance in the group.

Similarly, to alter prejudice against women and change the prevailing social norms that maintain prejudice (e.g., discrimination in jobs, wages, and education), we cannot simply place new participants in the social "experiment," since the new participants will be forced to adopt the existing norms for survival. Ultimately, the structure of the system must be altered to allow the development of new norms. In their study, Jacobs and Campbell found that a *"functionless* arbitrary belief" will eventually erode unless "latent functions . . . at the personal or societal level" support its retention [p. 637]. To change inequitable norms the latent functions that maintain them must ultimately be altered. Functions in education, such as the economic structure of funding for schools, may mediate against a woman becoming a school administrator. Because the economic structure is based on local funding, conservative communities can continue to block the hiring of women to administrative positions and thereby perpetuate the norm of discrimination. Under such conditions, merely placing new people in an unchanged situation would not lead to changes in norms.

As we have seen, behavior comes from the interaction between beliefs, attitudes, values, and norms. When the outcome of this interaction prevents the maintenance of a just society, someone must intervene to change behavior. Even though Americans believe in "justice for all," they generally give equality lower priority than they give other issues, as Schuman (1972) has shown (see also Myrdal *et al.*, 1944). To make social equality a top priority, agents of change must devise methods for intervening in the society that will alter the norms that maintain social inequities. But where should they begin their attempts to alter discriminatory behavior? Should they first try changing beliefs, attitudes, and values? or should their first efforts be directed toward changing how individuals behave?

BEHAVIORAL CHANGE

The attitudes people espouse do not necessarily indicate how they will behave. As the Schuman study (1972) showed, the value of nondiscrimination was easily superceded by the higher priority of economic stability and majority rule. In a study by Tavris (1973) a somewhat similar phenomenon was observed. Although over time the men in the study indicated more favorable attitudes toward hiring and working with the women in the study, the men's behavior toward women did not change. On the abstract level, the men displayed a socially desirable attitude, but on the concrete level of actually hiring women, they did not change their negative behavior. Tavris found that nondiscrimination was low in the value priorities of the sample group; and obviously, equality for women employees was not valued highly in the priorities of these men.

On a more general level, such inconsistencies between attitudes and behavior are "clashes of abstract values in concrete form (Schuman, 1972, p. 352)." When there is little reason for people to change their behavior, the attitudes they express in an abstract situation do not necessarily indicate how they will actually behave. Since behavior is not necessarily determined by people's attitudes, the question is whether individuals who wish to eliminate discrimination should try to change attitudes and value priorities first and assume that behavior will follow or should try to alter behavior first and hope that changes in attitudes and values will follow. For men such as those in the Tavris study, should their behavior be changed first by forcing them to hire women or should their attitudes toward women be changed first through such methods as consciousness raising?

Social psychologists generally agree that altering behavior will lead to changes in attitudes and that this is a more efficient means of changing behavior than an initial focus on values. Evidence for this position comes from Festinger's (1957) classic theory of cognitive dissonance, Bem's theory of self-perception (Bem, 1970), and research by Tajfel (1969). Although the causes of prejudice are not known with total certainty, evidence based on the processes of cognitive categorizations, cognitive consistency, and the assimilation of social beliefs, attitudes, and norms allows us to understand the possible causes of discriminatory behavior. Whether Festinger's, Bem's, or Tajfel's theory provides the best explanation for behavior is less important to agents of social change than the knowledge that behavior can dictate attitudes. As Triandis put it: "People do something first, then bring their attitudes in line with their behavior. Actually, it is best to think of attitudes and behavior as interacting in a reciprocal process, but the more powerful influence involves that from behavior to attitude; the less powerful, that from attitudes to behavior [1972, p. 127]."

Cognitive Consistency

According to Festinger's theory, when individuals engage in behavior that is inconsistent with their beliefs and attitudes, they experience a state of cognitive dissonance. The creation of this disagreeable situation will cause them to search cognitively for the reasons they are engaging in inconsistent behavior. Individuals will thus strive for a consistent state that is free of emotional conflict by developing a rationale for their behavior. In Festinger's theory, cognitive dissonance can occur only when individuals believe they have freedom of choice and are not unduly coerced. Should choice be absent, this lack of freedom may provide the rationale for behavior.

Since we are continually facing dissonant situations, there are many examples of cognitive dissonance. When offered an extra helping of a favorite dessert, an individual on a diet must resolve the conflict between enjoying the dessert (thereby gaining weight) and abstaining (thereby growing no fatter). This dissonant situation can be resolved by promising to maintain the diet the next day or by inventing some rationalization. Individuals engaged in behavior that is inconsistent with their attitudes or beliefs (whether eating, smoking, or discriminating), can seek to reduce dissonance by rationalizing their inconsistent behavior in a group context. That is, they can change their opinion so that it conforms more closely with the group consensus; they can attempt to persuade group members to alter their attitudes; they can distort the meaning of the group's attitudes; they can discredit the group; they can reduce the importance of their own attitudes; they can attempt to obtain support for their own attitudes from inside or outside the group (Adams, 1961).

An example of cognitive dissonance that supported Festinger's theory is provided in a study by Brehm and Cohen (1962) of individuals' rationalizations for changes in their behavior and attitudes. Different monetary sums were used as inducements, in asking university students to write an essay supporting the conduct of police in a clash that had recently occurred between themselves and the police on campus. Brehm and Cohen found that the less money the students were offered, the more favorable their essays were toward the police. Students who were not induced by monetary rewards changed their attitudes and wrote a pro-police essay. This would be predicted by cognitive dissonance theory. That is, while students who were paid a larger sum for writing the pro-police essay could justify their behavior with the high monetary reward, students paid a low amount needed a different rationale for their inconsistent positive attitudes toward the police. Poorly paid students engaged in some form of dissonance-reducing behavior, rationalizing perhaps that the riot was really the students' fault or that it was not really a serious incident or that the police actually handled the situation well.

Pettigrew's finding that southern whites were prejudiced against blacks not because of inherent prejudice, but because the social norms dictated discrimination, is another example of cognitive dissonance. Whites adopted attitudes to justify their behavior in a manner similar to that of the students in the Brehm and Cohen study. The students attained consistency through various rationalizations about the riot; and the southern whites attained consistency with the logic that they were following the social norm. Likewise with the Schuman study regarding the black engineer: discrimination was justified on the basis of economics. In all these situations, cognitive dissonance was relieved by developing a rationale for engaging in behavior that was not entirely consistent with earlier beliefs and attitudes.

Bem (1970) also offers a theory of self-perception that provides evidence of attitudes, following behavior. He suggests that because we use what we see of others' behavior to determine their inner state, we also use our own behavior to infer our own internal states [p. 57]. According to Bem's theory, students in the Brehm and Cohen study changed their attitudes by observation of their own behavior. They inferred, unconsciously, that the pro-police behavior must have reflected their own attitudes since the small amount of money could not have been responsible for changing their behavior.

Causal Attribution

The concept that behavior precedes attitudes is supported in Tajfel's (1969) research on the concept of causal attribution. Tajfel explains that because our social environment is so complex, we constantly make causal attributions to adjust to changing stimuli. According to Tajfel, these attributions are based on three processes: "categorization," "assimilation," and "search for coherence." Categorization is the process of stereotyping people, things, and events so that we may cope with them in the social environment. Assimilation concerns the "learning of evaluations (or preferences)." Because our social identities are formed from cultural membership, we each have beliefs and attitudes that dictate our reactions to stimuli. From our family, peers, teachers, the mass media, and other sources we assimilate or learn what others consider to be appropriate social behavior. The search for coherence is similar to processes posited by cognitive dissonance theorists. That is, individuals seek consistency between causal explanations for events and the categorizations and assimilation processes they have learned and developed.

The desire for consistency leads to a preference for members of one's own group (see Tajfel, Flament, Billig, and Bundy, 1971), and the preference is so strong that individuals have been found to value their own group members most highly even when group membership has been randomly assigned (Billig & Tajfel, 1973). From these findings, Billig and Tajfel conclude that social and cognitive theories of intragroup behavior should consider the role of affiliation on group behavior. Although much prejudice has been based on hostility and aggression (see Allport, 1958), the significant effect of affiliation has mostly been overlooked.

Determinants of Behavioral Change

Because behavior can alter attitudes, change agents must identify as many social determinants of behavior as possible in order to create the most effective change strategies. The most notable of these determinants of behavior are social pressures exerted by family, peers, valued leaders, religious affiliations, mass media, and any other social contingency or norm that dictates behavior. Because certain behavior is expected from individuals who are members of a group, it is extremely difficult for change agents to alter one individual's behavior unless the group's pressure for confirmity is removed. Social pressures from the family and peer groups greatly influence how an individual will behave. Meaningful change cannot be accomplished until strategies are developed that alter the pressures exerted by a significant number of such social determinants.

Social determinants of behavior also effect change through their interaction with an individual's cognitive predispositions and personality. For example, the degree to which an individual is emotionally attached to an issue determines the ability to alter behavior. The firmer the hold individuals have on their beliefs and the stronger the social pressure, the more emotionally attached they will be to the beliefs. As Katz (1960) explains, the "simpler the attitude in the cognitive structure, the easier it is to change"; but when beliefs have high emotional involvement and ego attachement, it is less likely that change can be induced from external sources. Strong pressure to change emotionally attached beliefs from low-status sources, such as change agents, for example, may cause an individual to protect these beliefs in an even more zealous manner.

Another factor that affects behavioral change is the "latitude of acceptance" held by an individual. The beliefs an individual possesses have boundaries that act as barriers to the acceptance or rejection of new information. This "contrast and assimilation effect" (explained by Hovland, Harvey, and Sherif, 1957), depends on the proximity of an advocated position to an individual's attitudes and beliefs. If an advocated behavior falls within an individual's latitude of acceptance, the position will be assimilated; if the position appears too extreme (outside the latitude of acceptance), it will be rejected. For example, integration of the races might be too extreme for bigoted individuals because it falls outside their latitude of acceptance; the integration of blacks into professional sports might fall within the latitude of acceptance and thus be considered appropriate.

These determinants that affect the likelihood of behavioral change cannot be considered inclusive because total accuracy in the prediction of human behavior is impossible. A completely deterministic theory of behavioral change cannot be developed because human behavior does not always follow rational predictions. We know that certain factors do affect behavioral change, however, and from our understanding of these we can predict that individuals will be motivated to the greatest extent to change their behavior and beliefs, under the following conditions: when the change advocated comes from a valued source, possesses the least emotional attachment, is cognitively simple, falls within the latitude of acceptance, and creates a dissonant situation with perceived choice and minimal coercion.

Since, as Bem has stated (1970), sufficient evidence exists that attitudes do follow behavioral changes, how then do change agents intervene in the social environment to change discriminatory behavior with the eventual hope of changing attitudes? We will now investigate these methods of instituting social change.

INTERNAL AND EXTERNAL SOCIAL INTERVENTION

Social change can be accomplished from inside or outside the social system. Hornstein (1975) listed four methods of intervention used by change agents. These focused on "outside pressure," "people changes," "organizational development," and "analysis for the top." Our discussion uses two categories: external intervention and internal intervention, which includes all of Hornstein's items other than outside pressure.

Internal Interventions

Internal interventions include attempts to change individuals through "sensitivity training" or "behavior modification" and attempts to improve problem-solving capabilities within an organization "by changing the norms and values regulating behavior [Hornstein, 1975, p. 219]. Internal analysis for the top levels of an organization is identified by Hornstein as an intervention to provide feedback and advice to the top management of a system or an organization. In order for change to occur through internal intervention methods, the members of a social system must open their system for inspection. The change agent must be *invited* into the system and given the power to institute change. The necessity for invitation is a major disadvantage of the internal method, especially when change agents are not empowered to implement the treatments they recommend. They may be unwelcome should their diagnosis or treatment be contrary to the wishes of the leaders. In any of the internal methods of intervention, change agents have a limited capacity to institute large-scale changes. Additionally, interventions are typically limited to relatively autonomous organizations. However, invited change agents engaged in internal intervention are endowed with a certain amount of authority, since their intervention has been approved of. This is often not true of external change agents.

External Interventions

Whereas internal methods require acquiescence from within, external methods are imposed from outside the social system. By expanding the basic definition of Hornstein (1975), which included "mass demonstration, civil disobedience, and violence", external intervention can be viewed as extending from the extremes of violence (making change

Violence   Goodwill

_____

(Making change happen)   (Waiting for change)

FIGURE 6.2   External intervention continuum.

happen) to goodwill (waiting for change). The placement of external methods of intervention on a continuum such as that in Figure 6.2 will provide a more complete view of the range of choices available to change agents. At one end of the continuum change is aggressively pursued through physical means, while at the other extreme external agents passively wait for change because of their religious or social beliefs. For example, in the women's movement we have seen the leftist extreme of violence as advocated by Marxist revolutionaries, the more moderate civil disobedience pursued by the National Organization of Women, and the waiting-for-change position of conservative women who feel that change will come of its own accord.

A major advantage of externally instituted change is that invitation is not needed to begin the intervention process. Should individuals who have no internal access to the social system view change as necessary, they need not wait for members of an internal system to invite an intervention. Individuals without invitations can initiate change by choosing one of the methods for outside pressure. The two distinct disadvantages associated with external interventions are danger of physical harm and polarization. Change imposed upon a social system by severely coercive methods often lead to violent resistance and reaction from individuals within the system. In addition, the use of physical force does not create dissonance, since individuals can directly attribute their changed behavior to the coercion. In accordance with cognitive consistency theories, change in attitudes would not be expected under these coercive conditions.

External intervention may also polarize individuals within the system. When change is advocated from a dubious source (e.g., "radicals"), traditionalists may reject any attempt at change and hold more firmly to their beliefs. Sympathetic individuals within a system may also move away from the positions advocated because of the tactics used by change agents. Although they may favor change, sympathetic individuals may not condone coercive tactics (e.g., civil disobedience, destruction of property); they may become polarized in the opposite position. On the other hand, polarization can serve a positive function by increasing the awareness of apathetic individuals within a system. Simply by forcing people to become involved with social issues, regardless of their position, change is accomplished. The hope is, of course, that apathetic individuals will choose the mantle of social justice.

External intervention has been the method used by black leaders to fight racial discrimination. Because no individuals were invited by the southern white power structure to inspect or alter social conditions, civil rights leaders selected strategies to induce change externally. Through civil disobedience, these change agents were able to intervene and in many cases usurp the maintenance of the status quo in the south. Although the interventions in the south were imposed externally upon the social system, the leaders also used change strategies to work *along with* the federal government to lobby for civil rights legislation. In a similar manner, individuals opposed to discrimination against women are often forced to intervene externally. Because inspection of the inequitable situation in employment and education has generally not been invited by the individuals in power, some form of external intervention has been necessary.

In the selection of strategies for change, violence is often viewed as too extreme and waiting for change has appeared to be too slow. For change agents who are forced to choose an external strategy, the most appropriate intervention appears to be those that fall along the middle of the external-intervention continuum. These middle-ground strategies include efforts such as civil disobedience, boycott, protest, legal action, and fiat from a higher governmental authority.

CHANGE THROUGH LEGISLATION

Legislation prescribes normative behavior through law. Because social science research has indicated that attitudes will be altered to coincide with changes in behavior, the legislation of behavior can be one of the most effective methods in changing inequitable social situations in our democracy. Legislation falls between the extremes of violence and the hope of good will (see Figure 6.3), and it is often seen as a most useful way to implement social change.

Legislation and Dissonance

Since the legislation of behavior is less coercive than violence, legal requirements that dictate nondiscrimination can create a dissonant situation for individuals who are opposed to such behavior. The legal system is governed by the majority group in our society, and thus a behavioral

Violence	Legislation	Goodwill

| (Making change happen) | | (Waiting for change) |

FIGURE 6.3 Intervention continuum.

change requiring nondiscrimination legislated by the peers (lawmakers) of this majority group can create dissonance. Legislation, therefore, provides the two requisite factors necessary for creating a dissonant situation: minimal coercion (as opposed to violence) and perception of choice (election of legislators). Because nondiscriminatory legislation can create dissonance for some individuals, these individuals may rationalize their behavior by engaging in one of the dissonance-reducing methods outlined by Adams (1961). For example, equal-rights legislation might cause prejudiced individuals to rationalize that it was because of the liberals that their legislators voted for equal rights; or that the legislation will not affect them since they have no prejudice; or that the equal-rights condition is only temporary and will soon fade; or that they always knew their legislators were scoundrels and that new ones should be elected. In a similar manner, bigoted individuals rationalize the nondiscriminatory behavior in which they are engaged: "The government made us do it." By being able to blame a legitimate external agents (the federal government), norms and behavior will change; but stubborn pride can remain.

Value Change

For legislation to be effective, the law must accomplish more than behavioral change. To create social reform and alter attitudes, legislation must also change the value order of the target group. Since individuals order their values (Schuman, 1972), any rationale for behavioral change must be linked to a high-ordered value. Legislative action alone may not alter attitudes if these attitudes are not part of the highest order of values. With the linkage of a proposed behavioral change, such as nondiscrimination, to a high-priority value, such as economic rewards, individuals can be shown the benefits of a new behavior. For example, legislation that offers economic incentives for hiring minorities may induce individuals who value economic gains to adopt the proposed hiring behavior; and legislation that dictates economic penalties for noncompliance (e.g., loss of federal funds) may induce economically minded individuals to change their behavior. In our avaricious society, this linkage of behavior to economic rewards or penalties certainly offers one of the best methods to induce behavioral change. Legislation that can demonstrate economic advantages for compliance can be extremely effective in a capitalistic society.

Socially Shared Autism

Title IX and other laws that prohibit discrimination in education are examples of legislation to induce change. Such legislation also serves to break down the "socially shared autism" that defines the role of women in the educational arena. Deutsch and Collins have explained this concept (originated by Murphy, 1947) as follows: "A vicious circle or a 'socially shared autism' is established whereby without personal experience with members of a minority group, contact with the prevailing attitude toward them provides the 'experience' to support a prejudice [1952, p. 585]." This socially shared autism assists in the development and maintenance of prejudice that results from a lack of knowledge or contact with other groups or individuals.

Deutsch and Collins (1952) and Hamilton and Bishop (1976) studied the dynamics of socially shared autism where different racial groups were integrated in housing projects. Both sets of researchers found that socially shared autism can be altered through integration of the prejudiced group (whites) with the object of the prejudice (blacks). A statement typical of the support for the findings of Deutsch and Collins is from a white woman in the integrated housing project: "I had always heard things about how they [blacks] were . . . they were dirty, drank a lot . . . were like savages. . . . Living with them, my ideas changed altogether. They're just people . . . they're not different [1952, p. 591]." Although Amir (1976) has viewed the results of the housing-integration studies as equivocal, research by Tajfel et al. (1971) and Billig and Tajfel (1973) found preferences for one's own group, and this should encourage change agents to devise strategies to integrate diverse groups.

Prejudice against women is an excellent example of socially shared autism. Although males have contact with females in society, neither men nor women often see women performing in roles traditionally held by men. This lack of professional contact has maintained ignorance and created stereotypes of women, such as the perception that women are incapable of being a principal or superintendent. Through the integration of men and women in professional roles and nonstereotypic work situations (where women are not always subordinant to men), Title IX exposes the socially shared autism that defines a woman's abilities in education. Title IX forces men and women into contact with women who are engaged in professional roles once reserved only for men. Such social integration forces both sexes to confront their stereotyped beliefs about women's social roles. Since psychological theory and evidence (Tavris, 1973; Schuman, 1972) explain that attitudes do not necessarily indicate behavior, Title IX does not rely on abstract attitudinal affirmation; it attempts to effect nondiscrimination by requiring a concrete integration of the sexes in education. The effects of Title IX will be limited, however, unless a sufficient number of females are integrated into the educational system to alter the status quo. In a study of public prejudice against women in administration Stockard (1979) explained that "having only a small number of minority group members available for contact may produce little challenge to previous attitudes because those members are simply viewed as exceptional." Unless Title IX can infuse a sufficient number of women into education to alter the norm of male administrators, the status quo will remain the status quo. Single, isolated individuals can do little to alter norms; however, the integration of a large number of women to challenge the present nature of educational administration can induce changes in attitudes.

Title IX is attempting to erase sexual discrimination in a manner similar to that of civil rights legislation, which required racially prejudiced individuals to engage in nondiscriminatory behavior towards blacks. The legal requirements for racial integration have helped mitigate the socially shared autism that exists about blacks. Through civil rights legislation, prejudiced whites have been forced to deal in a concrete form with their stereotyped ideas of the capabilities and social role of blacks, and prejudiced attitudes toward blacks have dramatically declined (Light & Keller, 1975). Civil rights legislation has also provided an additional rationale for engaging in nondiscriminatory behavior. After integration became law, whites could no longer fear contempt from their peers for humane overtures to blacks because these gestures were now legally required. Since nondiscrimination in the past was considered deviant behavior and a violation of the social norm, whites engaging in such behavior were ostracized from society. Civil rights legislation has not only induced behavioral change; it has provided a convenient rationale for humane treatment of blacks.

Change in Social Norms

Legislation can be an excellent social intervention method because it also has the capacity to change social norms. Although simply placing new people in an unchanged structure cannot assure change (Jacobs & Campbell, 1961), legislation can assist in altering the system's structure by placing new people in new social roles. When members of society who were once excluded from full participation in the social system are integrated into new roles, new norms can emerge; and old norms must be abandoned as inappropriate in the new and changed system. For example, the hiring of women for managerial positions has become a new social norm in some organizations. For these organizations, the failure to hire women exposes them as prejudicial among those that do employ women. In this situation, discrimination against women is not only illegal, but contrary to the new social norm of hiring women. Although nondiscrimination in employment was initially forced by legislation, this induced behavior is slowly leading to a change in the social norm. Legislation changes social norms by operating in a cyclical manner, as illustrated in Figure 6.4. First, legislation dictates a change in behavior, which causes attitudes to become consistent with the new behavior. The changed behavior and attitudes create new social norms, which in turn, cause further behavioral change.

An example of this cyclical process is the manner in which Title IX legislation has affected sports. The dictated behavioral change of nondiscrimination against women has begun to alter public attitudes toward the participation of women in varsity athletics at the college and university level. Because women cannot be discriminated against in sports participation, the social autism that fosters the inability of women to engage in such activity has begun to change. By seeing that women can actively participate in sports, the public has changed its attitudes, and these new attitudes have created, in turn, the new norm of women in sports. Because of this new norm, behavior has changed even more, and we now see competitive recruitment for top female athletes. This recruitment of the best female athletes changes attitudes even further about the appropriateness of women in varsity sports, which changes norms still further, and so forth in a cyclical manner.

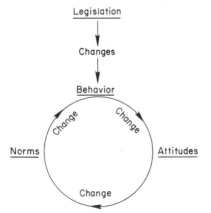

FIGURE 6.4 Cyclical effect of legislating change.

Advantages and Disadvantages of Legislative Changes

Although civil disobedience, boycott, and protest may be necessary antecedents of change, these external interventions cannot alter the behavior of the target group in the manner that legislation can. The target groups can ignore protests and remain unaffected by civil disobedience and boycott; but target groups cannot ignore as easily legislation, executive orders, and court injunctions from a higher-power authority (the federal government), and therefore these can be most effective nonviolent strategies for inducing behavioral changes. The legislative process may last several years, however, and change induced in this manner does have several disadvantages. In addition to the time required to lobby and to create, pass, and enact a law, a supportive climate for legislation must exist. Before lawmakers will even consider passing laws, alliances must be formed between change agents and legislators who are willing to impose change on a target group. People attempting to effect behavioral changes through legislation are at a most significant disadvantage when all members of the highest-powered authority wish to maintain the status quo. When this condition exists, other forms of external methods to induce change must be used. Such a social climate can lead to violent social upheaval.

Change through legislation is also disadvantaged by the effect of law enforcement. When physical coercion is needed for legislative enforcement, the hope of attitudinal change may be lost because target groups use physical enforcement as a rationale for their behavior and no dissonance is created. However, legislation can create a dissonant situation when economic or other noncoercive methods are used for enforcement. In summary, while the legal process may be more time consuming than other methods for bringing about change, legislation exposes socially shared autism by changing social norms, requires no invitation by the target group, accomplishes change more quickly than waiting for good will, and is preferable to violence. Legislation basically includes the requisites for behavioral and attitudinal change because it uses minimal coercion, provides the perception of choice through elected lawmakers, and can appeal to highly ordered values by providing an economic rationale.

CHANGES IN THE SOCIAL SYSTEM

Although legislation can alter behavior, it cannot comprehensively alleviate discriminatory conditions unless the social system is also restructured. The one major disadvantage of legislation, previously discussed, is that change must occur within a system amenable to such change. In addition, it is difficult for legislation to alter societal problems that are basic to a system's structure.

The Work Pyramid

The inherent dissatisfaction in our industrial society, which was identified by Drucker (1964), is one basic problem not easily remedied by legislation. Because Americans are socialized to become "number one" in all endeavors, Drucker notes, "getting ahead is seen as the exclusive criterion for success". Unfortunately, only a small percentage of number-one positions are available in our society, and, "if, as is the case in our society, advancement is seen as the only social goal, if every other satisfaction is regarded as subsidiary, the majority must necessarily feel dissatisfied [p. 130]." In other words, dissatisfaction is inherent in our social system because not everyone can advance to the top. The pyramid in Figure 6.5 illustrates why this is so. Most vocational positions in society are found at the pyramid's base and few jobs are available that have high status, power and income. The small percentage of these highly sought number-one positions are found at the pyramid's peak, accessible to relatively few people in society. For instance, in education there are many more teachers than principals and many more principals than school superintendents.

The number one positions in society are not only few, but they are accessible primarily to white Anglo-Saxon Protestant males. Attempts to remedy this inequitable situation have been made through the passage of nondiscriminatory legislation. These laws have required that women and ethnic minorities be given access to professions, jobs, and schools previously open only to white males. Although this has theoretically opened access to top positions in society, the structures of the system remain unchanged. By opening positions to women and minorities, legislation has enlarged the pool of workers striving for the top positions, but it has not increased the number of positions. Negative reactions from the white males majority to legislation that has increased the working pool and therefore the competition are not surprising. Since only a small number can rise to the top positions, the percentage of

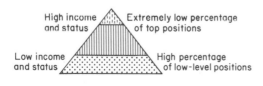

High income and status — Extremely low percentage of top positions

Low income and status — High percentage of low-level positions

FIGURE 6.5 The work-structure pyramid.

FIGURE 6.6 Accessibility to top positions for minorities.

people able to get ahead becomes even smaller when new groups are added. Even thought a white male may have little prejudice toward women or minorities, he will resent the intrusion of these individuals into the working pool because they reduce his opportunity to rise to the top of the social structure. Women and minorities who did not have access to top positions prior to equal-opportunity legislation (see left side of Figure 6.6) now have joined white males in the race for the top (see right of figure).

Getting Ahead

Although women and minorities now legally have access to top positions in society, the inherent dissatisfaction seen by Drucker still exists. Legislation has provided equal access to the top but has done little to alleviate the basic problem that not everyone can advance and become successful. Women and minorities enter the world of work as they did before and the social structure is unchanged. Although participants in the structure have changed, the system has not; getting ahead is still the criterion of success. Legislation has changed the participants, but the participants themselves must work to alter the structure. Through alternative methods of work, increased sharing of authority, expansion of responsibilities, and cooperative management and ownership, the quest for the number one position can be modified. By changing the principle that fulfillment can be attained only through economic gains and getting ahead, individuals should be able to derive greater fulfillment from their contributions to society, regardless of their position in the work structure.

Transformation of the Pyramid

From within organizations, with the use of Hornstein's three internal methods of intervention (personal, organizational development, and analysis for the top), individuals intent on erasing dissatisfaction and social injustices can begin to alter internal norms. Externally, intervention can be accomplished, for example, through legislation, which provides economic incentives for the implementation of alternative methods of work, organizational development, and rewards.

Equal access to all positions

FIGURE 6.7   Ultimate work structure of work system.

Ultimately, individuals should feel satisfied by reaping societal and economic rewards from positions other than number one. Positions of differing social and economic status will undoubtedly continue to exist, but personal advancement cannot be the only social goal in a system that must rely upon all members to provide an equitable and humane social structure. The pyramid could ultimately become an oval (see Figure 6.7), with all members of society having access to all positions and deriving satisfaction and rewards from their contribution to the social system. We agree with Drucker, however, that the "realization of human dignity, the achievement of status and fulfillment" still remains "the major unanswered question of industrial society [1964, p. 130]."

REFERENCES

Adams, F. S. (1961). "Reduction of Cognitive Dissonance by Seeking Consonant Information." *Journal of Abnormal and Social Psychology,* 62:74–78.

Allport, G. W. (1958). *The Nature of Prejudice.* Doubleday, Garden City, N.Y.

Amir, Y. (1976). "The Role of Intergroup Contact in Change of Prejudice and Ethnic Relations." In *Towards the Elimination of Racism* (P. Katz, ed.). Pergamon Press, New York.

Bem, D. J. (1970). *Beliefs, Attitudes and Human Affairs.* Brooks/Cole, Belmont, Calif.

Billig, M., and Tajfel, H. (1973). "Social Categorization and Similarity in Intergroup Behavior." *European Journal of Social Psychology,* 3:27–52.

Brehm, J. W., and Cohen, A. R. (1962). *Explorations in Cognitive Dissonance.* Wiley, New York.

Deutsch, M., and Collins, M. E. (1952). "The Effect of Public Policy in Housing Projects upon Interracial Attitudes." In *Readings in Social Psychology* (G. Swanson et al., eds.). Holt, Rinehart and Winston, New York.

Drucker, P. F. (1964). *The Concept of the Corporation.* New American Library, New York.

Festinger, L. (1957). *A Theory of Cognitive Dissonance.* Harper & Row, New York.

Hamilton, D. L., and Bishop, G. D. (1976). "Attitudinal and Behavioral Effects of Initial Integration of White Suburban Neighborhoods." *Journal of Social Issues,* 32:47–68.

Hornstein, H. A. (1975). "Social Psychology as Social Intervention." In *Applying Social Psychology: Implications for Research, Practice and Training* (M. Deutsch and H. A. Hornstein, eds.). Lawrence Elaum, Hillsdale, N.J.

Hovland, C. I., Harvey, O. J., and Sherif, M. (1957). "Assimilation and Contrast Effects in Reactions to Communication and Attitude Change." *Journal of Abnormal and Social Psychology,* 55:242–252.

Jacobs, R. C., and Campbell, D. T. (1961). "The Perpetuation of an Arbitrary Tradition through Several Generations of a Laboratory Microculture." *Journal of Abnormal and Social Psychology*, 3:649–658.

Katz, D. (1960). "The Functional Approach to the Study of Attitudes." *Public Opinion Quarterly*, 24:163–204.

Light, D., and Keller, S. (1975). *Sociology*. Knopf, New York.

Murphy, G. (1947). *Personality: A Biosocial Approach to Origin and Structure*. Harper & Row, New York.

Myrdal, G., Sterner, R., and Rose, A. (1944). *An American Dilemma*. Harper & Row, New York.

Pettigrew, T. F. (1959). "Regional Differences in Anti-Negro Prejudice." *Journal of Abnormal and Social Psychology*, 59:28–36.

Schram, S. R., ed. (1967). *Quotations from Chairman Mao-Tse-Tung*. Bantam Books, New York, p. 118. Originally from "On Practice," *Selected Works*, vol. 1, by Mao Tse-Tung (1937), p. 299.

Schuman, H. (1972). Attitudes vs. Actions *versus* Attitudes vs. Attitudes." *Public Opinion Quarterly*, 36:347–354.

Stockard, J. (1979). "Public Prejudice against Women School Administrators: The Possibility of Change." *Educational Administration Quarterly*, 15:83–96.

Tajfel, H. (1969). "Cognitive Aspects of Prejudice." *Journal of Social Issues*, 25:79–98.

Tajfel, H. Flament, C., Billig, M., and Bundy, R. (1971). "Social Categorization and Intergroup Behavior." *European Journal of Social Psychology*, 1:149–178.

Tavris, C. (1973). "Who Likes Women's Liberation—and Why! The Case of the Unliberated Liberal." *Journal of Social Issues*, 29:175–198.

Triandis, H. C. (1972). "The Impact of Social Change in Attitudes." In *Attitudes, Conflict and Social Change* (B. King and E. McGinnies, eds.). Academic Press, New York.

Chapter 7

LAWS PROHIBITING SEX DISCRIMINATION IN THE SCHOOLS

Peg Williams

[We] might say that those with similar abilities and skills should have similar life chances. . . . In all sectors of society there should be roughly equal prospects of culture and achievements for everyone similarly motivated and endowed [Rawls, 1971, p. 73].

It is impossible to ignore the importance of legal issues in education. Courts are expanding the rights of students, state laws are requiring collective bargaining, and federal legislation is demanding special programs and services for disadvantaged children. Educators often feel overrun by so many federal and judicial requirements. Recent legal requirements address inequities based on race, sex, handicap, and other innate characteristics. The legal system, through legislation, has become the tool for changing unwanted social attitudes by demanding changes in behavior. Changes, however, may be slow. For example, while legislation has opened doors traditionally closed to blacks and women, it has not made an appreciable impact on the income gap between white males, on the one hand, and women and minorities, on the other. As a result, overcoming the increasingly complex and subtle forms of sex discrimination will require the law's never-ending vigilance.

MODEL OF THE LEGAL SYSTEM

Legal efforts to address inequities regarding the status of sexual and minority groups have taken a variety of forms. Presidents have signed executive orders; legislators have passed statutes; government agencies have issued regulations; and courts have interpreted governmental actions. To assist in understanding this multitude of legal actions, we will first give a model for understanding the legal system and then review the development of laws against sex discrimination. Following this we will discuss in detail the current legislation prohibiting sex discrimination in the schools.

The legal system is represented in Figure 7.1 by a larger circle with five major components representing five sources of the law: statutes, executive orders, regulations, case law, and the United States Constitution. The following sections of this chapter describe the relationships among these five components.

The Constitution

The United States Constitution, the basic component of the model, is at the core of the legal system and superior to all other forms of law. The Constitution is composed primarily of principles established by the founders of our country. These principles are abstract concepts that allow for flexibility in their interpretation. The principle found in the Fourteenth Amendment to the Constitution, which has been central to legal advances in the area of civil rights, is "equal protection of the laws." In 1896 this principle was interpreted to mean that "separate but equal" facilities for blacks and whites were constitutional (*Plessy* v.

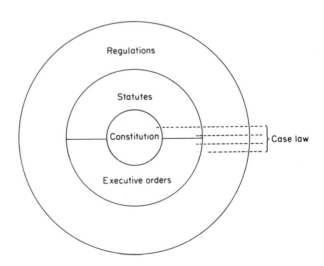

FIGURE 7.1   Model of the legal system. This model was inspired by John Snowden, Professor of Law, College of Law, University of Nebraska.

Ferguson, 1896). In 1954, however, the landmark decision of *Brown* v. *Board of Education* interpreted the same principle to mean that "separate but equal" facilities were inherently unequal and therefore unconstitutional.

The central importance of the Constitution affects the legal system in two ways. First, all other laws must conform with the Constitution, and second, judges are reluctant to interpret the Constitution because their decisions can have a far-reaching impact on other laws. Judges attempt to base their decisions on other less centralized and more specific laws, and therefore courts more frequently rely on statutes rather than on the equal-protection clause of the Constitution when reaching decisions in cases of sex discrimination.

Some court cases have interpreted the meaning of the constitutional principle of "equal protection of the laws," and judges find that different types of discrimination require different types of judicial review. To date, Supreme Court justices have refused to give people suffering from sex discrimination the same protection given to individuals claiming racial discrimination (Seitz, 1977). For instance, it is not a denial of equal protection of the law to maintain a state college "for women only" when other state-supported schools are available for men and when there is no "special feature" connected with the sex segregated college; but a similar state college for blacks only or whites only would violate the equal-protection clause (Babcock, Freedman, Norton, & Ross, 1975, citing *Williams* v. *McNair*).

Courts view some types of discrimination as "suspect"; that is, discrimination that deserves the greatest amount of protection. Racial discrimination is suspect in the eyes of the law, and it is treated differently from the way sex discrimination is treated. To date, sex discrimination has not been considered "suspect" (Seitz, 1977). As a result, proponents of the Equal Rights Amendment (ERA), wish to prohibit sex discrimination by an additional constitutional amendment that would specifically require equal treatment of males and females. With such an amendment in the Constitution, the courts would in all likelihood be required to treat both sex and racial discrimination as "suspect."

Statutes

A layer of statutes surrounds the Constitutional component of our model. A statute, or act, is passed by a legislature and results in a rule that defines the law more specifically and narrowly than the Constitution does. A statute gives a clear indication of what actions are legal and what illegal and therefore gives a better notion of what citizens must do in following the law. One illustration of a statute is Title IX of the Education Amendments of 1972. The words of this act clearly and concisely forbid discriminating by sex in any school program or activity that receives federal money: "No person in the United States shall, on the basis of sex, be excluded from participation in, be denied benefits of, or be subjected to discrimination under any education program or activity receiving Federal financial assistance ... [Title IX of Education Amendments of 1972, §901, 20 U.S.C. §1681(a) (1976).]"

Executive Orders

Because they resemble statutes, executive orders are also in the second layer of our model of the legal system. They too are specific rules for behavior rather than abstract principles; and they are generally equal to statutes in power and authority. However, executive orders originate from the president, within the executive branch of government, rather than from congress, within the legislative branch of government. Two important executive orders (EO) in the area of civil rights are EO 11246 and its amendment EO 11375, which were signed by President Johnson in 1965 and 1967. Together, these orders forbid employment discrimination on the basis of sex, race, religion, color, or national origin by employers receiving contracts from the federal government totalling more than $10,000. One requirement of these executive orders requires employers receiving federal contracts of $50,000 or more to develop affirmative action plans for guaranteeing equal employment opportunity.

Regulations

Regulations, which form the third layer of our model, are detailed guidelines for implementing statutes and executive orders. When congress passes a law and when the president signs an executive order, directives are sent to federal agencies that write the guidelines for implementing acts and orders. The regulations for Title IX were written by the Department of Health, Education and Welfare (HEW); the guidelines for EO 11246 and EO 11375 originated from the Office of Federal Contract Compliance of the Department of Labor. These guidelines are quite lengthy and comprehensive and took several years to write. While Title IX was passed in 1972, the regulations for Title IX did not appear until 1976.

Case Law

The last component of our model is case law, which cuts across all the layers of the legal system. Case law includes the long series of court decisions and judicial precedence. There are numerous instances of case law in the sex-discrimination area, for example, the *Romeo* decision on Title IX, the *General Electric* case on Title VII, and the *Reed* decision on the equal-protection clause. Case law affects the legal system because court decisions interpret the language in constitutions, statutes, executive orders, and regulations. In addition, case law ensures that components of the legal model appropriately interrelate. Judges determine the meaning of the law when interpreting Title IX, which forbids discrimination in any school program or activity receiving federal money. For instance, judges have been asked whether Title IX must be followed by all portions of a university or by only those departments or programs within a university that actually receive federal money (Status, 1978). Judges also ensure that the components of the legal system are correctly interrelated. They decide whether regulations drafted by an agency such as HEW correctly interpret the act from which they emerge (e.g., see *Romeo* v. *HEW*, 1977).

Two factors limit the effect of case law. First, basing a court decision upon a specific set of facts limits the legal effect of the decisions on similar situations. One illustration of how a ruling is limited is the *Brown* decision. This decision resulted in the court-made law that "separate but equal" facilities for blacks and whites are inherently unequal. The effect of this ruling is limited to cases of discrimination on the basis of race, and the ruling does not set a precedent for cases of sex discrimination. In fact, having a separate but equal athletic program for each sex is legal in certain instances (Kadzielski, 1977, citing *Ritacco* v. *Norwin School District*). The power and jurisdiction of the particular court also limit the effects of a court's decision. Decisions of the United States Supreme Court apply to all citizens; lower federal courts affect those people who reside in the judical district, or circuit; state courts control the actions of citizens within a state. The *Brown* decision was reached at the Supreme Court level and therefore binds all citizens covered by the Fourteenth Amendment of the Constitution.

Much of the current law prohibiting sex discrimination is found at the state level as well as at the federal level. A model can also be constructed for understanding a state's constitution, statutes, executive orders, regulations, and case law. There are times when the model of the federal legal system interrelates with models at the state level, but a thorough discussion of this relationship is beyond the scope of this chapter.

DEVELOPMENT OF LAW PROHIBITING SEX DISCRIMINATION

Laws against sex discrimination have gradually developed over the years. In the following sections we examine attitudinal barriers that exist within the court system; we summarize the legally recognized forms of discrimination; we give a historical overview of the development of the laws; and we provide specific reviews of the laws that affect schools.

Attitudinal Barriers within the Courts

Although since its ratification in 1868 the Fourteenth Amendment of the Constitution has promised "any person" the equal protection of the law, until recently, little has been done to guarantee those rights to women (Levin, 1975). The reasons for this inaction stem from societal notions of a woman's appropriate role. In 1873 the justices of the United States Supreme Court reflected these expectations of a woman's place: "Man is, or should be, woman's protector and defender. The natural and proper timidity and delicacy which belong to the female sex evidently unfits it for many of the occupations of civil life. . . . The paramount destiny and mission of women are to fulfill the noble and benign offices of wife and mother. This is the law of the creator [*Bradwell* v. *Illinois*, 83 U.S. 139 (1873)]."

There is some evidence of change from these early notions. In 1975 justices on the bench of the Supreme Court wrote: "No longer is the female destined solely for the home and the rearing of the family, and only the male for the marketplace and world of ideas. . . . The presence of women in business, in the professions, in government and, indeed, in all walks of life where education is a desirable, if not always a necessary antecedent, is apparent and a proper subject of judical notice [*Stanton* v. *Stanton*, 421 U.S. 7, 14 (1975)]."

The paternalistic notions of 1873 persisted into modern times, however, for in 1966, a Mississippi court upheld a state statute that excluded women from serving on juries. The judge wrote: "The legislature has the right to exclude women so they may continue their service as mothers, wives, and homemakers, and so to protect them (in some areas they are still upon a pedestal) from the filth, obscenity, and obnoxious atmosphere that so often pervades a courtroom during a jury trial [*State* v. *Hall*, 187 So. 2d 861, 863 (1966); appeal dismissed, 835 U.S. 98 (1966)]."

As late as 1971 a Connecticut court was reflecting traditional sex-role expectations in a decision that excluded girls from a high school cross-country running team: "In the world of sports, there is ever present as a challenge, the psychology to win. With boys vying with girls in cross-country running and indoor track, the challenge to win, and the glory of achievement, at least for many boys, would lose incentive and become nullified. Athletic competition builds character in our boys. We do not need that kind of character in our girls, the women of tomorrow

[Babcock *et al.*, 1975, citing *Hollander* v. *Conn. Interscholastic Athletic Conf., Inc.*]."

Because of decisions within the legal system that simply reflect and perpetuate traditional societal attitudes about sex roles, efforts to change discriminatory practices are continuing (e.g., see *Griggs* v. *Duke Power Co.*, 1971). Understanding these efforts requires a general overview of the ways discrimination occurs.

Legally Recognized Forms of Discrimination

In general, discrimination burdens a particular group of people but not others. Its various forms can be grouped into two general types: intentional and unintentional. Frequently, initial efforts to prohibit discrimination focus on intentional discrimination. Judges often use the Latin phrase *de jure* to refer to intentional discrimination (Reutter, 1976), the form that occurs when a governmental action willfully discriminates on the basis of sex, race, or other immutable characteristics. Intentional discrimination may occur (*a*) in the wording of statutes and policies from a governmental body or agency, (*b*) in governmental application of statutes and policies with unbiased wording, and (*c*) in the motive of legislators when they pass seemingly unbiased statutes.

For instance, one state law that is worded in a discriminatory manner explicitly gives a preference to men over women as administrators of an estate (*Reed* v. *Reed*, 1971). An example of discrimination in the application of an unbiased statute or policy can be seen when school administrators intentionally draw attendance lines around the predominantly black areas of the community for the purpose of segregating the schools. The seemingly unbiased statute regarding attendance lines is being applied in a discriminatory manner (*Keyes* v. *School District No. 1, Denver, Colorado*, 1973). An example of a discriminatory motive in passing an unbiased statute is for legislators to use their legal power to close public facilities and vote to close public schools in order to avoid racial desegregation (*Griffin* v. *County School Board*, 1964).

Judges often use the Latin term *de facto* to refer to unintentional discrimination (Reutter, 1976). This form of bias is often more subtle and more difficult to detect. It results when a governmental action that is nondiscriminatory in its terms, intended application, and motive still has a discriminatory effect. For example, public officials may propose a city boundary change that is nondiscriminatory in its wording, application, and motivation; but if the net effect of the change is to remove virtually all black voters from the city, then the boundary change has a discriminatory effect (*Gomillin* v. *Lightfoot*, 1960).

Historical Overview

Judges, legislators, presidents, and other public officials have addressed both intentional and unintentional forms of discrimination at various points in history. In the early 1960s civil rights legislation was passed prohibiting sex discrimination. In the mid-1960s the president signed executive orders concerning sex discrimination. In 1971 with the *Reed* decision, the justices on the Supreme Court actively began using the equal-protection clause of the Constitution to prohibit sex discrimination. Although several laws prohibiting sex discrimination existed, their effect was not felt in the schools until around 1972. Until that year, the law largely exempted the educational institutions of this country from legislation against sex discrimination, with the exception of EO 11375 and the equal-protection clause of the Constitution, which was not actively used by the Supreme Court to prohibit sex discrimination until 1971. EO 11375 concerned the then few schools that were federal contractors of more than $10,000. The legal system's involvement in addressing sex discrimination in education begins around 1972. In that year, Title IX was passed by Congress, and existing civil rights legislation was amended to prohibit sex discrimination in the schools.

Laws That Affect Schools

Within education, the numerous laws against sex discrimination guarantee two basic rights: equal educational opportunity, or the right of all persons to an education on the basis of ability and interest; and equal employment opportunity, or the right to work and advance on the basis of merit, ability, and potential (Russell, 1978). There are two legal means for guaranteeing these rights. Laws demand, first, general policies and practices that are nondiscriminatory, and second, affirmative action in addressing discrimination. Nondiscriminatory policies passively follow the law by developing neutral practices (Russell, 1978). A school board might adopt a policy on nondiscrimination in its district. In contrast, affirmative action takes a positive step towards remedying past discrimination by actively seeking out previously underrepresented groups. Affirmative steps to make up for past discrimination can be externally imposed on an employer by a court of law or internally initiated by an employer through self-evaluation studies and affirmative action plans (Russell, 1978).

Excluding interpretations of the equal-protection clause, there are four laws against sex discrimination that have a significant impact on the schools: Title VII of the Civil Rights Act of 1964, as amended in 1972; the Equal Pay Act of 1963, as amended in 1972 and again in 1974; Executive

Order 11246, as amended by EO 11375; and Title IX of the Education Amendments of 1972.

Title VII as Amended in 1972.

Title VII forbids discrimination against employees on the basis of race, color, religion, sex, or national origin. It covers all employers and is enforced by the Office of Equal Employment Opportunities within the Department of Labor. If an institution violates this law, a variety of remedies are available to the employee suffering from discrimination, including back pay, reinstatement, and/or money damages. The 1972 amendments to Title VII extended protection against employment discrimination based on race, color, sex, religion, and national origin to employees within state and local governments and educational institutions.

Equal Pay Act as Amended in 1972 and 1974

The Equal Pay Act prohibits discrimination against employees on the basis of sex while employers are paying them wages, including fringe benefits. From the 1971 amendments all employers are covered by this act. The Wage and Hour Division of the Department of Labor is responsible for enforcing the law. Employers who violate this law may be ordered to abstain from doing further unlawful acts and may have to give salary raises or back pay to employees suffering from discrimination.

EO 11246 as Amended by EO 11375

Executive orders that forbid discrimination against employees on the basis of race, color, religion, sex, or national origin require the development of affirmative action plans. All employers who are federal contractors of more than $10,000 are covered by these laws. Both the Office of Civil Rights within HEW and the Office of Federal Contract Compliance within the Department of Labor are responsible for enforcing the law. If a violation of this law occurs, federal contracts may be suspended or terminated, and future contracts may be barred.

Title IX

Title IX prohibits discrimination against students and educational employees on the basis of sex. All educational institutions receiving federal assistance are covered by this law. The law is enforced by the Office for Civil Rights of HEW. If an institution fails to comply with this law, federal money may be suspended or terminated, and future federal money may be denied.

EDUCATIONAL AREAS AFFECTED BY
CURRENT LEGISLATION

Title IX is of central importance in prohibiting sex discrimination in educational institutions. Its language specifically and comprehensively addresses both school employment and student programs and activities. The act defines an educational institution as any public or private preschool, elementary school, secondary school, or institution of vocational, professional, or higher education. Only two types of educational institutions are not covered by Title IX—military academies and those educational institutions controlled by a religious organization holding religious tenets (such as the belief that sex segregation is divinely ordained) inconsistent with Title IX. The following discussion of prohibitions against sexual discrimination addresses three areas of the schools: admissions, programs and activities, and employment.

Admissions

Title IX forbids the use of the following four types of admissions policies: (*a*) policies treating people differently on the basis of sex; (*b*) policies establishing fixed numbers or quotas on the number of either sex to be admitted; (*c*) policies for administering admissions tests that discriminate against one sex, unless the test correctly predicts successful school performance and no other less discriminatory alternative for screening exists; and (*d*) policies using lists for admissions that rank applicants separately on the basis of sex (Resource Center on Sex Roles in Education, 1977). Additional sections in Title IX explain how to treat information about an applicant's marital or parental status.

For public education, Title IX's requirement of nondiscrimination in admissions applies to all vocational schools at the elementary and secondary level. This results in vocational public schools taught only on a coeducational basis. Title IX's requirement of nondiscrimination in admissions applies only to those other public elementary and secondary schools which choose to admit members of both sexes. This allows some publicly supported schools to remain segregated by sex. Congress allowed this exception for two primary reasons. First, it recognized that the vast majority of public schools were coeducational and were therefore covered by Title IX's admissions requirements; second, it was uncertain whether the effects, below the college level, on education that segregated children by sex, would impede the ending of sex inequality (Buek & Orleans, 1973). Females might be more willing to pursue male sex-typed areas of learning in all-female classrooms. On the other side of the coin, a sex segregated education might be of no help in ending sex differences. For example, females who learn leadership skills in single-sex classrooms might be unwilling or unable to utilize their new skills in mixed-sex groups.

Programs and Materials

Ending sex discrimination in a school environment is a complex task because bias extends from the playground to the classroom reader. Title IX protects students' right to enroll in courses of their choosing and to be treated equally once in the class. Three specific illustrations of discrimination in course offerings provide a better understanding of the law's requirements. First, it is illegal to bar one sex from certain classes. For example, shop classes may not be restricted to males (Dunkle & Sandler, 1974). Second, school districts are not allowed to require the completion of a course by one sex and not the other. A graduation requirement of a course in home economics for females when one is not required for males is therefore considered discriminatory under Title IX. Third, courses offered to students must be taught on a coeducational basis. The only exceptions to this rule are vocal music, sex-education, and physical education courses involving contact sports or groupings by athletic ability (Malloy, 1976).

Vocational education provides students with practical skills and training. As we saw in Chapter 2, female students in this area are often channeled into stereotyped occupations as secretaries or homemakers, while males are placed in various skilled and semiskilled trades. Title IX forbids such "tracking" and demands equal treatment of the sexes in admissions, courses, services, and facilities. Recent federal legislation has added sex-equity specialists in vocational education at the state level (Women's Educational Equity Act, 1977). These specialists offer assistance in addressing the wide variety of sex-equity issues in the vocational education area.

Textbooks may help perpetuate society's stereotypic notions by casting men and women in traditional roles and by excluding important historical contributions by women. However, Congress decided not to include textbooks and curricular materials under Title IX because regulating the printed word could conflict with other laws guaranteeing freedom of speech (Dunkle & Sandler, 1974). Although Title IX does not directly regulate school publications, there are several alternatives available for addressing this form of sex stereotyping. Teachers can voluntarily examine textbooks and curricular materials before using them in the classroom. Local textbook commissions can provide lists of nonsexist texts for course adoption. Several federally funded projects under the Women's Educational Equity Act (WEEA) have developed nonsexist materials for use in the classroom.

Athletics

The law prohibiting sex discrimination in school athletics is controversial and much debated. The Title IX regulations require equal educational opportunity for members of both sexes in all aspects of a school's sports program. Providing equal athletic opportunity is a complex task, and therefore, schools were given an "adjustment" period for making changes in their athletic programs. Elementary schools were to have made the necessary changes by July 21, 1976, secondary and postsecondary schools by July 21, 1978 (Dunkle, 1976). Efforts to equalize athletic opportunity generally begin with an overall program evaluation. The changes a school will make largely depend upon two factors: whether or not the "type of sport" involves contact and whether the school has only a single team or separate teams for males and females. In general, Title IX allows separating the sexes when the activity is a contact sport, such as wrestling, football, or basketball. Noncontact sports may not be segregated on the basis of sex.

The changes schools must make in complying with this simple rule depend on the "team structure" of the school's sports program when the Title IX regulations went into effect. Schools have widely varying sports programs, depending upon such factors as student interest, public support, and financial capabilities. Some schools have sufficient money and interest for creating separate teams for both sexes. Other schools have only a single team for a particular sport. Therefore, there are Title IX requirements that apply to the four different combinations of "team structure" and "type of sport." Title IX allows schools to separate the sexes for contact sports such as wrestling and football. For these sports, it allows schools to prohibit women from trying out for the men's team and men from trying out for the women's team (Dunkle, 1976). Schools provide separate and identical teams if there is adequate student interest. For example, if a sufficient number of women request the formation of a football team when one exists for males, it may be necessary to create a separate football team for the women. But if insufficient female interest exists for football, schools are not required to create a separate football team (Fabri, 1975).

However, Title IX does require schools to provide equal athletic opportunity for both sexes. While schools may not need to create separate and *identical* teams for all contact sports, they may need to provide separate and *comparable* teams for both sexes (Fabri, 1975). For example, if insufficient interest exists for an all-female football team, but there is sufficient interest to form a women's field-hockey team, overall athletic opportunity may be guaranteed by providing football for men and field hockey for women.

Unfortunately, separate teams for both sexes create certain inequities. Separate teams are seldom identical in all respects. Frequently the varsity team is of superior quality, and the other team is of inferior quality (Kadzielski, 1977). Relegating an outstanding athlete to an inferior team simply because of his or her sex may inhibit athletic growth. For example, the outstanding female basketball player may be placed on a female team whose quality is below her level of excellence; but she may be prohibited from trying out and competing on the all-male varsity team. As a result of the situation, recent court cases have begun to question sex segregation for contact sports.

For example, the case of *Yellow Springs . . . Board of Education* v. *Ohio High School Athletic Association*, 443 F. Suppl 753 (1978), challenged the segregation of the sexes for contact sports. Two female students at Yellow Springs High School competed for and were awarded positions on the school's interscholastic basketball team; but because of their sex, the school board excluded them from the team, and created a separate female basketball team on which they could compete. The federal district judge in Ohio found that such an exclusion violated the women's constitutional rights, and the school rule that excluded them was struck down. This case permits outstanding athletes to compete at their level of excellence regardless of their sex. In addition, the court goes beyond the requirements under Title IX in correcting these inequities. The judge relied on the principles found in the Constitution to guarantee equal athletic opportunity for both sexes. In certain instances, Title IX may allow schools to provide a single team for one sex in contact sports areas, such as a single football team only for males. However, overall equal athletic opportunity must be provided, and if necessary, a *comparable* team for the other sex must be provided.

Court cases have also questioned whether school districts with a single team for a contact sport can exclude one sex. In the case of *Darrin* v. *Gould* 85 Wash 2d 859 (1975), two female athletes challenged a Washington Interscholastic Athletic Association rule prohibiting them from participating on the all-male football team. Wishkah High School in Washington provided no girl's contact football team, but they did have an all-male football team. The female athletes met all the eligibility requirements for the males' team, and they were permitted to play on the team during practice sessions. The Washington State Supreme

Court found that the girls' exclusion from playing in games violated both the Constitution and the Washington Equal Rights Amendment. The court found that the eligibility to play in athletic competition must be determined on an individual basis and without regard to the sex of the athlete.

As a general rule, Title IX does not allow segregation of the sexes for noncontact sports. However, in certain instances, it may be possible to find noncontact sports existing on a segregated basis. Title IX allows segregation of the sexes when the selection for the team is based on competitive skills. Therefore, if no athletes of a particular sex have the competitive ability to "make the team," sex segregated teams may result. In addition, although a school may provide integrated classes in a noncontact sport, segregation of the sexes can still occur. Courses may be divided into subgroups which are based on the individual's skill level. The net effect may be some groups which are composed of only one sex.

Some school districts may be able, because of size or financial constraints, to provide only a single team for a noncontact sport. Because Title IX does not permit segregating the sexes for noncontact sports, the single team must be open to members of both sexes. In certain instances, it may be possible to find a single team composed of members of only one sex because of a lack of competitive skill or a lack of student interest. However, a lack of expressed student interest must be investigated and efforts taken to increase the awareness of the underrepresented sex to the athletic opportunities available to them.

The above rules for contact and noncontact sports illustrate the purpose of Title IX, which is simply to remove existing sex barriers. Title IX is not demanding the complete integration of the sexes in all instances. By removing sex barriers and allowing athletes to compete at their ability level, it is hoped that both sexes will be encouraged to excel in all types of sports and that eventually a more complete integration of the sexes in all areas of athletics will result.

Counseling

School counseling assists students in course and career selection, and Title IX prohibits the materials and services provided by school counselors from being sex biased. Discrimination in this area is difficult to remove because it is often subtle (U. of Penn. Law Review eds., 1976). Counselors can inadvertently pass along the sex stereotypes of institutions and reflect their attitudes toward women (Dunkle and Sandler, 1974); and pamphlets and literature in the counselor's office may depict men and women in traditionally sex-typed occupations. To end discrimination, school districts can provide training programs for counselors that stress sex equity, and they can examine materials used by the counselors (University of Pennsylvania Law Review, 1976).

In general, while Title IX may produce changes in official policies regarding student admissions, access to courses, participation in athletics, and counseling, the law has a limited ability to affect the informal selection factor of student interest. Until students begin seeing nontraditional careers as options, the door to these nontraditional areas will remain unused. Title IX's requirements for ending sex discrimination in school counseling may help students begin redefining societal roles. Whereas Title IX prohibits certain discriminatory practices, some more recent court cases are even more radical in demanding changes in sex-role stereotyping.

Employment

When hiring employees, school districts must provide a valid selection procedure, equal opportunity for job security and advancement, fairly assessed fringe benefits, and equal pay for equal work. Portions of several laws guarantee these rights to nondiscrimination in employment. Two significant laws addressing employment in schools are Title VII and Title IX; the first prohibits segregation by sex within the labor force, and the second outlaws segregation by sex within the field of education. Recent court cases have questioned which of these federal laws should be used in interpreting employment decisions in education. An illustration of such a case is *Romeo Community School* v. *HEW*, 438 F. Supp. 1021 (E.D. Mich. 1977), which questioned the validity of certain parts of the employment section of Title IX. The judge reasoned that Title IX should protect only "those persons for whom the federally assisted educational programs are established, and this can only mean the school children in those programs [*Romeo Community Schools* v. *HEW*, id., at 1031.]"

Since the *Romeo* decision found that Title IX was intended to protect only students and not school district employees from discrimination; Title VII was thought to be more specifically designed to deal with employment discrimination in education. Consequently, in the federal district of Michigan, discrimination in educational employment is not prohibited by Title IX; and others laws, such as Title VII, must be used to address cases of discrimination. There is a disadvantage in not using Title IX to forbid employment discrimination. The enforcement powers under Title IX are much broader and therefore potentially more powerful than those under Title VII. Title VII gives relief only to the injured employee by such things as an award of back pay, reinstatement to the job, and money damages. Title IX permits withholding federal funds to the school district if an employee suffers from sex discrimination (Kahn, 1976). Advocates of efforts to end sex discrimination feel that Title VII may not sufficiently deter employers from discrimination because violation of Title VII would result in a smaller monetary loss to the school district than would a violation of Title IX. However, there are people who feel it is unfair to jeopardize an entire school program by one instance of employment discrimination when other, more specifically designed remedies are available to the employee under Title VII (Kahn, 1976).

The chance to be considered for a position without regard to sex or minority group status can be provided by a general policy and practice of nondiscrimination and additionally, by affirmative action plans to remedy discrimination. It is hoped that legislative mandates for equal employment opportunity will result in an equitable representation of minorities and women throughout the labor force. In the schools changes in present employment patterns will be necessary. While large numbers of women work in the schools, few are found in the administrative ranks. Legislators hope that because of equal employment opportunities, changes will occur in employment practices within the schools. Evidence of that change could include more female school superintendents and more male elementary school teachers.

Selection Procedures

Employers use selection procedures to make decisions concerning the hiring, promotion, and tenure of employees. The outcome of this process can determine a woman's upward career mobility or a man's entrance into the ranks of elementary teachers. Federal laws require school district employers to provide equal treatment for the sexes during the selection process (Title IX and Title VII). Generally, any test or criteria used in the selection process must not discriminate on the basis of sex. While it is possible to use a dicriminatory selection process if it is proven to be a valid predictor of successful job performance, any employer using such a selection device must meet federal requirements for validation and must guarantee that no other less discriminatory alternative exists for making employment decisions. An illustration of an instance in which an employer was permitted to continue using a discriminatory selection process is found in the Supreme Court case of *National Education Association* v. *South Carolina* 98 S.Ct. 756 (1978). The high court upheld South Carolina's continued use of the National

Teacher's Exam (NTE) in hiring and classifying teachers. Research had found that the test disqualified more black than white applicants and that it placed larger numbers of blacks in lower-paying classifications. The Court permitted the continued use of the NTE because a validation study of the test proved it to be a valid measure of success in teacher training courses.

Recruitment and Advertising

Federal law requires a neutral policy regarding the present and future employment of the sexes. A nonbiased recruitment policy may require changes in such areas as recruitment materials, word-of-mouth advertising, and internal recruitment practices (Russell, 1978). Written instruments including job advertisements, vacancy announcements, job descriptions, and applications must provide accurate and nonbiased information to job applicants. While not illegal, word-of-mouth advertising may exclude certain groups from the flow of information. The practice of promoting employees from within the system must include members of both sexes. For example, the large number of female teachers should not be ignored as potential applicants for presently male-dominated administrative positions.

Fringe Benefits and Pregnancy Provisions.

Title IX and Title VII forbid discrimination on the basis of sex in any benefit plan provided to employees, their spouses, and dependents. A benefit program may include medical, hospital, accident, and life insurance and retirement policies. Although employers are prohibited from discriminating in fringe-benefit programs, programs that unintentionally result in treating the sexes differently do not automatically constitute a case of sex discrimination (Flygare, 1978). This is because in cases of unintentional discrimination, the courts are concerned with equalizing the overall monetary value of the benefit plan to both sexes. Therefore, prior to establishing a case of unintentional sex discrimination, an employee must first show that on the whole, the benefit package is usually worth more money to one sex than to another. If the employee is unable to show this overall inequality between the sexes, the Supreme Court is unwilling to remedy the differences in treatment that are based on an employee's sex. The Court stated this standard in the case of *General Electric* v. *Gilbert* 429 U.S. 129 (1976) in which female employees claimed that excluding the coverage of pregnancy in an employer's benefit plan constituted sex discrimination. The high court ruled that in order to establish a case of unintentional discrimination on the basis of sex, the female employees first must show that the overall benefit plan was, in fact, worth more to men than to women. Because the female employees were unable to do this, the court dismissed their claim of sex discrimination.

A source of recent litigation is the employer's treatment of pregnant employees. Two issues of concern to school districts are whether paid sick leave must be granted to pregnant teachers and whether teacher tenure may be taken away during pregnancy leaves. Both Title IX and lower court interpretations of Title VII have regarded pregnancy as a temporary disability to be covered within the employer's insurance plans. But in the *General Electric* decision interpreting Title VII, an employer's failure to provide paid sick leave for pregnant employees was not an automatic case of sex discrimination. The Court reasoned that an insurance program that failed to treat pregnancy as a temporary disability did not necessarily raise issues of sex discrimination: "The program divides potential recipients into two groups—pregnant women and nonpregnant persons. While the first group is exclusively female, the second includes members of both sexes." [*General Electric Co.* v. *Gilbert*, id., at 135, quoting *Geduldig* v. *Aiello*, 417 U.S. 484, 496–497 (1974).]

In an attempt to address judicial reluctance regarding issues of pregnant employees, Congress passed a law that took effect on October 31, 1978, that prohibits discrimination against female employees because of pregnancy, child birth, and related medical conditions. The new law overrides the 1976 *General Electric* decision and makes it illegal to fire an employee because she is pregnant and to force a pregnant worker to take a sick leave at a specific time if she is able to continue working.

Although the Supreme Court refused to recognize a claim of sex discrimination by pregnant employees in the *General Electric* case, another Supreme Court case has upheld such a claim. In *Nashville Gas Co.* v. *Satty*, 434 U.S. 136 (1977), a female employee who worked as a clerk in an accounting department took an unpaid maternity leave to have a baby. Seven weeks later she returned to claim her old job but found that the position had been eliminated because of bona fide cutbacks in her department. After taking a temporary position, she unsuccessfully attempted to regain another permanent position. Each time, she failed because she was not given credit for the seniority that she had accumulated prior to her maternity leave. The court ruled that denying a female employee accumulated seniority because she took a maternity leave constituted sex discrimination and therefore violated Title VII. For schools, this decision could produce a similar result in cases involving tenure. The Court reached a different result in the *Satty* case because *Satty* involved a burden and *General Electric* involved a benefit. In *Gen-*

eral Electric an employer refused to give a benefit to pregnant female employees, but in *Satty* an employer substantially burdened a female employee by depriving her of an employment opportunity.

Salaries

Various laws also demand equal pay for substantially equal work. For highly skilled positions, such as those of professors, administrators, and teachers, this initial decision is further complicated by the individual nature of the professional position. For instance, males may be given more credit for prior work-related experience than females, with the result that males are placed higher on the salary schedule (Matthews, n.d.). The many intangible responsibilities of professional work often make it difficult to ascertain when two employees do equivalent work (Divine, 1976).

While laws regarding employment seem quite comprehensive in scope, present economic factors may be delaying their effect on education. Retrenchments or reductions in staff resulting from declining enrollments and inflation may be slowing down affirmative-action efforts. Although the statistics on the effects of layoffs and cutbacks on women and minorities are sparse, related data indicate that minority and female teachers in higher education who have been only recently hired are suffering from retrenchment efforts. Employment cutbacks because of certain seniority and tenure systems may find women and minorities, who are the last to be hired, the first to be fired (Abramowitz, 1978).

Summary

The above discussion has focused on guidelines for ending discrimination on the basis of sex in educational programs and employment. However, those areas of education presently evidencing an adverse impact on one sex deserve an additional and separate discussion. Legally, evidence of adverse impact exists when any area of school programs or employment has 80% or more employees in one sex group. For example, proportions of students in shop classes in some public schools are 99% male to 1% female. School management may have a low proportion of female as compared to male administrators. If evidence of adverse impact exists in any aspect of schooling, certain remedial steps are necessary. These steps include investigating the reasons for the disproportionate representation of one sex and the removal of any institutional barriers to the advancement of the underrepresented sex. For example, if certain counselors or teachers are discouraging female students from taking male-typed courses, then these employees must be contacted and advised to change their practices or risk a complaint of sex discrimination being filed against the school. Furthermore, if instead of institutional barriers to sex equity student interest or disinterest in certain course work is the cause of the disproportionate representation of one sex, schools may still need to take remedial steps to address issues of student motivation and interest. For example, schools might call convocations specifically designed to raise students' awareness about the opportunities available if they enroll in nontraditional course work.

In conclusion, the key to addressing sex inequities in education through the law appears to be through the provision of "opportunity"; and the means for providing such opportunity seem to be the removal of sex barriers both in training and in employment. In this connection, the legal system is being required to address increasingly more complex and subtle forms of discrimination. As society gains an increased awareness of sex-role discrimination, the law is reflecting this awareness—through court cases, legislation, and agency action. These are exciting times for advocates of change in sex roles. Only time will tell whether members of both sexes take the "opportunity" to change the nature of traditional sex roles. But nowhere is it more hoped that these efforts will be felt than within the field of education. For it is the attitudes and beliefs of our young people that will shape the future of tomorrow's men and women.

STATUTES

Title IX of the Education Amendments of 1972, §901, 20 U.S.C. §1681 (a)–(c) (1976).

CASES

Bradwell v. *Illinois*, 83 U.S. (16 Wall.) 130, 21 L.Ed.2d 442 (1873).
Brown v. *Board of Education of Topeka*, 347 U.S. 483, 74 S.Ct. 686, 98 L.Ed. 873 (1954).
Darrin v. *Gould*, 85 Wash.2d. 859, 540 P.2d 882 (1975).
Geduldig v. *Aiello*, 417 U.S. 484, 94 S.Ct. 2485, 41 L.Ed.2d 256 (1974).
General Electric Co. v. *Gilbert*, 429 U.S. 125, 97 S.Ct. 401, 50 L.Ed.2d. 343 (1976).
Gomillion v. *Lightfoot*, 364 U.S. 339, 81 S.Ct. 125, 5 L.Ed.2d 110 (1960).
Griffin v. *County School Board of Prince Edward County*, 377 U.S. 218, 84 S.Ct. 1226, 12 L.Ed.2d 256 (1964).
Griggs v. *Duke Power Co.*, 401 U.S. 424, 91 S.Ct. 849, 28 L.Ed.2d 158 (1971).
Hollander v. *Conn. Interscholastic Athletic Conference, Inc.*, No. 12497 (Super.Ct.Conn., New Haven County, March 29, 1971).
Keyes v. *School Dist. No. 1, Denver, Colorado*, 413 U.S. 189, 93 S.Ct. 2686, 37 L.Ed.2d 548 (1973).
Nashville Gas Co. v. *Satty*, 434 U.S. 136, 98 S.Ct. 347, 54 L.Ed.2d 356 (1977).
National Education Association v. *South Carolina*, 98 S.Ct. 756, 54 L.Ed.2d 775 (1978).
Plessy v. *Ferguson*, 163 U.S. 537, 16 S.Ct. 1138, 41 L.Ed.2d. 256 (1896).

Reed v. *Reed,* 404 U.S. 71, 92 S.Ct. 251, 30 L.Ed.2d 225 (1971).

Ritacco v. *Norwin School District,* 361 F. Supp. 930 (W.D. Pa. 1973).

Romeo Community Schools v. *HEW,* 438 F. Supp. 1021 (E.D. Mich. 1977).

Stanton v. *Stanton,* 421 U.S. 7, 95 S.Ct. 1373, 43 L.Ed.2d 688 (1975).

State v. *Hall,* 187 So.2d 861 (1966), appeal dismissed, 385 U.S. 98, 87 S.Ct. 331, 17 L.Ed.2d 196 (1966).

Williams v. *McNair,* 316 F.Supp. 134 (D. S.C. 1970), aff'd mem., 401 U.S. 951, 91 S.Ct. 976, 28L.Ed.2d 235 (1971).

Yellow Springs Exempted Village School District Board of Education v. *Ohio High School Athletic Association,* 443 F.Supp. 753 (S.D. Ohio 1978).

REFERENCES

Abramowitz, S., and Rosenfeld, S., eds. (1978). *Declining Enrollment: The Challenge of the Coming Decade.* Department of HEW, Washington, D.C.

Babcock, B. A., Freedman, A. E., Norton E. H., Ross, S. C., (1975). *Sex Discrimination and the Law: Causes and Remedies.* Little, Brown, Boston.

Barrer, M. E., ed. (1976). *Journal of Reprints of Documents Affecting Women.* Today Publications and News Service, Inc., Washington, D.C.

Buek, A. P., and Orleans, J. H. (1973). "Sex Discrimination, A Bar to a Democratic Education: Overview of Title IX of Education Amendments of 1972." *Connecticut Law Review,* 6:1–27.

Divine, T. M. (1976). "Women in the Academy: Sex Discrimination in University Faculty, Hiring, and Promotion." *Journal of Law and Education,* 5:429–451.

Dunkle, M. C. (1976). *Competitive Athletics: In Search of Equal Opportunity.* Department of HEW, Washington, D.C.

Dunkle, M. C., and Sandler, B. (1974). "Sex Discrimination Against Students: Implications of Title IX of the Education Amendments of 1972." *Inequality in Education,* October, pp. 12–35.

Fabri, C. J., and Fox, E. G. (1975). "Female High School Athlete and Interscholastic Sports." *Journal of Law and Education,* 4:285–300.

Flygare, T. J. (1978). "A Legal Embarrassment: Paid Sick Leave for Pregnant Teachers." *Phi Delta Kappan,* April, pp. 558–559.

Kadzielski, M. A. (1977). "Title IX of Education Amendments of 1972: Change or Continuity?" *Journal of Law and Education,* 6:183–203.

Kahn, J. Z. (1976). "Title IX: Employment and Athletics are Outside HEW's Jurisdiction." *Georgetown Law Journal,* 65:49–77.

Levin, B. (1975). "Recent Development in the Law of Equal Educational Opportunity." *Journal of Law and Education,* 4:411–447.

Malloy, M. (1976). "The Regulations of Title IX: Sex Discrimination in Student Affairs." *Houston Law Review,* 13:734–752.

Matthews, M., and McCune, S. (n.d.). *Complying with Title IX: Implementing Institutional Self-Evaluation.* Department of HEW, Washington, D.C.

Rawls, J. (1971). *A Theory of Justice.* Harvard University Press (Belknap Press), Cambridge, Mass.

Resource Center on Sex Roles in Education (1977). *Implementing Title IX and Attaining Sex Equity in Education: Participant's Notebook.* National Foundation for the Improvement of Education, Washington, D.C.

Reutter, E. E., and Hamilton, R. R. (1976). *The Law of Public Education*, 2nd ed. Foundation Press, Mineola, N.Y.

Russell, G. (1978). *Sex Discrimination in Educational Employment*. Unpublished paper, University of Oregon.

Seitz, W. J. (1977). "Gender-Based Discrimination and a Developing Standard of Equal Protection and Analysis." *University of Cincinnati Law Review*, 46:572–582.

The Status of Title IX in Region IX (1978). Miller and Associates, Inc. (available at 711 S. Capital Way, Olympia, Washington)

University of Pennsylvania Law Review, editors. (1976). "Implementing Title IX: The HEW Regulations." *University of Pennsylvania Law Review*, 124:806–842.

Women's Educational Equity Act, Second Annual Report (1977). Department of HEW, Washington, D.C. September.

Chapter 8

CONTEXT OF CHANGE: THE WOMEN'S MOVEMENT AS A POLITICAL PROCESS

Patricia A. Schmuck

Each time large numbers of women become conscious of their situation conflict follows. It has never been enough for women to point out the ills they observe. More often than not, change has involved the development of a conflict between feminist movements and organizations on the one side and counter movements and organizations on the other; in other words, a public social conflict. Change does not seem to occur without the development of both consciousness and social conflict [Sapiro, 1980, p. 1].

Education institutions never have been the forerunners of social change; schools are the mirror of the society they serve, and their purpose is to socialize the young into the prevailing adult culture. Public school people, by and large, are in the main stream of American society and do not hold radical political or social ideologies. Changes in sex equity in schools emanate from movements in the larger society. While Chapters 6 and 7 described change from the perspective of the social sciences and the law, this chapter focuses on the political processes inspired by the women's movement that are the backdrop for changes in schools.

Throughout this book, we have attempted to document inequities in our educational institutions and to unravel the multiplicity of conditions that may have brought them about. We have relied heavily on the published research and the compilation of findings from various sources. This chapter, however, is different from the rest of the book; we are yet too embroiled within the current women's movement to have a complete analytical literature from which to draw knowledge. Although some social analyses of the movement have been completed, such as Freeman's *The Politics of Women's Liberation*, Fishel and Pottker's *Sex Discrimination Law and Federal Policy*, Hole's and Levine's *Rebirth of Feminism*, and Klein's "Rise of the Women's Movement: A Case Study in Political Development", they are unfinished and incomplete because the movement is not yet complete. The twentieth century movement has not yet had careful scrutiny nor relatively objective study, and most of the authors have also been participants in the movement itself. Despite this lack of "seasoned" research and knowledge, we attempt to review the demands for change that have energized and mobilized women to focus on their limited opportunities within the society and the schools.

HISTORICAL VIEW OF FEMINISM AND EDUCATION

Only a decade ago the word *sexism* was not in common parlence, and some dramatic changes have occurred during the 1960s and 1970s. Laws prohibit sex discrimination in schools, a new feminist literature has been created, and some men and women are forging new careers and new images of themselves. What has inspired these changes? Primarily women have led the movement, and the focus has been on women. Although there have always been a handful of men involved in the feminist cause, and men certainly will be affected, women have been the catalysts for change. Women, however, do not constitute a singular or monolithic movement. The answer to the question "What do women want?" is perhaps not any clearer now than it ever was. Perhaps the strength of the current rebirth of feminism is its diversity. Women from different places, with different problems and different demands for change have simultaneously worked on different segments of the society and toward a variety of social solutions. The women's movement has focused on attitudinal change, on production of new knowledge, on organizational change, and on legislation. Energy has not yet been funneled into one sphere, such as it was in the early nineteenth century when suffrage became the common unifier and swallowed the energy of a diverse movement into a single issue.

Feminist activists have always believed that knowledge is power, and organized groups of women who sought social and political change have also sought equal access to education. The right to education is only one example of the similarity in agenda for feminists of the nineteenth and twentieth centuries. Schooling for females was a major issue among feminists then and it has carried over into our own time.

Feminism and Education in the Nineteenth Century

The 1848 Seneca Falls Convention described by Elizabeth Cady Stanton as "the first organized protest against the injustice which had brooded for ages over the character and destiny of half the race," included demands for educational opportunities. One part of the Declaration of Statements read: "The history of mankind is a history of repeated injuries and usurpations on the part of the man toward women—he has denied her all the facilities for obtaining a thorough education, all colleges being closed to her [Martin, 1972, pp. 43-44]." And in 1849, Lucretia Mott said: "The demand for a more extended education will not cease until girls and boys have equal instruction, in all departments of useful knowledge [Martin, 1972, pp. 59]." Susan B. Anthony, abolitionist, militant agitator, and dean of women, the highest position in education that a woman could obtain, took her message to the teacher's convention and demanded for women all the privileges that male teachers enjoyed. Education was clearly a political issue for nineteenth-century feminists, as it would be a century later.

No one really doubted that women should be educated; the debate was over the content and the goal of such an education. The debate is probably best typified by two eighteenth-century books. Jean-Jaques Rousseau's *Emile* argued that the female education should impress upon women that the aim of their existence was to please and be useful to men; Rousseau's objective was that women should be educated so that they would be willing to "submit uncomplainingly." In contrast, Mary Wollstonecraft's *The Vindication of the Rights of Women* argued that education was the path to personal and social freedom and independence. To "submit uncomplainingly" has never been an objective of feminism, and education has always been a powerful weapon that political activists understood.

Vinovskis and Bernard (1978) point out that the educational experiences of a vast majority of women (and men) in the nineteenth century remain an undeveloped field for historical investigation. Historical investigation has relied primarily on diaries and personal letters of the literate population. Using federal census data available from 1840–1860, Vinovskis and Bernard tried to fill the historical void. They showed that approximately 60% of the white people aged 5–19 attended school; female representation was about 58%, whereas male representation was 62%. About 19% of the free blacks attended school. Among blacks, female participation was again somewhat lower than males. Schooling was most common in the New England region and lowest in the south.

Interestingly enough, however, the percentages are reversed for college attendance. While about 3% of the students in the south attended college, in the northern and mid-Atlantic states, less than 1% of the students were enrolled in college. Most students had only a primary education, the next level of schooling (grammar schools and academies) and the colleges accounted for less than 10% of the student population.

Yet even within the one-room schoolhouse, sex segregation was apparent. Specifications of the ideal schoolhouse included a physical separation of the sexes. Each sex was often assigned to a different part of the room, a different playground, and a different cloakroom. Instruction apparently was also segregated, and there were male departments and female departments. Young men were trained for college or careers in business, and young women were trained to be daughters, sisters, wives, mothers, companions, and teachers who would determine the manners, morals, and intelligence of the community (Barnard, 1850, p. 28 quoted in Vinovskis and Bernard, 1978, p. 865).

Vinovskis and Bernard describe the incongruity developed by women's entrance into teaching during this period and note its probable effects on both girls and boys. Whereas the presence of female teachers probably encouraged young girls to seek learning activities for females, it probably "discouraged boys from seeing teaching as a viable and worthy profession for themselves [1978, p. 866]."

Gribskov (1980) in her analysis of women in educational administration in the west during the nineteenth century points to the women's movement as an important contributor to the numerous women who were county superintendents and heads of schools. Gribskov argues that western feminism provided an "old girl's network" of politically active and powerful women. Women ran schools, were active practicing medicine and dentistry, were involved in community political life, and supported each other. Upper- and middle-class women in the urban east formed benevolent societies and helped provide community services for their less fortunate sisters. Such societies included the Society for Employing the Poor of Boston, the Female Orphan Asylum, the Society for the Relief of Poor Widows, and the Boston Female Education Society (Berg, 1978).

It would, however, be historically unjust as well as historically inaccurate to suggest that nineteenth-century feminists had a profound impact on schools. They never gained the power for legal and political change. The organization, character, and structure of public schooling were probably more influenced by the social and economic forces of a growing and developing country. Yet at the turn of the century, many women became educators and had a profound effect on the character of public schooling.

Feminism and Education in the Twentieth Century

Females' numerical supremacy was an established fact in the educational profession by the 1930s. Frances Donovan's 1938 book *The School Ma'am* provides a thorough description of the life of the school ma'am, her private life, career mobility, place in the community, and economic condition. Her economic condition was not secure, as Donovan notes: "To be sure the majority of teachers are women while the majority of those in other professions are men, and men are generally accepted as more valuable in dollars and cents than women, no matter what the profession." Regarding the school ma'am's future, Donovan predicts "that teaching tomorrow should be a field difficult to enter. [It will] carry with it responsibility and win for its followers more distinction than it has in the past. . . . But when these conditions prevail perhaps the school ma'am will have more male competition in the classroom than she does today [1938, pp. 265–266]."

Although women actively participated in the community and the labor force during World War II, a feminist consciousness was missing. Day care centers were formed within industry and sponsored by federal legislation; women performed jobs in factories, provided medical care, service, and leadership in many phases of life. This participation was prompted, however, largely by the absence of men. Women again faded from roles in the society and from being the breadwinner when the men returned from the war and families were reunited. After World War II, many "male competitors" entered the teaching force, as predicted by Donovan; and today women's proportional representation as teachers is about where it was a century ago.

Within the last decade, however, those dormant seeds of feminism germinated, and a new generation of women took to the streets and to the courts in the spirits of their grandmothers and great grandmothers. The new generation of women spent their young years in the quiet time after World War II and the militancy of the 1960s; this new generation of women were those who adopted the major role of wife and mother, participated in the picket lines demanding civil rights, entered the universities, and pursued their own professional interests. They all began to question, again, the inevitability of "women's place" in the society.

Freeman (1975) described the precipitating social and psychological conditions of the feminist movement, "the roots of revolt," in her book,

The Politics of Women's Liberation. First, she notes the important factors of public development and active implementation of equalitarian values, the legitimization of rebellion as a process of social change, which was apparent in the antislavery movement of the nineteenth-century feminists, and the civil rights struggles of the twentieth century. Second, she suggests that industrialization had drastic consequences for the social and psychological well-being of women. Industrialization deeply affected women's functions in the home; the home was no longer productive economically, and women's valued and needed functions became superfluous for the well-being of her family. Goods, entertainment, and pleasures were bought on the marketplace by the wage-earning member of the household, the man. Psychologically, the situation created women's increased dependence on men and "contributed to the feeling of many women that they were useless parasites."

Men had the access and the power to gain material resources, which created a "strain" impairing the relations of men and women in the home; the socially forced designations of the home and the marketplace also helped create a growing sense of relative deprivation, especially among women in the middle and upper classes. Freeman suggests that this sense of deprivation was more pronounced among middle-class women than among their less economically secure sisters. She notes that relative deprivation involves both psychological as well as objective conditions, and a person who is relatively deprived need not be objectively deprived. These two factors, the emphasis on equality and the feelings of deprivation, provided the basis for the development of the contemporary feminist movement.

INFLUENCE OF CURRENT FEMINIST MOVEMENT ON EDUCATION

Five groups make up the major cornerstone of the current women's movement: (*a*) militant activists scathed by the civil rights and peace movements; (*b*) women searching for personal meaning; (*c*) employed middle-class managerial and professional women, especially those working in the federal government; (*d*) academic women who have begun to alter our knowledge concerning sex roles; (*e*) political pressure groups. These five groups are not discrete in membership, and over time probably most feminists have participated in two or more of such groups. Each group has had different problems and has adapted different strategies to solve them. Each has had a different perspective, identified different problems, and suggested different solutions. Independently, yet simultaneously, they have acted upon their own particular concerns and have brought momentum and energy to a movement labeled "the women's movement." While this is probably an appropriate label, it may oversimplify the diversity of complaints and demands that emerge from the needs and motivations of different groups who had the common ingredient of being women. We now discuss the motives and change strategies of each of these groups and how their demands have affected sexism in the schools.

Militant Activists and the Goal of Equality

The hallmark of the 1950s and 1960s civil rights movement was equalitarian values and protest as a legitimate means for change. In 1963 the March on Washington occurred and Martin Luther King made his famous "I have a dream" speech. Blacks and whites left the security of their universities and took leaves to sit-in at lunch counters, picket state governments, and conduct voter registration. Protest was a legitimate tool, and going to jail became a badge of honor rather than a social embarrassment. Women were part of that movement; they belonged to the Students for a Democratic Society, the Congress for Racial Equality, and the Student's Nonviolent Coordinating Committee. They ran mimeograph machines and staffed the free schools.

Except for identified women's groups, such as Women Strike for Peace and Women's International League for Peace and Freedom, women were not the leaders of the protest movement. Like the rest of society, women were second-class citizens who made sandwiches and coffee, took care of the children, and implemented policy. Perhaps the most flagrant example of women's status in the civil rights movement was Stokeley Carmichael's response to the question of where women belong in the movement: "prone" (Fishel & Pottker, 1977; Freeman, 1975). However, in addition to learning how to feed an army and organize day care programs and run mimeograph machines, women learned political strategy and how to organize meetings and implement policy. Finally, they turned their attention to another group in the society who were deprived of their legal and moral rights—themselves. Female social revolutionaries had been created and they provided an important source of knowledge and ideology for the women's movement.

There is little evidence about what has happened to the women who were civil rights workers, but several authors note that their participation was important in the formation of the women's movement. Freeman (1975) calls these women the younger branch of the movement;

at least in the early 1970s they were predominately under 30. (See also Fishel & Pottker, 1977; Mitchell 1973.) The women civil rights activists, however, are not a visible group today. They went in a variety of directions; they married, had children, became full-time housewives, became employed, went to graduate school. Today they are clearly over 30, and the new group of women under 30 are in many ways a different species from their sisters only a decade or two older.

Personal Meaning: Changing Attitudes and Values

In 1963 Friedan's *The Feminine Mystique* was published. Although several important events occurred prior to 1963, her book has been labeled by some as the beginning of the movement. While the actual origins of the women's movement may be forgotten or distorted, the naming of "the problem that has no name" certainly resonated in the minds of many. Friedan introduced it this way: "The problem lay buried, unspoken, for many years in the minds of American women. It was a strange stirring, a sense of dissatisfaction, a yearning that women suffered in the twentieth century in the United States. Each suburban wife struggled with it *alone*. As she made the beds, shopped for groceries, matched slipcover material, ate peanut butter sandwiches with her children, chauffeured Cub Scouts and Brownies, lay beside her husband at night, she was afraid to ask even of herself the silent question—'Is this all?' [p. 15]" Friedan's statement certainly echoes the sentiments expressed by a nineteenth-century sister: "The greatest trial . . . is that I have nothing to do. Here I am with abundant leisure, and capable, I believe, of accomplishing some good, and yet with no object upon which to expend my energies. . . . I am weary of life [Berg, 1978, p. 112]." "Woman belle" was freed from the everyday household and child care chores of our contemporaries, but her sense of self was as dismal as that of her more active counterpart a century later.

These personal statements support Freeman's assertion that women's displaced economic functions in the home created a feeling of dependence, powerlessness, loss of self worth, and relative deprivation. An economically secure situation could not make up for the deprivation of spirit and worth that comes from feeling that one has accomplished some good. Although *The Feminine Mystique* was read by women who were not wives and mothers, its central theme resonated around these roles of women. Sexism was not yet part of the lexicon, and women in the isolation of their homes in the suburbs, with their nuclear families, suddenly let out a collective sigh of relief: "I am not mad, I am not neurotic, there are others who feel stilted and thwarted by child care, chauffeuring, and baking the endless rounds of chocolate chip cookies."

The public acknowledgement of a common problem may have saved many women who might have made an appointment with a therapist, no doubt a male who would have helped them accomodate to their "feminine role." As Chesler has pointed out, the only two socially approved institutions for women are marriage and therapy (1972).

It was different from belonging to one of the socially active women's groups or the benevolent societies of the nineteenth century. It was a collective search for personal meaning; there were no agendas, except for what individuals brought with them. There were no tasks to perform, except to be in touch with oneself and others. Consciousness raising (CR) groups formed everywhere, from Scarsdale to Dubuque, from Seattle and its suburbs to Bullock, Texas. They were formed by organizations such as NOW (National Organization of Women), and they were formed spontaneously by women getting together to "rap."

Bernard (1976) points out that the bonds between females were broken when societies became mobile and the nuclear family arose as the basic social unit. Women were physically and psychologically isolated from each other. Plainly and simply, they were *alone*, as Betty Friedan pointed out. CR groups in suburbs and cities provided a process for female bonding; they provided intimacy and sharing among women who were isolated in their respective collectivities. This was a valuable function and the only purported task, but they did more. Most individuals spent only two or three years at most in such CR groups and then became involved in something else. Their individual concerns extended to others—daughters, sons, husbands, schools, communities. Many a divorce has been attributed to women's participation in CR groups, as illustrated in the movie *Tell Me Where it Hurts*, but the purpose of CR groups was not to break up families or move women into the work force. Consciousness raising groups were focused on women's learning to be in touch with themselves and other women. Many of the fluid spontaneous groups lived only a short time; others developed into more structured training sessions (Kravetz & Sargent, 1977).

Consciousness raising groups are difficult to document. They rose and disbanded when the need was no longer apparent. They occurred in people's homes, kept no minutes, had no agendas; membership was fluid and unrecorded. They were important unto themselves, but perhaps their greatest contribution was that they prepared women psychologically to participate in other planned and deliberate strategies for change. Consciousness raising groups changed attitudes and values of participating women and provided support for women to take risks in their lives. Today there are some male CR groups—not to solve the problem of physical isolation between men, but to define new patterns of relationships (Farrell, 1974). Men's CR groups energetically emphasize personalness and intimacy as opposed to the more prevalent modes of male interaction.

The grassroots CR groups of women focused on personal meanings, attitudes, and values; they became an important factor in legislation, political organization, and strategies for changing the educational experiences of students. Active citizens had their "consciousness" raised. Parents became concerned about a nonsexist education for their children. They became concerned about sex biased curricula, about girls opportunities in sports and career counseling. Parents spoke to school board members about equal educational opportunities and began creating new classes and materials for students. Probably the most relevant impact these groups had on schools was the creation of active citizens. *Sexism in the Schools: Unlearning the Lie* (Harrison, 1973) was written, and in many communities, small study groups of citizens and educators developed classes and materials for students. In response to the requirement of Title IX that schools create equitable opportunities, committees of teachers, administrators, and parents have become actively involved. Materials on the subject are now available from several sources, in published and unpublished form, and those are appearing in schools and classrooms.[1] Parents have become aware of the damaging effects of sex-role stereotyping in their own lives, often through CR groups, and they have taken an active interest to make sure their children receive the benefits of equality in education.

Working Women in Professional and Managerial Positions

In general, work experience is a primary factor in women's political participation. A strong positive relationship exists between their employment and their attitudes toward equality (Klein, 1976). Working women are more likely to favor equal roles for both sexes. Through direct experience, they are attuned to their lack of power and influence in the society. Without being psychologically deprived, they can see the objective reality of deprivation. They make less money than men and usually do not hold high positional status within an organization; and when their position is similar to a man's they face apparent sex discrepencies.

An awareness of such differences may be even greater for women employed professionally and in managerial roles. Many such women played an active role in addressing women's issues prior to publication

[1]For more information contact Women's Educational Equity Communications Network, Far West Lab., 1855 Folsom Street, San Francisco, Calif. 94103.

of *The Feminine Mystique*. Freeman (1975) refers to them as the older branch of the movement. It was these women who were called upon to join the President's Commission on the Status of Women established by President Kennedy in 1961 and chaired by Eleanor Roosevelt. Its 1963 report, *American Women* recommended the establishment of state commissions on the status of women. Most such state commissions had little budget or staff provisions, and their direct contribution to the resolution of problems was small; yet they laid the groundwork for research and for public awareness of inequality in the society. Most important, it was a communications network, a critical variable in a social movement (Freeman, 1975). In 1966 NOW (National Organization of Women) was formed and became the first formal pressure group; it arose out of this group of women. This group is discussed more fully in a later section.

While research in the early 1970s clearly documented the fact that employed women were more favorably disposed toward the women's movement than unemployed women, there are of course exceptions. Some employed professional women support backlash efforts such as those put forth by proponents of "the total woman" (Decter, 1974). (We prefer to think of it as the "totalled woman.") We would hypothesize, however, that employed women today are even more inclined to support the aims of the women's movement than they were only five years ago. Epstein's dissertation (1970) on women lawyers, written in 1968, noted the active antipathy of women who had "made it" toward other women in the field; they had adopted a male standard. Having worked so hard to achieve a position in a man's world and in a male-dominated profession, some women were concerned about losing their credibility by being viewed as "token women." Schmuck's study in 1975, however, did not find such antipathy among women school administrators. It is our distinct impression that the antipathy of many professional women for the activism of the women's movement has changed significantly in this decade. It has been our experience that there are actually many "closet feminists"—women who did not voice such equalitarian views earlier in the decade but who, with the growing acceptance of women's legitimate demands, have grown more vocal about their opinions.

Women who had achieved status within a male-dominated organization, like it or not, were often put in the position by their male colleagues of being the spokeswoman for the movement. Even if they wanted to ignore the issues, even if they believed they had not been discriminated against, and even if they disagreed with the strategies employed by the various factions of the movement, they often were asked, "What do women want?" Thus, many women were driven into the movement or made to sympathize with it by their male colleagues. As one woman administrator said: "It used to be when I walked into a room full of men and only one woman I would tend to ignore her. Now when I walk into a similar situation the woman and I at least have eye contact. There's too damn few of us women; we found out we need to support each other. If there were more of us, we would be free to act just as folks, but because there are so few of us, there is the common bond of being women [Schmuck, 1976, p. 81]." The visible women's movement and male colleagues inadvertantly colluded to prompt employed professional women to question their role as women.

Significantly, some women in professional or managerial roles, educated and with some knowledge of the political process, have been driven into the movement by a situation that called upon them to assert their rights. Fishel and Pottker (1977) reviewed the case of a teacher that brought the issue of pregnancy before the courts; but Susan Cohen was not inspired to establish justice for women; she simply believed that she, as an individual, had been treated unfairly. Feminism was not the inspiration for her suit; she was an educated woman who began demanding fairness for herself. This is perhaps a good illustration of how our judicial is based on the protection of the individual. Similarly, Barbara Hutchison, an Oregonian, sued her school district about pregnancy because she believed she was treated unfairly. She claims the experience from that suit clearly drove her into the feminist movement; she began asserting her rights as an individual and came to understand the larger implications of her demands.

Such cases of individual protection have had implications for the larger population. Certainly, acts of individuals on their own behalf have inspired social movements. The Montgomery bus boycott, which became a rallying cry for the civil rights movement, was begun by Rosa Parks because her feet hurt. Coretta Scott King recollects the incident this way:

> The fuel that finally made that slow-burning fire blaze up was an almost routine incident. On December 1, 1955, Mrs. Rosa Parks, a forty-two year old seamstress whom my husband aptly described as a "charming person with a radiant personality," boarded a bus to go home after a long day working and shopping. The bus was crowded, and Mrs. Parks found a seat at the beginning of the Negro section. At the next stop more whites got on. The driver ordered Mrs. Parks to give her seat to a white man who boarded; this meant she would have to stand all the way home. Rosa Parks was not in a revolutionary frame of mind. She had not planned to do what she did. Her cup had run over. As she said later, "I was just plain tired, and my feet hurt." So she sat there, refusing to get up. The driver called a policeman who arrested her and took her to the courthouse [King, 1969, p. 112].

The accumulation of several routine incidents often provides fuel for a fiery issue; a full-burning blaze has led to the formation of coalitions of women who want their message to be heard. Puerto Rican, black, and professional women in New York, for example, formed a group to study women's economic condition in New York City (Girard, 1978). Women in educational administration have joined together in statewide organizations in Washington, Oregon, and California and in Long Island, New York (Timpano, 1976; Schmuck, 1980). Whereas the past decade focused on individuals and independent groups of women, the future strength of the movement appears to be generating in collective coalitions of women asserting their rights within their own profession. Women have formed caucuses in most professional associations, such as in the American Educational Research Association, the American Association of School Administrators, and the teachers' unions. Women employed as professional educators have made inroads by coalescing and demanding rights for themselves and for female students as well, serving as internal agents of change within their own professional organizations. Women teachers have gotten on the programs in their local and state conventions and addressed the issue: a concern with "what's good for kids, boy kids and girl kids." Courses of study on subjects about women in history, literature, and other areas are available in many high schools; men as well as women educators have actively worked in their own school districts to help provide equal educational opportunities.

Because coalitions of women are stronger now than they were a few years ago and because they are working on legitimate and lawful issues, they have attracted many women who in years past might have been "turned off" by such militant feminism. In Oregon, for example, only three years ago there were only about 30 women in the entire state who belonged to a women's group in educational administration; and some women actively avoided associations with such a "militant" group. Yet in 1978 200 women traveled to a remote part of the state to participate in the First Annual Conference of Oregon Women in Educational Administration; and 300 are expected in 1979. Having seen the damaging effects of sexual stereotyping in their own lives and in the lives of children, many men have also made equality of opportunity a priority in education. Given all the federal and state mandates for equalizing opportunity, it is clear that the implementation of policies rests in the hands of local people who use their mandated power for change.

Women in the Content of Academic Subjects

Feminists of the twentieth century have gone further than the demand for equal educational opportunity. They are questioning the male bias of available knowledge itself. Bernard (1973) asked; "Can science transcend sex? Can [sociology] be a science of society rather than a science of male society?" Historians are being faulted for their neglect of women's role, psychologists are being questioned about the assumed truths of male–female differences, and feminist sociologists are "modifying, correcting, sharpening, or refining the classic paradigms and analyses of traditional sociology, often with the effect of exposing their male bias [Bernard, 1973, p. 16]." Knowledge of our world and of ourselves is necessarily distorted and inaccurate when it ignores one-half of the human species. Knowledge is power, and Weisskopf points out the implications of the male dominance of knowledge: "Evidence suggests that the natural and social sciences have out of self-interest, hubris, and ignorance, participated in the systematic oppression of women [1978, p. 269]." The "truisms of earlier works, such as as female dependency, are being questioned only a decade later [Maccoby, 1966; Maccoby & Jacklin, 1974]."

Books such as Chodrow's *The Reproduction of Mothering*, Chesler's *Women and Madness*, and Kanter's *Men and Women of the Corporation*, among the many that have questioned traditional analyses and provided a new perspective about women, are transforming the content of knowledge. A concerted effort has been made to assure women of a place in the content of university curriculum through Women's Studies programs. Howe (1976) reports that since 1970 more than 270 such programs have been organized on as many campuses; and some 15,000 courses have been developed by 8,500 teachers at 15,000 different institutions. Women's Studies appear in prison projects, YWCAs, adult education programs, and women's centers. In 1976 Feminist Press issued a directory listing 4,900 such programs in the United States (Berkowitz, 1976). Originally seen as a major route to providing information about women who were excluded from the content of the traditional curriculum, these programs now have an additional goal: "to transform disciplines, through a consideration of women, with regard to curriculum, research focus, and methodology [Howe, 1977, p. 16]."

Whether or not women's studies programs continue to flourish, many young people have already been exposed in their college experience to concepts and ideas that were unknown only a decade earlier. There is little empirical evidence concerning the impact of such courses on students; in fact, there is little empirical evidence regarding the influence on any college courses on students (Sanford, 1962). One limited study of the University of Cincinnati reported that less stereotyped sex-role attitudes resulted from enrollment in women's studies courses (Rey & Russell, 1978). Certainly, the active politics of the women's movement is a continuing necessity for the eventual acceptance of gender as a legitimate pursuit of inquiry within the domain of knowledge.

Feminist Political Activists

The 1964 passage of Title VII of the Civil Rights Act affirmed non-discrimination in employment, and although its inclusion of women was not treated seriously by the general public at that time, there were women who took it seriously. Freeman (1975) and Fishel and Pottker (1977) both suggest that Title VII was as important in the genesis of the women's movement as the publication of *The Feminine Mystique*. Women working with the Equal Employment Opportunities Commission, the regulatory agency for Title VII, began to form "some sort of NAACP" for women. Martha Griffiths, the representative from Michigan, also took the legal provisions seriously (Freeman, 1975; Griffiths, 1976). Important political pressure was exerted by her and other women and significant legislation emerged after 1964. The most important pieces of legislation directed at education were Title IX and the first federal fundings source devoted to sex inequity, the Women's Educational Equity Act (WEEA). Fishel and Pottker, in their book *Sex Discrimination Law and Federal Policy*, provide an excellent accounting of the political process involved in the passage of Title IX and of WEEA.

Although formal political pressure groups, such as the NOW Legal Defense Fund Project on Equal Education Rights (PEER) and Women's Equity Action League (WEAL), were formed and actively working, Fishel and Pottker point to the additional labor and energy among the female "faceless bureaucrats" of Washington, D.C. These skilled and capable women, who were often "underemployed" within the federal government, did not remain faceless for long. They looked to their own shop and in 1972 produced a publication that described women's roles in federal educational agencies, the National Institute of Education and the Office of Education (U.S. OE, 1972). Groups of women formed informally; significantly, they were women who knew the political ropes, and they applied that knowledge to their own problems. Certainly this group of women must have credit for the passage of laws against sex discrimination.

The passage of Title IX of the Educational Amendments has direct and profound implications for schools. Although the final regulations by HEW to implement the law took four years to develop, this is viewed by some as "incredibly speedy" (Fishel & Pottker, 1977). Yet implementation of these regulations is another problem, and the attitudes of educators will no doubt be a critical variable in providing equal opportunities for both sexes. One study illustrated that in the Northwest, attitudes and willingness to comply were the most important ingredients in successful implementation of Title IX (Miller & Associates, 1978). The change in federal policy is well illustrated by the following example. In 1975, the first proposal for the project called Sex Equity in Educational Leadership was written. The director of the project spent a week in Washington, D.C., to find resources to fund the proposal. No resources were available, even though there was already a network of interested women who were eager to hear about such a project. The overwhelming response of funding agencies was a disinterested and polite refusal: "This does not fit into our guidelines for funding." In 1976 WEEA was formed, and the first federal dollars were allocated for projects regarding the issues of women's education. Since 1976 additional sources of funding have been provided within the federal government and by private foundations. Enough sources of funding were available to prompt the publication of a booklet called *Finding Funds for Programs Relating to Women's Educational Equity* (Ekstrom, 1978).

The first meeting of the WEEA project directors was held in Washington, D.C., in October, 1976. It was a highly charged meeting. Eighty-two projects dealing with women were represented. For the first time, many women had the experience of being in a room crowded with capable, influential individuals, over 90% of whom were women. It was also a unique experience for the few men represented. Bernice (Bunny) Sandler, one of the instigators of the legislation, ebulliently greeted the audience: "This meeting proves it. The hand that rocks the cradle can also rock the boat." Today women's issues are a part of federal policies and regulations. The female of the species now has lobbyists, legislation, advocates, and detractors. Women's issues are now a legitimate part of the bureaucracy, along with those of farmers, oil interests, minorities, small business people, and consumers. That, in our view, is a worthy accomplishment. In addition, a few women are making it to management positions in the federal agencies.

Today, diverse groups of women have formed in loose and tight coalitions; the women's conference in Houston in 1978 reflected the diversity of women, their problems, and solutions. The Houston conference also had a good representation of the backlash—women involved in the move to halt the passage of the Equal Rights Amendment (ERA). The ERA is, of course, a prime political target for feminists. It is a critical symbol and a critical piece of legislation for the full guarantee for both women and men equality under the law. Alice Paul, who wrote the ERA and first submitted it to Congress in 1923, died in 1977. The intensity of the ERA movement is reflected in dollars and cents; many cities and counties have adopted formal boycott resolutions so they will not pay expenses for any employee attending conferences in a non-ERA-ratified state. In May 1978, *MS.* magazine indicated that Chicago had lost $15 million, Kansas City $4 million, Miami Beach $9 million, and New Orleans $8 million due to convention boycotts by organizations such as the League of Women Voters, the American Association for the Advancement of Science, the United Methodist Church, the National Education Association, the American Psychological Association, and the American Association of University Women. Many cities have adopted formal boycott resolutions for employees.

The five categories of women's groups have been responsible in one way or another for many of the dramatic changes toward social equality over the last two decades. They display the characteristics described by Freeman: a network of communications both formal and informal (see Footnote 1) and the willingness to redefine goals and tactics when necessary, respond to crises, and form coalitions. Whether or not the twentieth-century feminist movement will be more successful than the movement a century earlier is not yet clear. The current movement is diverse; its goal is equality; its process is dialogue, information, and pressure. Today's movement represents all levels of change; it has focused on attitudinal and behavioral change, on developing knowledge, on altering organizations, and on providing legislation. It will take no less than all these to root out the sex inequities and stereotypes that are deeply embedded within our psyches, our institutions, and our legal system. We believe that only the concerted efforts of people on all these fronts will allow our future generations to be released from the inequalities that have plagued us.

REFERENCES

American Women (1963). Report of the Presidents Commission on the Status of Women. Washington, D.C., Government Printing Office.

Barnard, H. (1850). *Fifth Annual Report of the Superintendent of Common Schools of Connecticut to the General Assembly.* New Haven, Conn.

Berg, B. (1978). *The Remembered Gate: Origins of American Feminism.* Oxford University Press, New York.

Berkowitz, T., Mangi, J., and Williamson, J. (1976). *Who's Who and Where in Women's Studies.* Feminist Press, New York.

Bernard J. (1973). "My Four Revolutions: An Autobiographical History of the ASA." In *Changing Women in a Changing Society* (J. Huber, ed.). University of Chicago Press.

Bernard, J. (1976). "Homosociality and Female Depression." *Journal of Social Issues,* 32:209–247.

Chesler, P. (1972). *Women and Madness.* Doubleday, New York.

Chodorow, N. (1978). *The Reproduction of Mothering.* University of California Press, Berkeley.

Decter, M. (1974). *The New Chastity and Other Arguments against Women's Liberation*. Putnam, New York.

Donovan, F. (1938). *The School Ma'am*. Frederick Stockes, New York.

Ekstrom, R., and Wehren, A. (1978). *Finding Funds for Programs Related to Women's Educational Equity*. Womens Educational Equity Act Communication Network, San Francisco.

Epstein, C. (1970). *Woman's Place: Options and Limits of Professional Careers*. University of California Press, Berkeley.

Farrell, W. (1974). *The Liberated Man*. Random House, New York.

Fishel J., and Pottker, A. (1977). *Sex Discrimination Law and Federal Policy*. Lexington Books, New York.

Freeman, J. (1975). *The Politics of Women's Liberation*. McKay, New York.

Freeman, J. (1979). *Women: A Feminist Perspective*. Mayfield, Palo Alto, Calif.

Friedan, B. (1963). *The Feminine Mystique*. Norton, New York.

Girard, K. (1978). Symposium presentation at the American Educational Research Association meetings. Toronto, Canada.

Gribskov, M. (1980). "Feminism and the Woman School Administrator." In *Women and Educational Leadership: A Reader* (S. Bicklin, ed.), Lexington Books, New York.

Griffiths, M. (1976). "Can We Still Afford Occupational Segregation? Some Remarks." In *Women and the Workplace* (Blaxall and Reagan, eds.). University of Chicago Press.

Harrison, B. (1973). *Unlearning the Lie*. Liveright, New York.

Hole, J., and Levine, E. (1971). *Rebirth of Feminism*. Quadrangle, New York.

Howe, F. (1977). *Seven Years Later: Women's Studies Programs in 1976*. National Advisory Council on Women's Educational Programs, Washington, D.C.

Kanter, R. (1977). *Men and Women of the Corporation*. Basic Books, New York.

King, C. (1969). *My Life with Martin Luther King, Jr.* Holt, Rinehart and Winston, New York.

Klein, E. (1976). "The Rise of the Women's Movement: A Case Study in Political Development." In *New Research on Women and Sex Roles* (D. McGuian, ed.). University of Michigan Press.

Kravetz, D., and Sargent, A. (1977). "Consciousness Raising Groups: A Resocialization Process for Personal and Social Change." In *Beyond Sex Roles* (A. Sargent, ed.). West, San Francisco.

Maccoby, E. (1966). *The Development of Sex Differences*. Stanford University Press.

Maccoby, E., and Jacklin, C. (1974). *The Psychology of Sex Diifferences*. Stanford University Press.

Martin, W. (1972). *The American Sisterhood*. Harper & Row, New York.

Miller and Associates, Inc. (1978). *The Status of Title IX in Region X*. Department of HEW, Washington, D.C. (available at Miller and Associates, Inc., 711 S. Capitol Way, Olympia, Wash. 98501).

Mitchell, J. (1973). *Woman's Estate*. Random House (Vintage Books), New York.

Rey, P., and Russell, D. (1978). "Some Proof That Women's Studies Courses Can Raise Consciousness." *Phi Delta Kappan*, June, pp. 716–777.

Sanford, N. (1962). *The American College*. Wiley, New York.

Sapiro, V. (1980). "News from the Front: Inter-Sex and Inter-Generational Conflict Over the Status of Women." *Western Political Quarterly*, June.

Schmuck, P. (1976). *Sex Differentiation in Public School Administration*. National Council of Administrative Women in Education, Washington, D.C.

Schmuck, P. (1980). "Changing Women's Representation in School Management. In *Women and Educational Leadership: A Reader* (S. Bichlin, ed.). Lexington Books, New York.

Schmuck, P. (1980). *Sex Equity in Educational Leadership: The Oregon Story*. Newton, Mass., Education Development Center.

Timpano, D., and Knight, L. (1976). "Sex Discrimination in the Selection of School Administrators: What Can Be Done?" National Institute of Education papers, *Education and Work*, no. 3, Washington, D.C.

U.S. Office of Education (1972). *Report of the Commissioner's Task Force on the Impact of Office of Education Programs on Women*. Washington, D.C.

Vinovskis, M., and Bernard, R. (1978). "Beyond Catherine Beecher: Female Education in the Antebellum Period." *Signs*, 3(4):856–869.

Weisskopf, S. (1978). "Essay Reviews." *Harvard Educational Review* 48 (2):269–278.

Chapter 9

EDUCATIONAL EQUITY: CURRENT AND FUTURE NEEDS

Jean Stockard

Women's liberation will . . . inevitably bring with it, as a concomitant, men's liberation. Men, no less than women, are imprisoned by the heavy carapace of their sexual stereotype. The fact that they gain more advantages and privileges from women's oppression has blinded them to their own bondage, which is the bondage of an artificial duality. This is the male problem: the positing of a difference, the establishment of a dichotomy emphasizing oppositeness. Men are to behave in this way; women in that; women do this; men do the other. And it just so happens that the way men behave and act is important and valuable, while what women do is unimportant and trivial. Instead of identifying both the sexes as part of humanity, there is a false separation which is to the advantage of men [Roszak, 1969, pp. 303 -304].

The sex inequities students face in education range from differences in achievement, to stereotyped curricula, to segregation in school activities and academic areas. Males suffer especially in the early years of schools, and females in the later years. We have suggested that these unequal experiences can be eventually traced to the division of sex roles in our society. While some of the inequities, especially those involved in learning disorders, may have a biological basis, most of them stem from cultural distinctions between appropriate roles. These cultural definitions and the greater valuation of the male roles can also account for segregation and discrimination in the advancement opportunities of professional educators. From a review of the relevant psychological literature we have suggested that the most effective way to produce social change is to alter the structures in which people live and work. Chang-

185

ing the situation and the required behaviors, if this change is not viewed as coercive, will generally lead to changes in beliefs and possibly even greater changes in behaviors.

Based on the United States Constitution and its elaboration by various laws and court decisions, there is now a legal basis for banning sex discrimination in the employment, promotions, and salaries of workers and also to prohibit sex segregation in school activities. Many of the recent changes in the law have been promoted by activists in the current women's movement. The energy and commitment shown by these women and men indicate that pressure to end inequities in education will probably not soon disappear.

We will now review current attempts at removing sex inequities in schools, and after examining their effectiveness, we will suggest how to meet future needs.

CURRENT ATTEMPTS AT CHANGE

The most far-reaching attempts to promote sex equity today generally come from the federal government. Individual states can develop programs and laws with similar and sometimes even more far-reaching goals, but only the federal government has both the nationwide authority and the widespread enforcement mechanisms to promote compliance. The fact that most schools in the United States now receive some form of federal aid means that any threatened cut-off to this financial support will probably promote compliance with the law. Current changes in education generally focus on students, employment, and the development of new policies and programs.

Change for Students

Title IX regulations were reviewed in Chapter 7. Generally, these regulations focus on discrimination in access to education, sex segregation in classrooms and extracurricular activities, and discrimination in testing and counseling. They do not consider sex stereotyping in curricular materials, nor do they focus on possible sources of sex inequities in achievement. While it is probably too early to assess the long-range impact of these regulations, changes are already apparent, especially in school sports programs at the precollege levels. While only a few years ago most of the extracurricular sports involved only men, now there are both men's and women's teams, and in a few instances, males and females may compete together.

Educators have been concerned for many years with boys' special learning and behavior problems in school. Most attempts to cope with these difficulties have not focused on issues related to sex roles, and we know of no contemporary effort that leads in that direction. In contrast, and even though the Title IX regulations carefully avoided dealing with curriculum materials, publishers and school officials have made concerted efforts to rid textbooks, tests, and other materials of stereotyped representations. Publishers give authors explicit instructions on how to avoid both racial and sexual stereotypes, and local school advisory committees often scout for offensive materials and ask that they not be used. Because, however, any move to ban literature from the classroom can border on censorship and violation of constitutional rights, extreme care must be taken in determining whether material is actually offensive.

In the late 1970s more women entered college, and the proportion of women attending schools in traditionally male areas such as business, law, and medicine increased rapidly. (See Chapter 2 and Gappa & Uehling, 1979.) It appears that at least one important factor in this increase is active recruitment of women students. Studies of recruiting strategies have documented success in increasing women's enrollment in schools of engineering (Sproule & Mathis, 1976) and dentistry (Nyre & Xhonga, 1975), both areas that have traditionally had few women students. It is unclear, however, how widespread such recruiting efforts are or the extent to which they are the main factor responsible for the changes in enrollment.

Change for Employees

Title IX regulations as well as various equal-pay acts, affirmative action programs, and civil rights laws all apply to professionals in education. These laws and regulations require that men and women be considered equally for hiring and promotions and that policies that specifically discriminate against women, such as those regarding maternity, be altered. The enforcement of these laws and regulations can be promoted through appeals to the various local, state, and federal bureaucracies. In 1979 the Supreme Court ruled that individuals seeking redress for sex discrimination in education can also file suits directly in courts. Whichever method is used, however, the procedure is often both time-consuming and costly. (See Appendix B for a description of how to file a complaint under some of these systems).

While enforcement can be eventually obtained through the withdrawal of federal funds and by court orders after the successful completion of the complaint process, groups of educators in local areas also promote enforcement through lobbying efforts and attention to school policies. City, district, and statewide groups of educators interested in promoting equity for professionals in education are becoming more common. People in these groups encourage women to aspire to nontraditional jobs in education and call attention to discriminatory practices that prevent equal access. (See Schmuck, 1980 and Smith, Schmuck, Kalvelage, Starling, 1980 for descriptions of such efforts.)

Research and Program Development

In addition to its direct attempts to promote sex equity for students and professionals, the federal government has also promoted the development of new programs and research work which deals with sex inequities in education. One key element in these areas was the formation of the Women's Educational Equity Act (WEEA), which was passed as part of the Education Amendments of 1974. WEEA authorizes the support of a broad range of activities whose targets are the many areas of education that involve sex bias. Programs financed through the Office of Education (OE) include the development, evaluation, and dissemination of curricula, textbooks, and other educational materials; preservice and inservice training for educational personnel, including guidance and counseling personnel; research, development, and other educational activities designed to advance educational equity; guidance and counseling activities, including the development of tests that do not discriminate on the basis of sex; educational activities to increase opportunities for adult women, including continuing educational activities and programs for underemployed and unemployed women; and the expansion and improvement of programs and activities for women in vocational education, career education, physical education, and educational administration. Public agencies, private nonprofit organizations, and individuals have applied for contracts and grants to carry out these authorized activities. One WEEA project funded by the OE focused on the development of a career model for the transition of women offenders from correctional institutions into the community. It developed classroom materials, counseling techniques with individuals, job-placement strategies and follow-up seminar materials. Another project developed materials to encourage young women to enter agricultural careers and to encourage faculty members to have more accepting attitudes toward women students in agriculture. Other projects have helped women's centers in colleges gain organizational skills, provided leadership training for aspiring administrators, and aided parents and teachers interested in nonsexist child rearing.

While the OE traditionally supports projects that develop practical materials and programs, the National Institute of Education (NIE) within HEW supports programs of basic research that try to develop an understanding of social and psychological processes underlying sex inequities. In recent years, NIE has financed research aimed at understanding more about differences in mathematical achievement, the experiences of women who have returned to education after an absence of several years, and influences on women's achievement in nontraditional scientific areas.

POTENTIAL EFFECTS OF CURRENT PROGRAMS

In assessing the possibility of altering sex inequities in education, we must consider the potential effects of current programs and policies and areas in which further work in the research and development of policy needs to be done.

Current programs and policies are obviously a start toward attaining greater sex equity in education. The current situation is far beyond that even envisioned a decade or two ago. Females and males are guaranteed equal and nondiscriminatory access to most educational facilities and programs. Schools are required to assess their program offerings continually to make sure they are free of sex bias. These provisions could provide the basis for important changes in the future. For instance, as the proportion of women in professional schools grows, eventually the number of women in the job-applicant pool for related positions will also increase. If the demand for these professionals continues, eventually change may occur in occupations that now suffer strongly from sex segregation.

We noted in Chapter 6 that the most effective way to promote social change is probably to change behavior, not attitudes. To the extent that affirmative action programs, the prohibitions of sex segregation of students by Title IX, and legal suits seeking greater equality in pay and the advancement of professionals require changes in situations and behaviors, they may produce changes in attitudes that will lead to even further future changes in behaviors. Already it is apparent that the inclusion of girls in school athletics has led to more liberal attitudes toward female participation in sports, and even greater changes toward equality of school programs may then eventually develop. In contrast, most of the programs sponsored by the OE focus on changing beliefs and attitudes. For instance, many programs develop awareness programs or new curricular materials. Extensive social change may not be forthcoming from these projects, at least with their current focus.

While changes in student participation in extracurricular activities, especially in sports, may be noted, the affirmative action programs regarding employment have not met such rapid success, perhaps because there are no immediate sanctions placed on employers for noncompliance. Moreover, strict timetables for enforcement have only rarely been enforced. Changes in job compositions ultimately require moving some people out of jobs while others move in. The fact that the relatively slow economy in recent years, especially within education, has not provided many new job opportunities may also have contributed to the lack of change.

Yet it is possible, if not probable, that affirmative action goals in employment are not being met because those in power do not want to meet them. They may not be motivated to promote change. We noted in earlier chapters that in recent years more men have entered elementary teaching, but more women have not entered administrative posts. In fact, the proportion of women entering administrative posts may be declining. Certainly over the past half-century women have become much less common in both school administrative posts and as secondary teachers. Since the passage of the Civil Rights Act in 1964, the gap between the median annual income of all blacks and that of all whites has actually widened. Even though blacks have been assured equal access to jobs, they may be even further from equality than a few years ago. Similarly, even though more women have entered the labor market in increasing numbers, the gap between their average full-time wages and those of men has continued to grow wider. Even though blacks and women have been guaranteed their legal rights to equality in employment, equality appears to be no nearer than it was earlier. White men still control the gates to occupational success, and until they are willing to accept women and minorities as equals, it may be unrealistic to expect changes.

Just as affirmative action and equal employment have not altered motives that may underlie the perpetuation of sex segregation and discrimination in the educational profession, Title IX and various school district policies have probably not dealt with the underlying basis for many of the inequities students face. Until policies and programs deal with issues that involve cultural definitions of masculinity and femininity and the development of individuals' self-definitions as males and females, many of the inequities students face will probably remain.

Future Needs

If we look to the future it is possible to envision the additional policies that will be needed as well as the additional research that must be completed if the policies are to be successful.

Policy Alterations

In altering policy to make it more effective, the various enforcement procedures associated with the current regulations should be streamlined and tightened. If sanctions for violating affirmative action or Title IX regulations were more readily available, enforcement would be easier. This would require changes in the regulatory bodies charged with enforcing these provisions.

It will be necessary, however, to deal with the motivations that underlie the maintenance of segregation and discrimination and the patterns in other social institutions that reinforce inequities in education. Education is an institution that responds to other parts of the social system; it tends to reflect discrimination in other institutions and respond to the sex-role socialization that first occurs in other areas of the society. The segregation in schools reflects that in the economy and in the family. The attitudes and beliefs that children bring with them to school reflect early experiences in the family. Changes in education alone cannot alter these institutions, except perhaps through some eventual effect over a very long period of time.

To bring full sex equity about in education, it will be necessary to have changes occur in other social institutions. Changes in the family should involve greater participation by both the father and mother in early child care; changes in the economy should assure equal access to males and females in all occupational areas. Changes in family structure could promote a greater acceptance by males of that which is now seen as feminine, including success in schools (Stockard & Johnson, 1979). Our cultural definitions of schooling could change so that if a boy were a scholar or abided by school regulations he would not be in danger of being deemed a "sissy;" if a girl were a scientist or mathematician, she would not fear being called unfeminine. Changes in the economy could alter the sex-segregated occupational and vocational aspirations of boys and girls as they see that more fields are open to them. These changes could also provide the basis for lessening the motivations currently supporting segregation and discrimination in the education profession by making the prospect of a more equally balanced representation less threatening to men who currently control the hiring process.

Finally, in formulating new policies, especially in regard to the profession of education, new structures of employment and the organizational work force should be considered. In Chapter 6 we described the pyramidal structure of occupations and the notion that success requires "making it to the top." Because in reality only a few people can achieve the highest positions, this structure of occupations may waste the skills and talents of many people and bring inevitable disappointment to some. Perhaps, instead of trying to move more women into the few administrative posts in the schools, policymakers could also consider altering the school structure so that more people, both men and women, participate in decision making and school governance. These policies could also focus on minimizing the differences in the levels of prestige attached to teaching at different levels and to administration as compared with teaching. A major way to accomplish this task would be to alter the pay scale. Such changes would entice both men and women to aspire to the various positions and would also use more of the available talent on school staffs.

Research Needs

All policy, if it is to be effective, should be based on well-established research results and theoretical understandings. There are many areas where our knowledge is yet incomplete or even minimal and where continued research is necessary in order that we understand the sources and nature of sex inequities in education. For instance, much work remains to be done in the area of academic achievement and aspirations to understand possible physiological influences on verbal and mathematical skills; to explore how different teaching styles can best accomodate male's skills and female's skills; and to examine the impact of sex-stereotyped materials on children's achievement and aspirations. Careful follow-up studies are also needed to examine the long-range impact of the enforcement of Title IX.

With respect to professionals, further research is needed to explain more thoroughly why such extensive sex segregation persists in education. Further research could also focus on what it is that aids those few women who do attain nontraditional posts.

With both the research on students and on professionals, it is important to examine variations by class, race, and region. Coleman's (1961) work indicates that working-class boys are less threatened than middle-class boys by girls who achieve academically. Other writers have suggested that urban blacks in the United States have less sex-typed personalities than whites (e.g. Tanner, 1974). Rural students often have fewer available educational resources than urban students, especially when the influence of social class is controlled. Do these variations then indicate different patterns of sex differences in achievement and aspirations among various race, class, and geographic groups? Do they suggest varying remedies for ending sex inequities in different demographic groups?

Research is also needed on the relationships between sex inequities of students and those of professionals. For instance, researchers could ask under what situations does the sex of the teacher influence sex differences in achievement? Do male and female teachers have different teaching styles and do these influence sex differences in achievement patterns? How does altering sex segregation in the profession of education affect the achievement of students and their occupational aspirations? How do boys and girls perceive the hierarchy in the education profession, and how are their perceptions related to their own future aspirations and plans?

Finally, future research could focus on how linkages between the social institutions of the economy, the family, and education affect sex inequalities. For instance, historical analyses could help clarify the extent to which changes in education such as in the sex composition of students in various programs affect the sex composition of related occupations at a later date. Other studies could examine the extent to which experiences in schools reinforce and/or work against experiences in the family in the development of sex roles.

Hopes for the Future

Education can be a humane and a nonsexist institution. Both boys and girls can like school, both boys and girls can achieve. Boys can learn languages, girls can learn mathematics. Curricular materials can represent males and females fairly. Males and females can both have access to school programs, classes and activities. Males as well as females can be elementary teachers; females as well as males can teach in all areas of the secondary schools. Both males and females can be college professors. Both males and females can participate in school management. We can and should value the work of male and female elementary teachers in preparing young minds as much as we value the managerial skills of administrators or as much as we value technical and advanced knowledge in specialized scientific areas.

The beginnings of these changes are found in our present laws as well as in the motivation and aims of the current women's movement. Much work remains to be done. The changes will not be easy, and they cannot occur by altering education alone. However, with careful attention to the nature of the problems, analyses of why they occur, knowledge of the most effective ways to promote change, and a willingness to examine unique solutions, greater equity can be achieved.

REFERENCES

Coleman, J. S. (1961). *The Adolescent Society*. Free Press, New York.

Gappa, J. M., and Uehling, B. S. (1979). *Women in Academe: Steps to Greater Equality*. American Association for Higher Education, Washington, D.C.

Nyre, G. F., and Xhonga, F. A. (1975). "Graduate and Professional Education: An Incisive Look at Dentistry." In *Meeting Women's New Educational Needs*. Clare Rose (ed.) Jossey-Bass, San Francisco.

Roszak, B. (1969). "The Human Continuum." In *Masculine/feminine* (B. Roszak and T. Roszak, eds.). Harper & Row, New York.

Schmuck, P. A. (1980). *Sex Equity in Educational Leadership: The Oregon Story*. Education Development Center, Newton, Mass.

Smith, M. A., Schmuck, P. A., Kalvelage, J., and Starling, C. (1980). *Sex Equity in Educational Leadership: Getting Out and Getting Ahead*. Education Development Center. Newton, Mass.

Sproule, B. A. and Mathis, H. F. (1976). "Recruiting and Keeping Women Engineering Students: An Agenda for Action," *Engineering Education*, 66:745–748.

Stockard, J., and Johnson, M. (1979). "The Social Origins of Male Dominance." *Sex Roles*, 5:199–248.

Tanner, N. (1974). "Matrifocality in Indonesia and Africa and Among Black Americans." In *Woman, Culture, and Society*. (M. Z. Rosaldo and L. Lamphere, eds.). Stanford University Press.

APPENDIX A

Mary Ann Smith
and
Sakre K. Edson

EXERCISES: EXPERIENTIAL LEARNING ABOUT SEX ROLES

All learning has a cognitive component, the contents of the information about a subject, and an emotional component, the feelings and beliefs about the subject. Often the cognitive component is the only area recognized as important and legitimized in academic classes. In some subject areas, such as calculus, it may be the only area of importance. Few people have strong emotional feelings about what calculus *ought* to be. However, some subject areas have values and feelings intertwined with facts, as in the area of sex roles, and learning the facts only provides partial understanding. Classroom activities that stress active participant involvement can help people learn about their feelings and values and explore the intellectual content as well (Pfeiffer & Jones, 1977).

Experiential Methods

As humans we use selective perception. We have learned to reject certain inputs from our environment and to accept others. Part of the experience of learning about sex roles is to understand what it is we subconsciously filter out and ignore and what it is we accept as true. Often we do not realize the most powerful influences on our perceptions. Until we are forced to challenge the subconscious and untested assumptions upon which we base our perceptions, large blind areas will inevitably develop in understanding complex emotional issues (Napier, 1973).

A male professor who was involved in research about sex roles recently described his experience as the lone man at a workshop: "All of a sudden, it was as if I didn't exist. I would say something and no one would even hear me! It was a powerful lesson suddenly to feel the way many women must feel. Now I really listen to someone who is in the minority because I have learned how it feels to be ignored." This professor was describing learning from experience—the process of changing his behavior based on his emotional experience, rather than only on his cognitive knowledge.

195

Cognitions or thoughts are usually taught through information in readings and lectures in which the learners are passive. However, the emotional or affective aspects of learning are more often taught by *experiential* methods, such as role playing or structured experiences, in which the learners are encouraged to be *active*, to take the responsibility for their own learning. Pfeiffer and Jones (1977) suggest that experience precedes learning and that the meaning derived from any experience comes from the learners themselves. They describe five revolving steps in the experiential model that is fully addressed in a later section (see Figure **A.1**).

1. **Experiencing:** Participants become involved in an activity. They act and behave in certain ways and they perform, observe, see, and say something. This initial experience is the basis for the entire process of experiential learning.
2. **Sharing:** Following the experience itself, the participants share their reactions and observations with others who have experienced or observed the same activity.
3. **Debriefing:** Participants must integrate their sharing of the experience. They explore, discuss, and evaluate the dynamics between participants that emerged during the activity.
4. **Generalizing:** After the debriefing, the participants need to develop principles, or abstract generalizations, from the experience. Verbalizing about what is learned in this way can help participants further define, clarify, and elaborate it.
5. **Applying:** Participants complete the experiential cycle when a new learning is used and tested behaviorally. Application becomes an experience in itself, and with a new experience the cycle begins anew.

We hope this model will be helpful in experiential learning about sex roles in the classroom. Since the exercises included may be a new teaching activity to some users of the book, we explicitly describe guidelines for how to proceed in the next section. We include both procedures and cautions for teachers using the class exercises. It is our firm hope that the information and the personal experiences resulting from the exercises will generate questions, insights, and understanding about what it means to be male or female in our society.

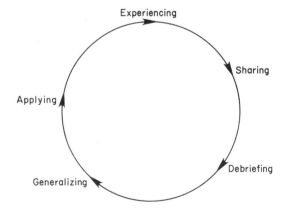

FIGURE A.1 Model of experiential learning.

HOW TO LEAD EXPERIENTIAL LEARNING

This section includes discussion of the characteristics of a group leader and group participants, examination of expectations, goals, and contracts, consideration of the problems of logistics in group activities, and a summary of the sequence of events in the group process.

Group Leaders

Group leaders must ask themselves three questions when they are about to use experiential learning: What is my role? What is my style? What are my skills? Group leaders' **roles** are simplified by legitimate authority in the group. You, as a professor, have the right to ask students to do things, and your task will be simplified if when you introduce yourself, you make clear your role as a leader. If you do not have legitimate power, ask the group to join with you in experiential learning and use yourself as an example by participating first.

Group leaders' **styles** vary greatly. If you have the reputation of being very authoritarian or traditional, you have two choices in working with experiential learning. The first is to explain to the group that you are learning along with them and want feedback both when you facilitate and when you hinder the process. The second is to look for a co-leader with a complementary style. For example, two professors in a class decided to cooperate when one said, "I just want to teach. I don't want to do any of that exercise stuff and I hate it when they fight." The other said, "That's the interesting part—I'd love handling that, as long as you lecture and cite references. I get scared when I have to do that!"

Group leaders' **skills** also vary greatly. If you feel that you lack skills in dealing with groups, you have the same two choices. You can choose to expand your skills and try leading the exercises. In most cases, inexperienced group leaders should be careful to structure the exercise well and control the amount of emotion generated. All of these exercises have been designed so that beginning group leaders can handle them without awkward amounts of emotion being generated. If you still have doubts about your skills, you can look for a co-facilitator who has had group experiences and work with the person as a team. In the exercises that follow there are guidelines for how to structure each exercise.

Group Participants

Leaders of experiential learning will want to think about group members' familiarity with each other, past experiences, roles, diversity, freedom, and about giving the participants encouragement during the process.

Consider the group members' **familiarity** with each other when planning early activities. We have found that the payoff from structured ice-breaking introductions (see exercises for Chapter 1) never fails to amaze us, especially in the degree of comfort provided for people who are unfamiliar with each other. For those who are already acquainted introductions also have dividends; they set the stage for uniting the group into a cooperative whole for this new learning task.

Learn about the **past experiences** of the group participants. Participants who have been a part of experiential learning before may be willing to lead in sharing their feelings and reassuring others who may be more reluctant.

Consider outside **roles,** especially when group participants are employer–employee pairs and people who work together. It is especially important for these people to agree upon guidelines such as confidentiality. Usually, the ice-breaking introductions will begin the process of relating to each other as peers learning together. Leaders can be models for equality in relationships and emphasize that all participants are equal.

Discuss the delights of **diversity** within the group. In experiential learning, the variety and richness come from varied age, background, experience, and status. Encourage younger, less experienced and lower-status people that they have much to contribute, and structure the exercise so that all are expected to participate.

Try to increase **freedom,** and keep participation voluntary. Emphasize that all have freedom of choice about joining activities, and that you will not penalize group members who choose not to participate although you do expect them to observe.

Finally, **encourage** group members to speak, to do the activities, to take individual stances, and to give constructive feedback. Remember that all feelings are valid information in experiential learning.

Expectations, Goals, and Contracts

Since experiential learning violates many of the norms of traditional learning, it is doubly important to examine people's expectations and goals and establish contracts between the leaders and the participants in the class.

The first step is to **elicit expectations**—namely, why they are here, what they want to learn, what they think will happen. Make a list of expectations, including readings, projects and assignments, and a personal journal. Discuss the equal importance of cognitive and experiential learning. Be sensitive to responses and explore which concerns are standard participant groans and which are legitimate concerns that need discussing. Both leaders and participants can discuss their expectations of each other and explore how they can mesh their expectations.

Next, the group must **set goals.** What do they want to learn, what do they want to be able to do or be when the group is finished, and how the goals mesh with the expectations. The group needs to discuss these questions and become clearer about their aspirations.

Finally, the group must **make contracts** and make these aspirations explicit. The first contract to be made might be that the teacher has a syllabus and a list of assignments and that the students agree to do these assignments. In experiential learning, teacher and students discuss the assignments and make sure all understand why they are important and which are most important.

A second contract might be about the role that experiential learning will play in the class. The following contract is a rather comprehensive model suggested as a guideline for thinking about what experiential learning really means. It is adapted from Johnson and Johnson (1975, p. 15):

Sample Contract

I understand that I will be taking a cognitive as well as an experiential approach to learning. I willingly commit myself to the statements hereunder:

1. I will use the structured experiences in this book to learn experientially. This means I am willing to engage in specified behaviors, and seek out feedback about the impact of my behavior on others in order to make the most of my learning.

2. I will make the most of my own learning by (a) engaging in specified behaviors and being open about my feelings and reactions regarding what is taking place in order that others may have information to react to in giving me feedback and in building conclusions about the area of study; (b) taking responsibility for my own learning and not waiting around for someone else to "make me learn"; (c) building conclusions about the experiences highlighted in the exercises.

3. I will help others make the most of their learning by (a) providing feed-

back in constructive ways; (*b*) helping to built the conditions, such as openness, trust, acceptance, and support, under which others can learn; and (*c*) contributing for the formulation of conclusions about the experiences highlighted in the exercises.

4. I will keep a journal each week, writing about my feelings and reactions to the group and to events outside the group, and I will discuss parts that I wish to share with others in the groups.

5. I will use judgment in keeping what happens among group members in the exercises appropriately confidential.

Signed: _____

The exercises for experiential learning are not just fun and games but a vital part of the whole learning process. Using a contract may help make that clear to the participants.

Problems of Logistics

In dealing with the practical matters of experiential learning exercises, consider the length of time available, the size of the group, the location and kind of physical facilities, and the materials to be used.

The **length of time** available will determine what exercises to use. Some require only 10 minutes; some require 2 hours. For example, with the 3-hour format, a teacher can vary the amount of time allotted to didactic and experiential learning, depending on the subject area and the needs of the participants. A 3-hour block also allows time to build more trust among the participants and have more time to process the data generated. However, experiential learning can also be used in the traditional 1-hour class time if the leaders plan to use the available time carefully.

Much of experiential learning depends upon the **size of the group.** Interaction with each other, as well as giving and receiving feedback, are of primary importance; these processes can occur more readily in small groups. If you have a group of over ten, divide it into subgroups of from four to six people (or whatever size the particular exercise suggests) to increase each person's active interaction with others.

The **materials** needed for experiential learning are: newsprint, felt-tip pens, and masking tape. It is also useful to have chalkboards with appropriate appurtenances and duplicating equipment; most educational environments already have the latter two as standard equipment. Newsprint can be used constantly for a number of the activities in the classroom.

Physical facilities are very important to experiential learning. If possible, have movable furniture, a moderate size space, and privacy. Movable furniture allows the leader to set up small and large groups, a big circle of chairs, or whatever is needed for each exercise. The moderate space is better than a gymnasium-like expanse that might tend to work against building rapport and warmth. Privacy is useful so that participants are not worried about non-participants watching, interruptions, phone calls, etc.

Sequence of Events

The following sequence of activities during experiential learning is adapted from Pfeiffer and Jones (1977).
1. **Getting acquainted:** The major need at the beginning of the class is for participants to establish some familiarity with each other, so that the initial caution with which people interact can be eased. An unfreezing process often begins in the middle of the first session and continues until participants are comfortable with each other.

2. **Closing expectation gaps:** It is important that leaders and participants make explicit their expectations of each other. When these expectations differ, both must clarify and negotiate until they agree upon explicit goals for the total learning experience.
3. **Legitimizing risk-taking:** Early in the experience, participants can test their willingness to know and be known by other people, to express their feelings, to explore how others are reacting to them, and to attempt new ways of behaving in relation to other people. At this point, risk-taking is legitimized and reinforced as a norm in the learning setting.
4. **Learning about roles and shared leadership:** Leaders need to introduce the concept of roles and shared leadership and to model this concept for the participants. As a result of this experimentation, perhaps participants will take home some new ideas about their roles as leaders and followers in relationship to others.
5. **Learning about feedback:** Leaders need to provide some kind of instruction in the feedback process so that effective sharing can occur during the experiential learning and so that feedback becomes expected and experienced freely.
6. **Developing an awareness of process:** As soon as the group begins to be comfortable with experiential learning, the leaders and participants need to explore the dynamic processes of how the group works together. Stop periodically to "debrief," to discuss the interaction and reactions to that interaction.
7. **Integrating the conceptual model:** Participants need to use continuously the steps of experiencing, sharing, debriefing, generalizing, and applying the diagramed conceptual model (Figure A.1). They are more likely to integrate their learning if they consciously use this model.
8. **Experimenting with self-expression:** One way participants can "stretch" their personal development is through the use of self-expression in a journal. By writing of their experiences and emotions, they will be able to integrate these experiences with the cognitive information they are receiving. This integration causes a much more powerful understanding of sex roles.
9. **Planning back-home application:** Ideally, plans for back-home application begin to develop from the first goal-setting activities and continue as the group progresses. Toward the end of the group experience, the leader can encourage participants to make definite plans for changes they want to institute in their back-home situation. These plans need to be evaluated by themselves and other group members.

"This general sequence does not imply a rigid structure. It is simply an attempt to highlight the needs of participants to develop an ability to talk with each other, to learn how to make sense out of the interaction that is occurring, and to heighten the development of ways that participants can use the experience in their everyday existence [Pfeiffer & Jones, 1977, pp. 22–23]."

Note about Format

The following exercises correspond to the chapters included in the book. We have included a short summary of the goals and rationale for each of the activities to clarify the background and the intent of the activity, both for the leader and the participants. Each exercise has several variations, from short discussion groups to structured exercises that take up to 2 hours. The leader is free to choose the variation that seems most useful to the group and best fits the allotted time. We also describe the materials, if any, needed for the activity, as well as the best structure or setting for the participants. Although we include step-by-step instructions for the exercises, the leader should feel free to adapt them to her or his own style and group.

Goals and Rationale

Aim: To become better acquainted with the members in the group.

We all function in our everyday lives by stereotyping or categorizing our environment and things in that environment. For example, we have an image of what a chair is and know that when we sit down in one, it will hold us up. We don't sit on stoves because we have a different image of the function of stoves. Developing impressions is helpful; in fact, it's a necessary task we do each day. Just as we have an impression or a stereotype of chairs and stoves in our society, we also categorize people. It is useful to think of stereotypes along a dimension; at one end they are impressions or categories, easily altered, at the other end they are prejudices and harder to change: impressions—stereotypes—prejudices. A stereotype ascribes the projected characteristics of a group upon an individual of that group. Impressions that plumbers are rich, redheads have fiery tempers, and girls are passive are all examples of stereotypes. Sometimes these impressions become deeply entrenched and we no longer differentiate the unique individual from the group prejudice. As we move into prejudices, we are less willing to change our psychological set. We need to be aware of when we are developing stereotypes and what we are gaining or losing by using them.

The exercises that follow can be fun and can bring about insights regarding what kinds of quick judgments people make with new acquaintances and how accurate they may be in those first impressions. The exercises grapple with the issues of stereotyping. Choose the one that seems appropriate for your group.

Variation 1

Time: Approximately 1 minute per group member with a short 5-minute wrap-up discussion at the conclusion.

Materials: None.

Structure: Participants should be sitting in a circle.

Instructions: Have the participants in the circle take turns telling their name and what they spend the major part of the day doing; e.g., working, going to school, caring for children, etc. Then ask each to give one stereotype or some judgment people in society often seem to have about what people in those daily activities are like. For example, if Mary says she works in Hollywood, the stereotype people have might be that people from Hollywood have glamorous jobs.

After everyone has had a turn, ask the group for general comments. Be sure everyone who wants to speak has a chance to do so.

1. Were they surprised by what other people's ideas of stereotypes were?
2. Were the stereotypes that were shared necessarily the truth about the participants?
3. Do different group members have different stereotypes about particular jobs mentioned?

Variation 2

Time: Approximately 2 minutes per person in the group with a short 5-minute wrap-up discussion at the conclusion.

Materials: None.

Structure: Participants should be sitting in a circle. They will need access to personal possessions in their pockets, purses, backpacks, briefcases, etc.

Instructions: Have the participants take a minute or so to find a personal possession that might lead people to form an impression or stereotype about them. Participants take 1 minute each to go around and say their name and show their object. Other group members say what conclusion might be drawn from the object, and the person can say whether these conclusions were correct or incorrect. For example, John might show several match boxes that he carries, the group might say that he is a smoker. In reality, he might pick them up for friends who smoke and for the fireplace at home.

After everyone has had a turn in the circle, take a few minutes to share what people might have learned during this exercise. Be sure there is a chance for everyone to speak.

1. Were there any surprises?
2. Was one person's impression or stereotypes of an object necessarily what others thought it might be?
3. Were the group members' impressions or stereotypes necessarily true of each group member?

Variation 3

Time: Approximately 30 minutes.
Materials: None.
Structure: Tables and chairs need to be pushed against the walls so that participants are free to move around the room.
Instructions: In this exercise, participants will spend time with three other people in the group that they don't know well or at all. The participants will spend 4 minutes a pair with 2 minutes of talking by each person in the pair. The leader will be the timekeeper, stating after 2 minutes that the speaker in the pairs should change, and stating after 4 minutes that group members can move on to a new partner.

In each pair, each person has 2 minutes to share his or her name and three impressions about the other person. When 2 minutes are called, the other person shares the same information. For example, I might say, "You are a sharp dresser, so I'd guess you are successful in your work." There should be time to tell each other how close to reality people were in their guesses.

After there have been three sharing periods, ask the participants to pull up a chair and sit in a circle. Have the group members talk about what they learned. Be sure that all those who wish to speak get a chance to do so.

1. Were they accurate in their impressions?
2. Was it difficult to share their first impressions with one another?
3. Was anyone surprised by how they were categorized by others?

(Note that for Variation 2 of the exercises in Chapter 2, the group members must complete a short questionnaire. Because the data are compiled by the instructor and presented as part of that exercise, the questionnaire should be completed at the end of the first session.)

EXERCISES FOR CHAPTER 2

Goals and Rationale

Aim: To understand the background and school experiences of group members.

We have all been in school and have felt the pressures from teachers, peers, and parents to conform to certain sex roles. We had aspirations for when we grew up, just as our parents had hopes for our futures. As we grew up in schools, some of us experienced discrimination of one sort or another. Some of these experiences were based on our gender. We can learn a lot by sharing these experiences from our backgrounds, and perhaps we can become a little more sensitive to how teachers may be affecting children with whom they come into contact in the schools.

Variation 1

Time: Approximately 30 minutes.

Materials: Blackboard and chalk. or newsprint; felt-tipped markers; masking tape.

Structure: Have the group split into small groups of three or four and move to a private space in the room.

Instructions: In the small groups, have participants choose a recorder to take down the group comments. Ask them to share the different experiences they recall boys and girls having in schools. For example, perhaps in one school only boys were allowed to play kickball during lunch and only girls got to work in the school office. Have the small groups compile lists to share with the larger group. This should take about 10 minutes.

Reconvene the larger group and have each group share their list. The leader may want to write the results up on the board or on newsprint in two lists: Experiences for Boys and Experiences for Girls. Conduct a general discussion of what the group's experiences were and how they feel about them. This discussion may take 15 or 20 minutes, and the leader should be sure everyone gets a turn to share.

1. How did group members feel about the different activities of boys and girls when they were in school?
2. Do group members feel there was any discrimination involved in what boys and girls were allowed to do in schools?
3. Do the group members feel that these different experiences have affected their lives in any way?
4. What do participants think happens in schools today?

Variation 2

This is a two-part exercise. As noted in the exercises for Chapter 1, the leader needs to hand out in the first session the questionnaire that follows and compile the data on newsprint before this meeting. The time needed to compile the data should be between 1 hour and 90 minutes, depending on class size.

Time: 60 minutes.

Materials: Questionnaire data either up on the blackboard or on newsprint.

Structure: Participants need to be seated so they can see the data and each other for discussion, perhaps in a semicircle around the board or newsprint.

Instructions: The leader shares the compilation of the data with the group, question by question, in whatever form seems appropriate for the group. A combination of percentages and listings of comments when appropriate seems helpful to group discussion. As the data are being presented, the leader can encourage group members to elaborate or comment on what the group has said in their answers to the questionnaire. At the end of sharing the data, have a few minutes of general discussion about what the group may have learned from this information. Be sure everyone has a chance to speak.

1. Were participants surprised at the answers of others?
2. Were womens' responses to the questions different from those of men?

3. Were womens' responses to the questions different from those of men?
4. How might or might not some of these *past* experiences be influencing the *current* experiences of group members?

SELF-EXPLORATION QUESTIONNAIRE

Do not put your name on this questionnaire. The responses you give to these questions will be used as a basis for the next class discussions. The questionnaires will be destroyed after that class meeting. You need not answer any question that you do not want to answer.

1. Are you a male___ or a female___?
2. Are you an undergraduate ___ or a graduate student ___?
   If you are a graduate student, what degree are you studying for?
   ___M.A. ___PhD ___EdD
3. What is your major field of study? _____
4. What is your current occupation? _____
5. When you were in high school, did your mother and/or father expect you to go to college?
   Mother: _____
   Father: _____
6. What were your parents' expectations for what you would do when you grew up?
   Mother's: _____
   Father's: _____
7. What things did your parents expect you *not* to do when you grew up?
   Mother: _____
   Father: _____
8. What kind of academic student were you in elementary school? _____
   _____
9. What kind of academic student were you in junior high and high school? _____
   _____
10. What kinds of trouble did you get into when you were in elementary school? _____
   _____
11. What kinds of trouble did you get into when you were in high school?
   _____
12. How did you generally feel about elementary school when you were a student? ___
   liked it very much ___ liked it ___ it was OK ___ mostly didn't like it ___ hated it
13. How did you generally feel about junior high when you were a student? ___liked it very
   much ___ liked it ___ it was OK ___ mostly didn't like it ___ hated it
14. How did you generally feel about high school when you were a student? ___ liked it
   very much ___ liked it ___ it was OK ___ mostly didn't like it ___ hated it
15. When you were in elementary school, what did you want to be when you grew up? ___
   _____
16. What is your occupational goal now? _____
17. If your goal has changed over the years, briefly explain why you changed plans. ____
   _____
18. Please rate how you see yourself on a scale from 1 to 5 for the following items (1 is hardly at all, 5 is a great deal).

	1	2	3	4	5
Tend to want to be around other people	—	—	—	—	—
Tend to be satisfied with myself	—	—	—	—	—
Tend to be driven for achievement	—	—	—	—	—

	1	2	3	4	5
Tend to compete	—	—	—	—	—
Tend to be aggressive	—	—	—	—	—
Tend to dominate others	—	—	—	—	—
Tend to care for others	—	—	—	—	—

19. Briefly describe an instance when you have experienced stereotyping or discrimination due to your sex. _____

EXERCISES FOR CHAPTER 3

Goals and Rationale

Aim: To understand how language can perpetuate sexism in our society and what the effects of language are, especially on students in school.

We have all grown up in a society that uses sexist language. The generic use of *he* and *man* excludes half the population and also severely limits, usually in an unconscious way, the career options for adults and children of each sex. Overcoming centuries of everyday language takes time. In many instances, using *she* along with *he* and saying *they* or *human* instead of *man* seem awkward and stilted. Nevertheless, the effort to change the language is necessary and critical in our culture. Language is incredibly subtle and powerful. In some sense, we *are* what we say, and we continually serve as a model to others as well.

Time: 25–30 minutes.

Materials: Dictionary; blackboard and chalk or newsprint; felt-tipped pens; masking tape.

Structure: Participants need to put their chairs in a semicircle around the blackboard or newsprint stand.

Instructions: Often people have a hard time defining the words they use in everyday language. Tell the group they are going to take a closer look at the words *feminine* and *masculine*. Take 60 seconds or so and let people in the group call out characteristics that they typically associate with *feminine* while one person writes the list on the board. Then do the same for *masculine*.

Look over the lists. Do they clarify an objective definition of the two words or do they indicate subjective judgments? Compare a dictionary definition of the words.

Make a large chart on the board resembling the following:[1]

	Enter + or −	
	Men	Women
Feminine Characteristics:		
Example: gentle	−	+
Masculine Characteristics:		
Example: competitive	+	−

Copy the words generated by the group into the chart, putting the feminine characteristics in the top left rectangle (example: gentle) and the masculine characteristics in the bottom

---

[1]This is an adaptation of an exercise from *Removing the Mask*, by Anne Grant, Newton, Mass.: Educational Development Center, 1978, p. 5.

left rectangle (example: competitive). For each item, rate whether this is typically viewed as a negative or positive trait for men as a group and for women as a group. For example, gentleness may be seen as positive in women, but negative in men. Likewise, competitiveness may be seen as a positive trait in males, but negative in females.

Take some discussion time to look at the group's chart and at the differences between entries for women and entries for men regarding these particular characteristics. When discussing the group's chart, make sure that everyone has a chance to participate.

1. Which characteristics would the group like people in general to exhibit most?
2. Are people surprised at the negative and/or positive characteristics that these two terms can conjure up?
3. What are the consequences for women and men when they are viewed as exhibiting a few or a lot of the characteristics on the chart?

EXERCISES FOR CHAPTER 4

Goals and Rationale

Aim: To understand the career choices of group members and to see how often these choices are a result of social roles rather than a true individual choice.

In this society we often are raised to think only of certain career aspirations for each sex. For example, men are often encouraged to pursue careers as principals, women as teachers. Why is this so? Certainly the answer is not dictated merely by people's skills or personal interests. We all know successful females who are principals and males who are teachers, yet we would generally stereotype them in other roles. This sex stereotyping of women and men occurs even in the teaching areas chosen by a person. For example, science and math teachers are usually men, while English teachers are typically women. If we understand our own current career choices, we may be freer in setting future goals.

(Note that Variation 2 may be especially appropriate for students in education.)

Variation 1

Time: 10–15 minutes.

Materials: Worksheet for each participant; blackboard and chalk or newsprint; felt-tipped pens; masking tape.

Structure: Participants will fill out worksheets at their places and then form a semicircle around the blackboard or posted newsprint stand.

Instructions: Have each member fill out the worksheet on career choices. Tell them to quickly go down the list and mark their first impression of whether a male or a female or both might hold each of these jobs. Tell them to move quickly through the list, marking without great deliberation, who typically holds these positions in our society.

Then compile a group chart on the blackboard or on newsprint. One person can write the data while group members raise their hands to tell choices they made in each category.

Then have a group discussion about what members may have learned that is new to them. Make sure every group member has a chance to address the issue if they wish.

1. Are there groupings of one sex or another around a certain job? If so, why?
2. How many jobs were marked for one sex and how many for the other?
3. What are the implications of these groupings for men and women?

Time: 10–15 minutes.
Materials: None.
Structure: Group members, perhaps in a circle, must be able to see all of the others for a group discussion.
Instructions: Ask the following questions and have group members stand in response:

1. Who intends to be (or is) an elementary teacher? a secondary teacher? a university teacher?
2. Who wants to be (or is) a principal at the elementary level? secondary level?
3. Who intends to enter (or is in) the field of special education?
4. Who has a teaching emphasis in English? physical education? math? home economics? science?

Lead a discussion group about what was discovered in this exercise. Be sure that everyone who wishes to speak gets a chance to talk in the group.

1. Did the group notice any breakdowns by sex around certain jobs or certain subject areas? Why would this be?
2. Does the group feel that career choices are personal choices, or are people often programmed into particular areas?
3. Can participants think of career changes or choices they might make now that they hadn't considered before?

(Note that Variation 1 in Chapter 5 is a two part exercise. A small bit of homework needs to be done by each participant before the next session. Please see the instruction on page 208–209 for further details.)

CAREER-CHOICE WORKSHEET

Quickly go down the list of jobs and mark whether a male or a female or both might hold these positions. Do not spend a great deal of time on any one job or choice.

	Male	Female	Both
High school principal	—	—	—
Janitor	—	—	—
English teacher	—	—	—
Superintendent	—	—	—
Head cook	—	—	—
Nurse	—	—	—
Counselor	—	—	—
Science teacher	—	—	—
Coach	—	—	—
Elementary principal	—	—	—

EXERCISES FOR CHAPTER 5

Goals and Rationale

Aim: To understand better the extent to which sexism operates in professional life and to learn more about what others are thinking and feeling about work and sexism.

We often don't know what others have experienced or think regarding sexism in the workplace because we just don't talk about these things, particularly between the sexes and rarely in a work situation. Likewise, we often *think* we know what others are feeling because we *assume* they feel the same way we do about these issues. In the workplace, males' feelings are often different from females'; children often experience schools differently from the way adults imagine they do. Sharing our different points of views and experiences can bring us all to a closer understanding of a variety of perspectives.

Variation 1

This is a two-part exercise. As noted in the previous exercise, there is a homework assignment to be given out at that time. The leader needs to ask each participant to do a small field study in which he or she will interview six people about their opinions regarding who should hold certain positions in education. The participants should be instructed to interview two adults who work or study in the field of education, two who are outside education, and two students. Ask each participant the following questions:

1. Who should be teachers, women or men? Why?
2. Who should be principals, women or men? Why?
3. Who should be superintendents, women or men? Why? (Young children may not know this occupation, so it may be eliminated.)

Each participant should record all responses and note what the sex of each respondent is. This information should be brought and shared with the group in the following exercise:

Time: Approximately 45 minutes.

Materials: Interview data; newsprint; felt-tipped pens; masking tape or blackboard and chalk.

Structure: Participants should be sitting so they may easily see the blackboard or newsprint.

Instructions: In a group discussion, ask the group members to share the information they gathered one by one. Write the responses up on the blackboard or on newsprint. The following breakdown might be helpful to fill in.

	Opinions regarding positions					
	Teacher		Principal		Superintendent	
Respondents	Male	Female	Male	Female	Male	Female
Male educators	——	——	——	——	——	——
Female educators	——	——	——	——	——	——
Male noneducators	——	——	——	——	——	——
Female noneducators	——	——	——	——	——	——
Male students	——	——	——	——	——	——
Female students	——	——	——	——	——	——

Discuss the various responses and the reasons given. Be sure that all members get a chance to share before you end the discussion.

1. Are the children saying the same things as adults?
2. Are people inside of education saying the same things as people outside the field?
3. What are the implications of what the group members found for men and for women in education?

Variation 2

Time: 2 hours, including a 10 minute break.

Materials: Newsprint; felt-tipped pens; masking tape.

Structure: Participants will break up into small groups of four or five people of the same sex for discussion, later reconvening to share information and discuss their experiences.

Instructions: Begin with a discussion of the importance of sharing similar and differing experiences and points of view. It may be helpful to use the model of Johari's Window, below, or to talk about the shared knowledge in more general terms. The main points to consider are as follows: There is a certain amount of information that is *public*, known by oneself and others; there is an area of knowledge that is *private*, information that may or may not be shared, as individuals choose; others may know things about us that we do not know, that we are *blind* to; perhaps none of us understands the area of the unconscious, or the *unknown*. By trying to share more of these private, blind, and unconscious areas, we all can grow in awareness and understanding. With this kind of sharing, the public area of knowledge can grow, and we can make decisions on the basis of understanding rather than pure conjecture.

JOHARI WINDOW[2]

	Known to self	Not known to self
Known to others	1. Open (public): areas of sharing and openness	2. Blind: area of blindness
Not known to others	3. Hidden: (private) area of avoided information	4. Unknown: area of unconscious activity

Now explain to the group that they are going to spend some time in small groups discussing several questions that the groups will record and bring back to the larger group. Divide the group into a number of all-male and all-female groups of four or five people each. Have each group go off into a space or room of its own for 1 hour to discuss the questions that follow. Have each group take a felt-tipped pen and some newsprint on which to record their responses to the questions. Ask them to use *one page of newsprint for each question and to write the question at the top of each page.*

1. Think of the other sex. What do you value about people of the other sex?
2. Think of the other sex. What do you think they value about people of your sex?
3. What behaviors exhibited by the other sex are *hindering* you in a work setting?
4. What behaviors exhibited by the other sex are *helpful* to you in a work setting?

After an hour call a break of about 10 minutes. During that time, the groups will need to tape the answers up on the walls of the room where everyone can see them easily.

[2]From J. Luft, *Of Human Interaction*, National Press Books, Palo Alto, Calif., 1969.

After the break, reconvene the larger group. An hour of discussion should ensue, with each group having someone read through its responses to the questions. Make sure that after all the reports are given, there is sufficient time for people to discuss the different responses, especially those regarding the other sex, and how they felt after being involved in this exercise. Be sure all participants get a chance to share their responses and feelings during this group discussion.

1. What did group members learn that had previously been hidden or private about the other sex?
2. Did individuals learn things they might have been blind to before the exercise?
3. Does the group believe these questions and sharing information with one another are useful?

EXERCISES FOR CHAPTER 6

Goals and Rationale

Aim: To understand the biases that may be at work in selection committees.

Hiring is one area that may show the influences of sex roles and sex-typed expectations in education. Predominately all-male and all-white school boards have traditionally hired superintendents much like themselves. With the change in the composition of school boards, and with increasing awareness, some of these old patterns are slowly changing. Personnel decisions in education, on *all* levels, have important ramifications for adults and children in the schools. If each sex is to share equally in the running of schools and the modeling for children, selection committees need to look toward hiring a more heterogeneous staff. In participating in this exercise, group members might become more aware of how stereotypes and role expectations can affect hiring practices.

Time: 90 minutes to 2 hours, including a 10-minute break.

Materials: Copies of the resumes that follow and worksheets; newsprint; felt-tipped pens; masking tape.

Structure: Participants will fill out worksheets individually and then form small groups for discussion. A discussion with the total group will ensue at the close of the session.

Instructions: First, hand out a resume and an individual worksheet to every participant. Tell them they are to read the resumes and each individual is to pick out a superintendent for their school district. (Further instructions are on the worksheet.) They have 15 minutes to complete this part of the exercise. This part of the exercise is done individually and group members should not discuss their choices at this point. Collect all of the worksheets. (During the next part of the exercise, the leader will want to compile the data on newsprint to share with the group later on in the exercise by making a sheet for each of the preferred choices, listing reasons, and tallying the number of preferences each person received.)

Put people into groups of four or five for 30 minutes. Tell them they are to be a screening committee. They will need to appoint a recorder and make a consensual choice for the most preferred candidate. This should be a choice that everyone in the group can "live with" even if they are not totally pleased with the choice of the group. If there is time, ask the groups to do the same thing with the least preferred choice.

Take a 10-minute break. (During this time the leader may still be putting the individual data up on newsprint.)

Reconvene the larger group for the next 30–45 minutes. Have each group report their choice(s) and why they made it. Then put up the individual data so the whole group can see easily.

1. Did group members or individuals choose a person much like themselves?
2. Did group members or individuals choose a person who fits the typical superintendent pattern?
3. What are the implications of the various choices for women and for men in education?

In the last 15–30 minutes, share any kinds of insights group members may have, making certain all have a chance to speak if they wish.

LIST OF RESUMES

All candidates have superintendents' credentials. The last position listed is their current employment. All people come with strong recommendations from employers.

Michael Fosberg

Age, 55. Married, two children, white. EdD in 1976 from local university.

Experience (all in state): Sixth-grade teacher for 3 years. Acting elementary principal for 2 years. District office director of elementary education for 3 years. Principal of elementary school for 4 years.

Memberships: American Educational Research Association, state education association, Phi Delta Kappa, Democratic Party, state school administrators association.

Educational Philosophy Statement. Students need to learn responsibility by being responsible. We should offer more choices to students.

Self-Identified Strengths: Interest in curriculum and alternative schools; democratic leadership style.

Reva Farrell

Age, 55. Married, four children, white. EdD in 1960 from out-of-state university.

Experience: Teacher of third, fourth, sixth, and eighth grades for 10 years in Kansas. Director of curriculum (Kansas) for 5 years and of high school social studies teachers for 3 years in Montana. Social studies department chairwoman for 3 years. Associate Superintendent of Montana State Department of Education.

Memberships: AASA, Women's Political Caucus, Republican Party, various Montana community and state organizations.

Educational Philosophy Statement: Students need to learn basic skills and have more equal opportunities; community should be involved in setting educational goals.

Self-Identified Strengths: Organizing abilities; community involvement; strong speaker.

Samuel Speers

In-district candidate. Age, 48. Divorced, no children at home, white. M.A. at local state university; some PhD work.

Experience: Military service. High school math teacher 5 years, department chairman 2 years. All the following in your district: high school math teacher 10 years, chairman 5 years, curriculum director 5 years, director federal program on math improvement.

Memberships: Lions Club, independent political registration, education and school administrators associations, various community groups.

Educational Philosophy Statement: Schools must do a better job of education by being more efficient. Educational problems result from poor use of resources.

Self-Identified Strengths: Fiscal responsibility; good organizing ability; strong community support.

Jeremy Hodgkins

Age, 48. Married, three children, black. PhD from Stanford in 1965.

Experience: High school teacher of social studies in local urban district for 8 years. Staff development in central office of local urban district for 4 years. Title I program director at San Francisco public schools for 4 years. Intern to superintendent and federal grants officer for 2 years in San Francisco.

Memberships: Phi Delta Kappa, Black Educators, NAACP, Republican Party, AFT, American Educational Research Association.

Educational Philosophy Statement: Schools should strive toward equal opportunities for all students. We must be responsive to the clients we serve.

Self-Identified Strengths: Successful in all positions. Good organizing and leadership abilities; strong commitment to public education.

Amelia Caron

In-district candidate. Age 43. Divorced, five children, white. PhD almost completed at local university.

Experience: State president of League of Women Voters. Preschool director, 6 years, high school science teacher, 5 years. All the following in your district: High school department chairwoman, educational association representative and state president, high school science teacher.

Memberships: Democratic Party, Phi Delta Kappa, American Association of University Women, League of Women Voters, educational association.

Educational Philosophy: Students need leadership, schools should create more opportunities for student leadership in decision making.

Self-Identified Strengths: Knowledge of school district and state; hard worker; good teacher.

Gabriele Friente

Age, 49. Married three children, Hispanic. EdD almost completed at local state university.

Experience: League of Migrant Workers organizer. High school physical education teacher and coach in local urban district. State Department of Education. Compensatory education for 5 years. Human relations director for 3 years in local city. Regional director locally for 4 years.

Memberships: Democratic Party, League of Migrant Workers, educators and administrators association.

Educational Philosophy: Community should be involved. More attention should be given to remedial work and basic skills.

Self-Identified Strengths: Fluent Spanish, good political relations, strong leadership.

Marjorie Stein

Age, 47. Single, no children, black. MA+.

Experience: Teacher of English for 5 years in junior high and 3 years in senior high school. English department chairwoman for 2 years. IED director, special education for 4 years. Director of special education in nearby city for 4 years.

Memberships: Educational association, Republican Party, Council for Exceptional Children, educational administration association.

Educational Philosophy: Students learn by direct experience. We need to address issues of students who are not college bound and students with special needs.

Self-Identified Strengths: Experience with mainstreaming special education students; fiscal responsibility.

Robert Nevrall

Age, 55. Married, four children, white. EdD in 1970 from local university.

Experience: High school social studies teacher and coach in Michigan, Iowa, California, and Oregon for 10 years. Social studies department chairman for 3 years. Assistant high school principal for 5 years, principal for 5 years, vice principal for 5 years, and superintendent for 10 years—all locally.

Memberships: AASA, Elks Club, Boy Scouts, several state and community volunteer organizations, education and administration associations.

Educational Philosophy: Education should provide students with basic skills and prepare them for college. Educational leaders should lead.

Self-Identified Strengths: Competent leadership; variety of positions; strong community leadership.

RESUME EXERCISE

Individual Selection

Directions for filling out individual forms: You hold a position in your own school district, and you are on a screening committee to select a new superintendent for the district. Eight candidates have been selected as finalists. In 15 minutes you will meet the other screening committee members, and you have been asked to do the following:

1. Identify your first choice, and give three reasons to defend your choice.
   Your choice: _____ (name of applicant)
   Three reasons for your choice:
   a. _____
   b. _____
   c. _____
2. Identify your two *least preferred* candidates and give two reasons.
   Least preferred candidate: _____ (name of applicant)
   Two reasons for the low rating:
   a. _____
   b. _____
   Least preferred candidate: _____ (name of applicant)
   Two reasons for the low rating:
   a. _____
   b. _____

RESUME EXERCISE

Group Form A (Large School District)

Directions: You are a screening committee for a large school district. Your school district has an average daily attendance of about 20,000. It includes 4 high schools, 8 junior high schools, and 30 elementary schools. There are no severe problems, although enrollments are declining. The school board has asked you to recommend a candidate. Your group decision should be by consensus. That does not mean the person selected is every individual's first choice but that it is a choice you can live with. Please assign a reporter to present the name and give three reasons for your selection.

1. Your committee choice: _____ (applicant's name)
   Three reasons for your selection:
   a. _____
   b. _____
   c. _____
2. Your least preferred choice: _____ (applicant's name)
   Two reasons for your low rating:
   a. _____
   b. _____

RESUME EXERCISE

Group Form B (Small School District)

Directions: You are a screening committee for a small school district serving 3000 to 6000 students. You have one high school that serves a large region, two junior high schools, and several elementary schools. There are no severe problems, although enrollments are declining. The school board has asked you to recommend a candidate. Your decision should be by consensus. That does not mean the person selected is every individual's first choice, but is a choice you can live with. Please assign a reporter to present the name and give three reasons for your selection.

1. Your committee choice: _____ (applicant's name)
   Three reasons for your selection:
   a. _____
   b. _____
   c. _____
2. Your least preferred choice: _____ (applicant's name)
   Two reasons for your low rating:
   a. _____
   b. _____

EXERCISES FOR CHAPTER 7

Goals and Rationale

Aim: To better understand the law and its implications.

Like civil rights legislation, the laws to equalize the sexes in their work, in hiring, and in schooling may have a large impact on society. Laws are significant, but people's attitudes and behaviors may run contrary to the laws and their implications. To change a society whose culture has been founded on the inequity of the sexes will take time. Meanwhile, we need to familiarize ourselves with the law and to monitor our own behavior as best we can. The following exercises will hopefully help expand awareness about the laws and their practices.

(Note that Variation 2 may be especially appropriate for teachers.)

Variation 1

Time: 1 hour to 90 minutes.

Materials: One preemployment inquiry and one copy of the law worksheet for every participant. (See pages 215–219.)

Structure: Each participant will complete a worksheet, and then the group will discuss it, preferably in a circle.

Instructions: Have the participants choose groups of five people to work in for the next 15–20 minutes. When people are in their groups, ask them to fill out the quiz individually first. Then tell them to take 15 minutes to come to a consensus (or a decision everyone can live with) on the answers.

Reconvene the larger group and discuss the questions in light of the law worksheets, which go over the legal and illegal kinds of employment inquiries. Note that Questions 5, 10, 14 and 16 are the only legal questions on the worksheet.

Time: 30 minutes.

Materials: Double-standard quiz for every participant. (See page 218.)

Structure: Individuals fill out quiz and then move into a circle for discussion.

Instructions: Hand out one quiz to each member. Tell them to take 5 minutes or so to answer the questions. Then as a group, go through the test question by question. Discuss each one as you go. Make sure all have a chance to add to the discussion.

1. How do the group members rate themselves?
2. Does the test make anyone more aware of changes they might make in their behavior and attitudes toward boys and toward girls?
3. What are the implications of this kind of behavior for boys and girls in schools?

PREEMPLOYMENT INQUIRY[3]

Questionable inquiries of applicants:	Legal	Conditional or illegal
1. Whether they are Mrs., Ms., or Miss	___	___
2. Request for proof of age on birth certificate or baptismal record	___	___
3. Birthplace or that of parents, spouses, or other close relatives	___	___
4. Religious affiliation, name of church or parish, or religious holidays observed	___	___
5. Whether they are citizens of the United States	___	___
6. The date they acquired their citizenship	___	___
7. Their plans for child care	___	___
8. Whether they plan to have more children	___	___
9. Names of relatives working for the district	___	___
10. What foreign languages they can read, write, or speak fluently	___	___
11. Whether they have ever been arrested for any crime, and if so, when and where	___	___
12. A list of all clubs, societies and lodges to which they belong	___	___
13. Request of a photograph with their application for employment	___	___
14. Whether they are able to work long hours	___	___
15. Height and weight	___	___
16. Their past working experience	___	___
17. What their plans are if their husband moves	___	___

Next, discuss the questions in terms of the next two pages—the legal and illegal kinds of employment inquiries.

[3]Adapted from "Pre-Employment Inquiry Quiz," by Jerry Gumbert, Kent State University, Kent, Ohio: KEDS General Assistance Center, 1976.

LAW WORKSHE

Area of inquiry:	Questions that are legal
1. Name	For access purposes, inquiry into whether the applicant's wo records are under another name
2. Address/housing	To ask for current and previous addresses and length of time applicant lived there and for phone number and how applican be reached
3. Age	To ask, after hiring, for proof of age by birth certificate
4. Birthplace/national origin	
5. Race/color	To indicate that the institution is an equal opportunity employ ask, after hiring, for affirmative action plan racial statistics
6. Sex	To indicate that the institution is an equal opportunity employe to ask, after hiring, for affirmative action plan sex statistics
7. Religion/creed	
8. Citizenship	To ask whether person is a United States citizen and, if not, wh person intends to become one; to ask whether residence is lega whether spouse is a citizen; to require proof of citizenship after h
9. Marital and parental status	For insurance and tax purposes, to inquire, after hiring, about m or single status and about number and ages of dependents an of spouse
10. Relatives	To ask, after hiring, name, relationship, and address of person notified in case of emergency
11. Military service	To inquire into service in the United States armed forces and branch of service and rank attained; to ask about any job-rel experience; to require military discharge certificate after hirir
12. Education	To ask what academic, professional, or vocational schools v attended and about language skills, such as reading and wr foreign languages
13. Criminal record	To request a list of convictions other than misdemeanors

[4]Adapted from Keser, Joyce, Jim Haggerty, and Cathy Eddy, "Legal and Illegal Areas of Inquiry in Hiring," Kent State University, Kent, Ohio: KEOS General Assistance Center, 1976.

Questions that are illegal	Legislation:
ask if a woman is a Miss, Mrs., or Ms or to request applicant ɡive maiden name or any other previous name he or she has ѳd	Title VII of the Civil Rights Act of 1964 as amended by the Equal Employment Opportunity Act of 1972 (Title VII); Title IX of the Education Amendments of 1972 (Title IX)
ask age or age group of applicant or to request birth ʳtificate or baptismal record before hiring	Age Discrimination Act of 1967
ask birthplace of applicant or of parents, grandparents, or ɔuse or make any other inquiry into national origin	Title VII
y inquiry that would indicate race or color	
ask applicant any inquiry which would indicate sex, unless ɑted to the job (in education, a locker room or restroom ɘndant)	Title VII, Title IX
ask applicant's religion, religious customs, and holidays or ʳequest recommendations from church officials	Title VII
ask whether person is native born or naturalized; to ask for ѳof of citizenship before hiring, whether parents or spouses ѳ native born or naturalized, or for date of citizenship	Title VII
ask marital status before hiring; to ask the number and ages ɕhildren, who cares for them, or if applicant plans to have more ɭdren	Title VII, Title IX
ʳequest names of relatives working for the same institution or ʳict (Nepotism policies that impact disparately on one sex are ɡal under Title IX.)	
ʳequest military service records; to ask about military service ɪny country other than the United States; to inquire about type ʟischarge	Title VII, Title IX EEOC interpretation of Title VII[a]
ask specifically about nationality, racial, or religious affiliation ʙchools attended; to ask how foreign language ability was ʊired	Title VII
inquire about arrests	

(*continued*)

The designated legislation is the primary statutory authority. However, the interpretive regulations of ʂ legislation are the basis for determining the finer points, and these regulations should be reviewed ʝetermine a question's legality.

Area of inquiry:	Questions that are legal
14. References	To request general and work references not relating to race, c⊘ religion, sex, national origin, or ancestry
15. Organizations	To ask organizational membership—professional, social, etc.– long as affiliation is not used to discriminate on the basis of r⊘ sex, national origin, or ancestry.
16. Photographs	Photos required after hiring for identification purposes
17. Work schedule	To ask willingness to work required work schedule and wheth⊘ applicant has military reservist obligations
18. Physical data	To require applicant to prove ability to do manual labor, lifting, other physical requirements of the job; to require a physical examination
19. Handicap	To inquire for the purpose of determining applicant's capabilit⊘ perform the job (burden of proof for nondiscrimination lies wit⊘ employer)
20. Other qualifications	To inquire about any area that has direct reflection on the job⊘ applied for

DOUBLE-STANDARD QUIZ: ASSESSING HOW WE TREAT KIDS

Rate yourself on the following questions:

1. Do you call attention to children's sex by calling them "boys and girls" or "ladies and gentlemen" when working with them in groups? __ Yes __ No
2. Do you use the male pronoun generically? __ Yes __ No
3. Do you ask boys to do heavy work and perform executive duties while girls do light work and secretarial chores? __ Yes __ No
4. Do you call attention to girls who are fashionable or pity those who are unable to unwilling to be fashionable? __ Yes __ No
5. Do you call attention to boys who are athletic or pity those who are unable or unwilling to be athletic? __ Yes __ No
6. Do you react negatively to boys who wear jewelry or long hair, or to girls who wear slacks and jeans? __ Yes __ No
7. Do you plan different activities or different adaptations of the same activity depending on whether there are boys or girls in the group? __ Yes __ No
8. Are the books you recommend for boys different from the ones for girls? __ Yes __ No
9. Do you ever arrange children by sex—for lines, activities, etc.? __ Yes __ No
10. Do your discussions with children involve more numerous or more exciting role models for males than for females? __ Yes __ No
11. Do you tend to direct verbal and artistic questions to girls and mathematical and scientific questions to boys? __ Yes __ No
12. Do you tend to think and speak to students about futures and careers more for boys than for girls? __ Yes __ No

Questions that are illegal	Legislation:
request references specifically from clergy or any other persons who might reflect race, color, religion, sex, national origin, or ancestry	Title VII, Title IX
request listing of all clubs to which applicant belongs or has belonged	
request photographs before hiring; to take pictures of applicants during interviews	
ask willingness to work any particular religious holiday	Title VII
ask height and weight, impairment or other nonspecified job-related physical data	Title VII, Title IX
exclude handicapped applicants as a class on the basis of their type of handicap (each case must be determined on an individual basis by law)	Title IX (sight provisions)
any non-job related inquiry that may present information permitting unlawful discrimination	

EXERCISES FOR CHAPTER 8

Goals and Rationale

Aim: To become more aware of differences between women and men as to how each functions in a group and to increase the behaviors available to each sex when working in groups.

In general, research data delineate how people's behavior differs depending on whether they are working in mixed-sex groups or groups of the same sex. This exercise is designed to help group members look at how they function in a group.

Time: 45–50 minutes.

Materials: One observation sheet per person in the observer group.

Structure: Four or six volunteers will work on a task in the center of the room, while the remainder of the participants form a circle around them to observe their behavior. A group discussion will conclude the session.

Instructions: Tell the group that you are going to look closely at how groups function. Ask for four or six volunteers to do a short task while the rest of the group forms an observation group. In choosing volunteers, try to select half males and half females. Have the volunteer group sit in a small circle in the middle of the room while the observer group forms another circle around them.

Tell the volunteers that they are a task force of teachers, appointed by their principal, who have been called together to work on a problem in the school. There have been a number of problems and complaints of stealing in the school, and the principal has asked the task force to come up with two or three concrete suggestions that could be implemented in the school. The group will have 15 minutes to discuss, narrow down, and choose their three suggestions. They can make up whatever incidences of stealing they think the principal might be referring to if they so desire.

While this group is discussing, the observer group will be watching their interactions. Hand out the observer form that follows as a guide to what these people might watch. They are not allowed to talk during the exercise but will be called upon for their observations in the group discussion afterward.

After 15 minutes, ask the volunteer group to stop and to reflect on how they functioned as a group.

1. Was there equal participation by all the members?
2. Did anyone emerge as a leader?
3. Were people pleased with how decisions were made?
4. Did the men and women participate in the same way?

Only after the volunteer group has had 5–10 minutes to discuss their ideas and feelings, ask the observer group to share with the total group, what they observed, using their observer forms if necessary. Let them discuss and interact with the volunteer group for 15 minutes or so using their observation worksheets as a guide.

The leader can share additional information about men and women in groups. In general, research data show that men and women behave differently when working in mixed-sex groups. Three general trends will probably emerge. First, men initiate more ideas in mixed-sex groups than women do, and they are therefore seen as group leaders. Second, women are more likely to give in to the suggestions of men, indicating that the perceived power of men is greater than that of women. Third, men are more task-oriented, while women may be more concerned with the socioemotional process in a group.

Before closing, check the implications of what happened in the group's task force. Be sure all participants get a chance to air their views.

1. Did women and men participate in the same ways?
2. Did anyone perceive the men as more powerful than the women?
3. Who was task-oriented and who took care of the social and emotional needs of the group?

GENERAL OBSERVATION WORKSHEET

It may be helpful to keep these questions in mind while observing the group:
1. Who, if anyone, is the leader in this group, and how does that person function?
2. How are decisions handled in the group?
3. Who talks to whom, and who listens to whom?
4. Do all members participate equally?
5. How do males and females function in this group?
6. What happened to ideas that got presented?
7. Does this relate to your own work and school situation? In what ways?

EXERCISES FOR CHAPTER 9

Goals and Rationale

Aim: To think back on what has been learned and to look toward the future.

We tend to think of the future as something upon which we may or may not have impact. In education, as in other fields, it is critical for us to see where we have been and to think about where we might go. By doing this, we will not only affect the present circumstances of education, but may also have an impact on the future.

Time: 15–20 minutes.

Materials: None.

Structure: Participants should be in a discussion circle.

Instructions: Take some time with the participants to reflect back on what has been learned in these sessions. Then ask these questions:

1. What will education be like in 50 years?
2. What will classrooms be like in schools and in universities?
3. Who will be holding the jobs in education? Is this any different from other areas of work within our society?
4. What will the family look like? What will students be like?

And, one last time, make sure every person gets a chance to share ideas of what has been learned and what the future of education might be.

REFERENCES

Grant, Anne. (1978). *Removing the Mask*. Newton, Mass: Educational Development Center.

Johnson, D. W., and Johnson, F. P. (1975). *Joining Together*. Prentice-Hall, Englewood Cliffs, N.J.

Keser, Joyce, Jim Haggerty, Cathy Eddy, and Jerry Gumbert. (1976). "Pre-Employment Inquiry Quiz and Legal and Illegal Areas of Inquiry in Hiring." Kent State University, Kent, Ohio: KEDS General Assistance Center.

Napier, R. W., and Gershenfeld, M. K. (1973). *Groups: Theory and Experience*. Houghton Mifflin, Boston.

Pfeiffer, J. W., and Jones, J. E. (1977). *Reference Guide to Handbooks and Annuals*, 2nd ed. University Associates, La Jolla, Calif.

APPENDIX B

Peg Williams

ALTERNATIVES AVAILABLE FOR CHANGING A SEX DISCRIMINATORY PRACTICE

If you are aware of a situation or condition within your school which is sex discriminatory, you have several alternatives for doing something about it. If the bias occurs within student courses, programs, or activities there are as many as six possible alternatives for changing the practice. If the issue is employment discrimination on the basis of sex, there are as many as seven available alternatives for remedying the situation.

Sex Discrimination in Student Courses, Programs, and Activities

1. Talk to the teacher, counselor, or other school officials about the situation. They may be able to rectify the problem quickly once they are aware of the unfair treatment.

2. Talk to the Title IX coordinator in your school about your concerns. Title IX requires schools to designate a person within the school system to handle Title IX complaints. This person may be able to informally remedy the situation.

3. File a complaint within your local district. Title IX requires all schools to have an internal grievance procedure for handling complaints of sex discrimination.

4. Check with appropriate state level officials about remedying the situation. Many states have passed their own anti-sex discrimination laws. Your rights under the state law may include a right to file a complaint with the appropriate state agency or department.

5. File a complaint with the Office of Civil Rights. The address is: Office of Civil Rights, Department of HEW, Washington, D.C. 20201. Your letter or complaint should include the following information:

   (a) The name and address of the person who is filing the complaint.
   (b) The name of the people or groups that you believe have been discriminated against.
   (c) The name and address of the school.

(*d*) The date of the discrimination.

(*e*) A description of the discrimination.

6. File a lawsuit through your attorney, in the appropriate court. The 1979 United States Supreme Court case of *Cannon* v. *University of Chicago* established the right of individuals to file a lawsuit alleging a violation of Title IX.

Sex Discrimination in the Employment of School Personnel

1. Talk with the employer or the personnel director about the situation. He/she may be able to rectify the problem quickly once notified of the inequitable situation.

2. Contact the employee's union to find out if you have any means of remedying the situation through the collective bargaining agreement.

3. File a complaint within your local school district. The law requires schools to have an internal grievance procedure for handling employment discrimination based on sex.

4. Check appropriate state level agencies which address issues of employment discrimination based on sex.

5. File a complaint with the Office of Civil Rights. The address is: Office of Civil Rights, Department of HEW, Washington, D.C. 20201.

6. File a complaint with the Equal Employment Opportunity Commission. The address is: Equal Employment Opportunity Commission, 2401 E Street NW, Washington, D.C. 20506.

7. For violations of the Equal Pay Act, file complaints with the Wage and Hour Division. The address is: Wage and Hour Division, U.S. Department of Labor, Washington, D.C. 20210.

8. Talk with an attorney about filing a lawsuit in the appropriate court of law.

INDEX

A

Abramowitz, S., 161, 163
Academic ability, 32, 33
Academic women, 170
Achenbach, T. M., 18, 49
Achievement
  adult, 109
  changing sex differences in, 72, 186
  concern with, 16
  explanations of sex differences in, 60–69,
    72, 192
  sex differences in, 11, 12, 20–23, 49, 185
Achievement motivation, 65–68
Achievement tests, 18, 25, 61, 62
Acker, J., 102, 113
Adams, F. S., 133, 140
Adolescence
  academic achievement in, 12, 17, 19–20,
    22, 65
  attitudes and interests in, 4, 16, 17, 58, 65,
    70
Adolescents, *see* Adolescence
Administration
  attitudes toward women in, 107–108, 135,
    175
  career patterns in, 104–105, 106–111
  changing women's representation in,
    111–113, 136, 189, 190, 193

  explaining sex discrimination in, 104–
    111
  in higher education, 91, 94
  in nineteenth century, 168
  in public schools, 6, 88–91
  and racial discrimination, 105–106, 149
  salaries in, 93–95
  sex segregation in, 5, 82, 83, 88–92, 104
  in women's professions, 101
  women's representation in, 6, 7, 88–91,
    112–113, 161
Administrative positions, *see* Administration
Administrators, *see* Administration
Admissions, 33–36, 72, 152–153
Adulthood, 6, 12, 22, 71
Affiliation, 128
Affirmative Action
  and blacks, 106
  legal basis for, 146, 150, 158
  and men as teachers, 87
  and possibility of social change, 161, 185,
    189–191
Aggression, 12, 52, 53, 61, 128, *see also*
  Behavior problems
Agriculture, 40, 42, 87, 88, 188
Aiken, L. R., Jr., 22, 23, 43
Alexander, K. L., 7, 8, 32, 33, 43
Algebra, 19, 23, 61

Ali, F. A., 17, 48
Allport, G. W., 120, 140
Almquist, E. M., 32, 43
Alper, T. G., 68, 74
American Association for the Advancement
    of Science, 181
American Association of Elementary
    Kindergarten–Nursery Educators, 85
American Association of School Adminis-
    trators, 177
American Association of University Wo-
    men, 181
American Council on Education, 37, 38, 43
American Educational Research Associa-
    tion, 177
American Psychological Association, 181
American School Board Journal, 83
American Women, 175, 181
Amir, Y., 134, 140
Analytic ability, 8
Anastasi, A., 22, 43
Anderson, J., 94, 95
Anthony, Susan B., 167
Anthropologists, 6, 51, 91
Anthropology, 49
Antislavery movement, 170
Anttonnen, R. G., 23, 43
Architecture, 42
Art, 17, 21, 41, 42, 88
Asher, S. R., 16, 20, 43, 63, 73, 74
Aspirations, 5, 108–111, 191
Associated Press, 42, 43
Astin, A. W., 19, 34, 35, 36, 43
Astin, H., 22, 26, 34, 43, 45, 94, 95
Athletes, 39
Athletic program, *see* Athletics
Athletics, 147, 154–156, 189, *see also* Sports
Atkin, C. K., 55, 70, 74
Atkinson, J. W., 65, 66, 67, 74, 76
Attitudes, 79, *see also* Prejudice
    changes in, 119, 120, 121–126, 129–132,
        136, 166, 172–174, 178, 189–191
    the law and, 147–149
    and learning, 8
    racial, 70
    regarding women administrators, 107–
        108
    regarding women's roles, 86, 103
    toward school and teachers, 15–17, 60, 62,
        63–64
    toward specific subjects, 17, 23, 64

Ausubel, D. P., 18, 43
Awards, *see* Scholarships
Awareness programs, 190

B

Babcock, B. A., 145, 149, 163
Bailey, M., 67, 77
Balow, I. H., 20, 43
Bardwick, J., 76
Barfield, A., 12, 43, 51, 74
Barnard, H., 168, 183
Barnes, T., 91, 95
Barrer, M.E., 81, 94, 95, 163
Barter, A. S., 108, 113
Barton, Sue, 70
Bayer, A., 19, 43, 94, 95
Behavior change, 125–130, 136, 137, 186,
    189
Behaviorism, 53
Behavior management, 62
Behavior patterns, 72
Behavior problems, 5, 11, 12–13, 60, 61, 62,
    63, 187, *see also* Aggression
Behr, A. N., 23, 43
Beliefs, 119, 120–125, 126, 129, 190, 191
Belief structure, 120–121, 124
Bem, D. J., 120, 125, 126, 127, 129, 140
Benet, J., 77
Bentzen, F., 12, 43
Berg, B., 168, 181
Berglund, G., 23, 45, 64, 75
Berkowitz, T., 178, 181
Bernard, J., 79, 95, 178, 181
Bernard, R., 167, 168, 183
Bias, 7
Bicklin, S., 182
Billig, M., 128, 134, 140, 141
Biological explanations, 50–52, 71, 185
Biology, 42, 50, 51, 52
Birns, B., 54, 74
Bishop, G. D., 134, 140
Blacks, *see also* Minorities
    discrimination against, 81, 143, 190
    educational attainment, 32
    prejudice against, 134–135
    school enrollment, 30–31, 167
    segration in education, 27, 32, 145
    and social change, 171, 177, 190
Blackwell, Alice Stone, 49

Black women, 81, 105–106
Blau, F., 81, 95, 100, 101, 113
Blau, P. M., 7, 8
Blaxall, M., 95, 182
Block, J., 54, 74
Blom, G. E., 12, 24, 43
Blumer, H., 58, 74
Boards of Education, *see* School boards
Bond, G. L., 20, 43
Books, 56, *see also* Curricular materials;
    Textbooks
Boruch, R. F., 19, 43
Boston Female Education Society, 168
Bradfield, L., 23, 45
Bradway, K. P., 18, 43
Bradwell, 148, 162
Bray, H., 13, 45, 62, 75
Breese, F. H., 18, 45
Brehm, J. W., 125, 127, 140
Britain, *see* England
Brophy, J. E., 20, 44, 63, 73, 74
Broverman, D. M., 7, 8
Broverman, I. K., 7, 8
Brown, 145, 147, 162
Bryn Mawr, 27
Buek, A. P., 152, 163
Bullock, Texas, 173
Bundy, R., 128, 141
Bureau of Education, 90
Bureau of the Census, 93, 94, 97
Business, 41, 42, 85, 187
Business education, 87, 88

C

Calderwood, A., 37, 44, 47, 95
California, 177
California Achievement Test, 25
Callahan, L. G., 23, 44
Callahan, R., 83, 95
Campbell, D. T., 124, 135, 141
Campbell, J. W., 28, 44
Canada, 21, 73
Career education, 188
Career patterns, 101, 104–106, 106–113
Carlsmith, L., 18, 44
Carlson, R. O., 105, 113
Carmichael, L., 48
Carmichael, Stokeley, 171
Carnoy, M., 46

Carpenter, J., 89, 90, 96
Carter, R. S., 18, 23, 44, 61, 63, 74
Case law, 144, 146–147
Cassell, F. H., 101, 113
Causal attribution, 127–128
Censorship, 185
Central administration, 5
Charters, W. W., Jr., 113
Chemistry, 59, 88
Chesler, P., 173, 178, 181
Chicago, 84, 181
Childcare, 34, 38, 51, 191
Childrearing, 74, 187
Chodorow, N., 57, 74, 178, 181
Citizenship, 21
Civil disobedience, 130, 131, 132, 137
Civil rights, 132, 135, 150, 169
Civil Rights Act, 150, 159, 190
Civil rights activists, 171–172
Civil rights laws, 185
Civil rights movement, 170, 171–172
Civil War, 84
Clark, R. A., 65, 76
Clarkson, F. E., 7, 8
Class, *see* Social status
Cleary, T. A., 34, 48
Clement, J., 90, 95
Clerical staff, 5
Clifford, M. N., 34, 48
Coaches, 39, 58
Coaching, 4
Cobbley, L., 108, 113
Cognitive consistency, 126–127
Cognitive development, 55, 58, 60, 62, 63,
    69
Cognitive dissonance, 125, 126–127, 128
Cohen, A. R., 126, 127, 140
Cohen, Susan, 176
Coleman, J. S., 18, 20, 44, 65, 74, 192, 194
College
    admissions, 33, 72, 169
    degrees, 29–32, 36, 41–42, 106
    dropouts, 34
    enrollment, 28–30, 32, 168, 187
    faculty members, 28, 29, 91–92, 94, 110,
        193
    financing attendance, 37–38, 72
    grades in, 18, 22
    graduates, 84
    presidents, 91
    students, 17, 18, 36

College *(continued)*
    and Title IX, 147, 154
    women's centers, 188
College prep classes, 88
Collins, M. E., 134, 140
Communications, 42
Computer, degrees in, 42
Condry, J., 68, 74
Congress, 146, 150, 180
Congress for Racial Equality, 171
Connecticut, 148
Conner, J. M., 51, 52, 74
Consciousness raising groups, 173–174
Constitution, *see* United States Constitution
Coordinators, 89, 101, 104
Counseling, 38, 156–157, 174, 186
Counselors, 4, 26, 89, 156–157
Coursen, D., 105, 113
Crandall, V. C., 67, 75
Creager, J. A., 19, 36, 43, 44
Crozier, M., 102, 113
Cruickshank, W., 12, 44, 61, 75
Cubberly, E., 83
Current Population Reports, 30, 44
Curricular materials, 93
    and sex segregation in education, 41
    sex typing in, 11, 24–26, 49, 69–71, 72
    and social change, 72, 73, 153–154, 174,
        186–187, 190, 193
Curriculum, 72, 174, 178, 185, 188
Custodians, 5

D

Daniels, A. K., 77
Darrin, 155, 162
Davis, J. A., 18, 44
Day care centers, 169
Decter, M., 175, 181
de facto discrimination, 149
de jure discrimination, 149
Dee, E., 93, 94, 96
deFleur, L. B., 33, 44
Degrees, college, 29–32, 36, 41–42,
    106
Dencker, E. R., 30, 48
Dental school, 41
Dentistry, 41, 42, 187
Department chairs, 4, 88, 101, 104

Department of Labor, *see* Labor, Department of
Depression, 28
Deutsch, M., 134, 140
Devaluation of women, 57, 58, 59, 60, 72
Dickson, W. J., 102, 115
Director, S. M., 101, 113
Disease, 50, 52
Dislike, *see* Attitudes
Dissonance, 132–133, 137
Divine, T. M., 161, 163
Doctors, S. I., 101, 113
Doeringer, P., 100, 113
Donlon, T. F., 26, 44
Donovan, F., 84, 95, 169, 182
Doppelt, J., 17, 46
Doran, B., 83, 95
Doughty, R. N., 81, 95
Dreger, R. M., 23, 43
Drew, D. E., 19, 43
Drew, Nancy, 70
Drucker, P. F., 138, 139, 140
Dubuque, 173
Duncan, B., 7, 8
Duncan, O. D., 7, 8
Dunkle, M. C., 153, 154, 156, 163
Dwyer, C. A., 73, 75
Dyer, S., 68, 74

E

Earnings, *see* Wages
Eckland, B. K., 7, 8, 32, 33, 43
Eonomics, 59
Economists, 6, 100
Economy, 6, 32, 59–60, 72, 74, 86, 191, 193
Eddy, C., 216, 221
Education, degrees in, 41, 42, 59, 108
Educational aspirations, 33
Education attainment, 7, 28–33, 37, 94, 107
Education Amendments, 145–146, 179, 188
Ekstrom R., 180, 182
Elementary school, 152, 168
    administrators, 89–91, 105, 107
    athletics, 154
    principals, 105, 107, 112, 113
    sex differences in, 3–4, 12
    teachers, 82, 85–87, 101, 193
Ellenburg, F. C., 86, 96
Emotional problems, 12, 15

Employment, 132, 152, 157–161, 179, 191
Engineering, 42, 59, 187
England, 21, 73
English, 59, 87, 88
Epstein, C., 75, 81, 96, 110, 175, 182
Epstein, S., 54, 77
Equal Employment Opportunities Commission, 179
Equal Pay Act, 150, 151, 187
Equal protection clause, 144–145, 147, 148, 150
Equal Rights Amendment, 145, 180–181
Ernest, J., 23, 33, 44
Estler, S., 106, 109, 114
Ethnicity, 71
Europe, 21, 69
Executive Order 11246, 150–151
Executive orders, 144, 146, 150
Executive positions, *see* Administration
Expectancies, 66–67
Extracurricular activities, 5, 11, 39–40, 71, 152, 153–154, 186, 190

F

Fabri, C. J., 154, 155, 163
Fagot, B., 54, 55, 58, 63, 73, 75
Family, 169
  and college attendance, 28
  and education, 28, 59–60, 191, 193
  and learning social roles, 3, 56, 128
  and social change, 6, 72, 74, 191
Farrell, W., 173, 182
Father, 57
Feather, N. T., 66, 68, 74, 75
Featherman, D. I., 7, 8
Feldman, D., 13, 16, 47, 62, 77
Felsenthal, H., 13, 15, 44
Female Orphan Asylum, 168
The Feminine Mystique, 172, 174, 179
Feminist movement, *see* Women's movement
Feminist Press, 178
Feminists, 7, 8, 59, 71, 165–181
Fennema, E., 22, 23, 44
Ferber, M., 17, 44
Ferree, M. M., 7, 8
Festinger, L., 125, 126, 140
Fiedler, L. A., 71, 75
Field dependence, 8

Field independence, 8
Financial aid, 34, 38
Finigan, M., 102, 109, 114
Finn, Huck, 71
Fishel, A., 3, 8, 82, 83, 96, 106, 108, 109, 112, 113, 114, 115, 166, 171, 172, 176, 179, 182
Fisher, K., 61
Flament, C., 128, 141
Flygare, T. J., 159, 163
Foster, B., 89, 90, 96
Fourteenth Amendment, *see* Equal Protection Clause
Fox, E. S., 163
Fox, L., 22, 26, 44, 45
Frazee, P., 93, 94, 96
Freedman, A. E., 145, 149, 163
Freeman, J., 38, 45, 47, 95, 166, 169, 171, 174, 175, 179, 182
French, 59
Freuh, T., 55, 75
Friedan, B., 7, 8, 172, 173, 182
Frieze, I. H., 66, 75
Fringe benefits, 159–160
Fry, L., 103, 108, 110, 115

G

Gaertner, K. N., 105, 114
Galenson, M., 69, 75
Gallup, G. H., 107, 114
Gappa, J. M., 30, 45, 187, 194
Garskof, M., 9
Gates, A., 20, 45
Geduldig, 160, 162
General Electric, 146, 159, 160–161, 162
Geometry, 22, 61
Germany, 21, 73
Gershenfeld, M. K., 221
GI Education Bill, 28, 84
Gifted, 13, 14, 18, 22
Gill, N., 17, 47, 64, 76
Gillman, D., 33, 44
Girard, K., 177, 182
Glennon, V. J., 23, 44
Goldberg, P., 17, 45
Goleman, D., 51, 75
Gomillin, 149, 162
Good, T., 20, 44, 63, 73, 74
Gootman, J., 20, 43, 63, 73, 74
Gornick, V., 48

Government employees, 170
Grade schools, *see* Elementary schools
Grades
    and college admission, 34, 35, 36, 37
    explanations of sex differences in, 60, 61,
      62, 63, 64, 68
    sex differences in, 4, 5, 12, 18–20
Graduate Record Examination, 35
Graduate schools, 30, 32, 35–36, 37, 111
Grambs, J. D., 108, 114
Grammar schools, *see* Elementary schools
Grant, A., 203, 219
Grant, W. V., 3, 8, 21, 27, 29, 30, 31, 32, 41,
    42, 45, 85, 86, 87, 91, 96, 112, 114
Greenberger, E., 33, 46
Gribskov, M., 91, 96, 168, 182
Griffin, 149, 162
Griffiths, M., 179, 182
Griggs, 149, 162
Grimm, J. W., 101, 114
Gross, E., 81, 96
Gross, N., 105, 114
Gumbert, J., 215, 221
Guttentag, M., 13, 45, 62

H

Hagen, R., 103, 114
Haggerty, J., 216, 221
Hall, K. P., 102, 115
Haller, A. O., 7, 9
Hamilton, D. L., 134, 140
Hamilton, R. R., 164
Hardy, Frank, 71
Hardy, Joe, 71
Harkess, S., 114
Harrison, B., 174, 182
Hart, J., 107, 115
Harvey, O. J., 129, 140
Harway, M., 26, 34, 43, 45
Hauser, R. M., 7, 8
Haven, E. W., 23, 45
Havighurst, R. J., 18, 45
Hawley, A., 105, 115
Health, 42, 88
Health, Education, and Welfare, Depart-
    ment of, 38, 48, 97, 146, 147, 151, 189
Hearing problems, 12, 14, 50
Heath, K., 84, 96
Henley, N., 59, 75

Herman, M., 20, 45
Hesselbart, S., 17, 45
Hetherington, E. M., 54, 75
Heuners, M., 24, 25, 45
Heuser, L., 52, 75
High mental ability, *see* Gifted
High school, 152
    administrators, 89–91, 101, 107, 109, 112,
      113
    athletics, 154
    graduates, 27–28
    sex differences in, 4–5, 18, 22
    students, 23
    teachers, 82, 87–88, 101, 193
Higher education, *see* Colleges
Hilton, T. L., 23, 45, 64, 75
Hinde, R. A., 52, 75
Historians, 178
History, 177
Hobson, J. R., 18, 45
Hoffman, L. W., 67, 68, 75
Hoiland, E. A., 21, 45
Hole, J., 166, 182
Hollander, 149, 162
Home economics, 40, 41, 42, 71, 83, 87, 88,
    153
Horner, M. S., 65, 67, 68, 75, 76
Hornstein, H. A., 130, 139, 140
Houston, 180
Hout, D. P., 18, 46
Hovland, C. I., 129, 140
Howe, F., 178, 182
Huber, J., 17, 44, 181
Humanities, 5, 71, 88, 91
Hunt, J. G., 74, 76
Hutchison, Barbara, 176

I

Illness, 50, 52
Income, *see* Wages
Independence, 8, 167
Industrial arts, 87, 88
Industry, 40, 85
Intellectual ability, 8
Intelligence tests, 17–18
Interactions, 13, 15, 60, 62, 72
Interdisciplinary degrees, 42
Intermediate schools, *see* Junior high
    schools

Internal Labor Markets, 100–101, 104, 108
Intervention, 73, 119, 130–132
Iowa Test of Basic Skills, 25
Iowa Test of Educational Development, 25
Ivy League, 27

J

Jacklin, C. N., 12, 20, 22, 23, 24, 45, 46, 47,
    51, 52, 53, 54, 55, 59, 61, 62, 66, 76, 178,
    182
Jackson, P. 13, 45, 109, 114
Jacobs, C., 24, 25, 45
Jacobs, R. C., 124, 135, 141
Janeway, E., 79, 96
Jenkins, W. J., 107, 114
Jo, 70
Johnson, D. D., 21, 22, 45, 73, 76
Johnson, D. W., 198, 221
Johnson, F. P., 198, 221
Johnson, G. S., 108, 114
Johnson, H. S., 108, 114
Johnson, M. M., 7, 9, 50, 52, 57, 59, 65, 67,
    72, 74, 76, 77, 100, 109, 110, 115, 191, 194
Jones, J. E., 195, 196, 199, 200, 221
Jusenius, C. L., 100, 101, 113
Junior high schools, 4, 18, 82, 88, 89–90

K

Kadzielski, M. A., 147, 155, 163
Kagan, J., 16, 45, 63, 76
Kahn, A., 103, 114
Kahn, J. Z., 158, 163
Kalvelage, J., 90, 96, 188, 194
Kaminski, D. M., 23, 45
Kane, R. D., 93, 94, 96
Kansas City, 181
Kanter, R. M., 102, 110, 114, 178, 182
Katz, D., 129, 141
Katz, P., 140
Kaufman, A. A., 17, 46
Keating, D. P., 43, 45
Keller, S., 135, 141
Kennedy, President John F., 175
Kent, R. N., 13, 15, 47, 62, 77
Keser, J., 216, 221
Keyes, 149, 162
Kindergarten, 92

King, B., 141
King, C. S., 176, 182
King, Martin Luther, 171
King, M. R., 34, 35, 36
Klein, E., 166, 174, 182
Klein, H., 22, 46
Knight, L., 183
Koch, H. L., 18, 46
Kohlberg, L., 55, 76
Konshuh, A., 22, 46
Kravetz, D., 173, 182
Kuhlena, R. G., 46
Kuhn, D., 68, 76

L

LaBarthe, E. R., 108, 114
Labor, Department of, 80, 97, 146, 151
Labor force participation, 80–81, 94–95, 169
Labovitz, S., 103, 108, 110, 114
Lahaderne, H. M., 13, 45
Lambert, H. H., 51, 76
Lamphere, L. 74
Lancaster, J. B., 52, 76
Languages, 5, 41, 42, 87, 88, 193
Latitude of acceptance, 129
Law, 32, 41, 42
Laws, *see* Legislation
Lawyers, 175
League of Women Voters, 181
Lear, F., 104, 114
Learning disorders, *see* Learning problems
Learning problems, 6, 11, 12–13, 60, 61, 62,
    63, 68, 185, 187
Legal system, 143–147
Legislation, 6, 80, 143–162
    and day care centers, 169
    and sex inequities, 33, 71, 166
    and social change, 41, 119, 132–137, 138,
        139, 174, 179, 186, 187, 193
Legislators, 149
Lesser, G. S., 46
Lever, J., 40, 46
Levin, B., 148, 163
Levin, H., 43
Levine, E., 166, 182
Lexington, Massachusetts, 88, 96
Librarians, 82, 85, 89, 109
Librarianship, *see* Library science
Library science, 41, 42, 83, 101

Library services, *see* Library science
Liebert, R., 69, 70, 77
Life cycle, 56
Light, D., 135, 141
Lind, C. G., 3, 8, 21, 27, 29, 30, 31, 32, 41, 42, 45, 85, 86, 87, 91, 96, 112, 114
Lindgren, H. C., 61, 76
Linton, D. L., 108, 114
Literature, 21, 177
Little Women, 70
Lockheed, M., 102, 115
Long Island, 177
Longstreth, C. H., 108, 115
Lord, F. E., 18, 46, 70, 76
Los Angeles, 90–91
Los Angeles Unified School District, 91, 96
Lowell, E. L., 65, 76
Luft, J., 217
Lutz, 18, 46
Lyles, T. B., 21, 46

M

Maccoby, E. E., 12, 20, 22, 23, 46, 51, 52, 53, 54, 55, 59, 61, 62, 66, 69, 76, 178, 182
Madden, J. F., 27, 46
Malkiel, B. G., 101, 115
Malkiel, J. A., 101, 115
Malloy, M., 153, 163
Malmquist, E., 21, 46
Managerial positions, *see* Administration
Managers, *see* Administration
Mangi, J., 181
Masculine bias, 7–8
Masculine perspective, *see* Masculine bias
Mansergh, G., 104, 107, 108, 110, 115
Mao Tse-Tung, 119
Marini, M. M., 33, 46
Markell, R., 16, 43
Marshak, W., 33, 44
Martin, R., 13, 46
Martin, W., 11, 46, 49, 76, 99, 115, 167, 182
Mason, W. S., 105, 114
Maternity leave, 160
Mathematics
    achievement, 4, 5, 20, 21, 22–23, 189, 193
    attitudes toward, 17
    explanations of differences in achievement, 60, 61, 63, 64, 192
    and sex segregation, 33, 41, 42, 71

teachers, 88, 109
textbooks, 24, 25, 69–70
Matheny, P. P., 107, 108, 115
Mathis, H. F., 187, 194
Matthews, E., 65, 76
Matthews, M., 161, 163
McCandless, B. R., 19, 46
McClelland, D. C., 65, 66, 76, 77
McClelland, L., 66, 77
McCune, S., 163
McEachern, A. W., 105, 114
McGhee, P. E., 55, 75
McGinnies, E., 141
McGuian, D., 182
McGuigan, W., 28, 46
McKuen, J., 19, 47
McLeod, B., 86, 96
McMillan, M. R., 104, 115
McNamara, P., 34, 43
McNeil, J. D., 16, 46
Mead, G. H., 56, 58, 76
Mead, M., 79, 80, 92, 96
Mechanics, 33, 71
Media, 5, 41, 69–71, 104, 128
Medical school, 41
Medicine, 32, 41, 42, 52, 69, 187
Mednick, M., 75
Mental deficiency, *see* Retardation
Merritt, K., 27, 46
Metropolitan Achievement Test, 25
Meyer, W. J., 13, 15, 16, 46
Miami Beach, 181
Michelson, S., 32, 46
Michigan, 179
Middle class compared to working class, 20, 28, 30, 31–32, 65, 71, 170, 192
Miller and Associates, Inc., 180, 182
Miller, H. P., 32, 48
Miller, J., 103, 108 110, 115
Miller, M. M., 69, 76
Millett, K., 7, 8
Millman, M., 114
Minnesota, 108
Minorities, 32, 100, 134, 138–139, 143, 158, 161, 190, *see also* names of specific groups
Minuchin, P. P., 16, 46
Mischel, H., 12, 46
Mischel, W., 12, 46
Mischell, H. M., 24, 25, 45
Mississippi, 148

Mitchell, D., 105
Mitchell, J., 172, 182
Mixed sex classes, *see* Single-sex classes
Modeling theory, 54–55, 62, 69
Monahan, L., 68, 76
Monday, L. A., 18, 46
Monetary rewards, *see* Wages
Montgomery bus boycott, 176
Moore, Mary Tyler, 70
Moran, B., 48
Morris, J., 21, 46
Mother, 56–57, 148, 168, 169, 172
Motive to avoid success, 67–68
Motive to dominate women, 57
Mott, Lucretia, 11, 167
Mount Holyoke, 27
Mumpower, D. L., 12, 15, 47
Murphy, G., 134, 141
Murphy, N., 94, 95
Music, 87, 88, 153
Myrdal, G., 124, 141

N

Napier, R. W., 195, 221
Nashville Gas Co., 160, 162
NAACP, 179
National Education Association, 85, 88, 89, 93, 96, 181
National Education Association, 158, 162
National Institute of Education, 82, 179, 189
National Organization for Women, 131, 173, 175
NOW Legal Defense Fund Project on Equal Education Rights, 179
National School Boards Association, 83, 96
National Teacher's Exam, 158–159
National Women's Rights Convention, 99
Native Americans, 27
Neale, D. C., 17, 47, 64, 76
Neidig, M. B., 108, 115
The Netherlands, 25
Neurological impairments, 14
New England, 167
New Orleans, 181
New York, 27, 177
Nigeria, 21, 73
Nineteenth century, 27, 166, 167–169, 170, 173

Norms, 80, 119, 120, 121, 123–125, 126, 127, 130, 135–136, 139
Norton, E. H., 145, 149, 163
Nursery schools, 52, 55, 152
Nurses, 89
Nursing, 101
Nyre, G. F., 187, 194

O

Oberlin, 27
Occupational aspirations, *see* Aspirations
Occupational choices, 6
Occupational world, *see* Occupations
Occupations
    and achievement, 68–69
    of adults, 5, 60
    and counseling, 26, 157
    and mathematics, 23, 64
    and schooling, 40–41, 60, 71–72, 88
    and social change, 112
    students' aspirations for, 5, 40–41
O'Conner, J., 85, 96, 113, 115
Oden, M. H., 18, 48
Office of Civil Rights, 151
Office of Education, 82, 90, 179, 183, 188, 189, 190
Office of Equal Employment Opportunities, 151
Office of Federal Contract Compliance, 146, 151
Ohio, 155
Ohlendorf, G. W., 7, 9
"Old boys' network," 107
"Old girls' network," 168
O'Leary, K. D., 13, 15, 47, 62, 77
Oppenheimer, V. K., 81, 96
Oregon, 82, 89, 107, 177
Oregon Women in Educational Administration, 177
Organizations, 100, 102–104, 109, 136, 175
Orleans, J. H., 152, 163
Orlow, M., 21, 22, 47

P

Paddock, S., 105, 108, 115
Parents, 32, 54, 55, 62, 71, 106
Parks, Rosa, 176

Parsons, T., 56, 57, 76
Pasternak, S. R., 22, 45
Patterson, G., 55, 58, 63, 75
Patterson, M., 37, 47, 91, 94, 96
Paul, Alice, 180
Peace movement, 170, 171–172
Pearson, K., 61
Peiser, N. L., 22, 45
Penning, J. M., 102, 115
Pettigrew, T. F., 123, 127, 141
Pfeiffer, J. W., 195, 196, 199, 200, 221
Physical abnormalities, 12, 15
Physical education, 88, 153, 188
Physics, 22–23, 88
Pietrofesa, J., 26, 47
Piore, M. J., 100, 113
Play, 4, 73
Plessy, 144, 162
Policies, 186, 191–192
Political pressure groups, 170, 179
Postsecondary schools, *see* Colleges
Pottker, J., 3, 8, 82, 83, 96, 106, 108, 109, 112, 113, 114, 115, 166, 171, 172, 176, 179, 182
Pregnancy, 159, 160–161, 176
Prejudice, 120, 121, 123, 124, 125, 134–135
Preschool, *see* Nursery schools, Kindergarten
Preschool children, 70
Preston, R. C., 21, 47, 73, 77
President's Commission on the Status of Women, 175
Prestige, 92–93, 99, 101, 102, 108
Prillaman, D., 12, 47
Primary schools, 25
Principals
  attitudes toward, 107, 134
  black, 105–106
  career patterns, 101, 105, 109–111, 138
  elementary, 3, 112, 113
  junior high, 4
  salaries, 93–94
  sex segregation, 5, 88–91
Priorities of values, 122
Professional schools, 30, 32, 41, 91, 152, 189
Professors, *see* College, faculty members
Promotions, 100, 102, 186
Psychoanalysis, 49, 53
Psychological explanations, 52–56, 62–63
Psychologists, 6, 65, 91, 178
Psychology, 41, 42, 49, 50, 53, 55, 62, 69
Puberty, *see* Adolescence

Public affairs, degrees in, 42
Publishers, 71, 187
Puerto Ricans, 177
Punishment, 16, 54
Pyramid, work, *see* Work pyramid

Q

Quantitative ability, 11, 18, 22
Quantitative skills, *see* Quantitative ability, Mathematics
Quattelbaum, C., 70–71, 77
Quotas, 152

R

Race, 19, 31, 71, 81, 106, 143, 147, 192–193
Raphelson, A. C., 68, 75
Rawls, J., 143, 163
Raynor, J. O., 66, 74
Reading, 16, 20–22, 62
  groups, 4, 16
  problems, 12, 14, 26, 50, 61
  readiness, 20
  texts, 24–25
Reagan, B. B., 95, 182
Recruitment, 100, 159, 187
Reed, 146, 149, 163
Reeves, B., 69, 76
Region, 192–193
Regulations, 41, 144, 146, *see also* Legislation
Relative deprivation, 170, 172
Remedial classes, 21–22
Resource Center on Sex Roles in Education, 152, 163
Retardation, 12, 14, 18, 50
Reutter, E. E., 149, 164
Rey, P., 178, 182
Richards, Mary, 70, 71
Richardson, G. T., 34, 35, 36
Ritacco, 147, 163
Rizzo, D., 25, 48
Roberts, A., 19, 46
Roberts, J. I., 46
Robbins, E., 68, 77
Robbins, L., 68, 77
Roby, P., 37, 38, 40, 47
Roethlisberger, F. J., 102, 115

Romeo, 146, 147, 157, 163
Roosevelt, Eleanor, 175
Rosaldo, M., 74
Rose, A., 141
Rosenberg, F. R., 59, 77
Rosenfeld, S., 163
Rosenkrantz, P. S., 7, 8
Ross, M., 23, 45
Ross, S. C., 145, 149, 163
Rossi, A. S., 37, 44, 47, 95
Roszak, B., 185, 194
Roszak, T., 194
Rousseau, Jean-Jacques, 167
Ruhlard, O., 66, 77
Russell, D., 178, 182
Russell, G., 150, 159, 164

S

Saario, T. N., 24, 25, 47
Salaries, *see* Wages
Sandler, B., 153, 156, 163
Sanford, N., 178, 182
Sapiro, V., 165, 182
Sargent, A., 75, 173, 182
Satty, 160, 161, 162
Sawyer, Tom, 71
Scarsdale, 173
Schackman, M., 51, 74
Schlossberg, N., 26, 47
Schmuck, P. A., 82, 87, 90, 93, 96, 107, 115, 175, 176, 177, 182, 183, 188, 194
Schnitzer, P. K., 68, 77
Scholarships, 33, 38, 72
Scholastic Aptitude Test, 35
Scholastic Aptitude Test-Mathematics, 26
Schone, F., 25, 47
School board members, 107–108
School boards, 82–84, 150
School programs, *see* Extracurricular activities
Schram, S. R., 119
Schuman, H., 122, 124, 125, 127, 133, 135, 141
Science, 178
    achievement in, 20, 21, 22, 61, 64
    attitudes toward, 17, 60, 63, 64
    courses, enrollment, in, 5, 33, 71
    degrees in, 41, 42
    teachers, 4, 87, 88, 91, 109

textbooks,, 24, 25
Scotland, 18
Scott, J. F., 55, 77
Scottish Council for Research in Education, 18, 47
Sears, P., 13, 16, 47, 62, 77
Seattle, 173
Secondary schools, *see* High schools
Secretarial staff, 5
Segregation, 26, 81
Segregation, sex, *see* Sex segregation
Seitz, W. J., 145, 164
Self-concepts, 59
Self-perception, theory of, 125, 127
Sells, L., 23, 37, 47
Seneca Falls Convention, 167
Sequential Tests of Educational Progress, 25
Serbin, L. A., 13, 15, 47, 51, 52, 62, 74, 77
Sewell, W. H., 7, 9, 32, 33, 47
Sex education, 153
Sex Equity in Educational Leadership Project, 86, 87, 97, 180
Sex segregation, 79
    and academic achievement, 65, 68, 71–72
    and access to education, 33
    in curricular areas 40–42, 49, 71–72, 168, 185, 186
    in education profession, 82–92, 99, 110
    explanations of, 57–60, 65, 68, 71–72, 110, 192
    in extracurricular activities, 39–40, 49, 156, 185, 186
    in occupations, 60, 65, 68, 71–72, 81, 100, 157
    and social change, 73–74, 189, 191
Sex stereotypes, *see* Stereotypes
Sexism, 166, 171, 172
Sexton, P. C., 12, 16, 47
Shah, V. P., 7, 9, 32, 33, 47
Shaver, P., 68, 76
Shaw, M., 19, 47
Sherif, M., 129, 140
Sherman, J., 18, 22, 47
Shop courses, 33, 71, 153, 161
Simmons, R. A., 59, 77
Single-sex classes, 20–21, 152–153
Six Millon Dollar Man, 56
Smith College, 27
Smith, C. P., 75
Smith, M. A., 188, 194
Smithells, J., 17, 48, 64, 77

Snowden, J., 144
Social class, *see* Social status
Social institutions, 50, 59–60, 69, 71, 74, 191, 193
Social learning, 53–54, 55, 62
Social psychologists, 125
Social psychology, 119
Social sciences, 42, 91, 165
Social scientists, 7, 11
Social status, 5, 7, 19, 31, 32, 33, 71, 192–193
Social studies, 4, 21, 24, 25, 87–88
Social systems, 56, 59–60, 68–69, 130, 135, 137–140, 191
Social work, 32, 101
Socially shared autism, 134–135, 136
Society for Employing the Poor of Boston, 168
Society for the Relief of Poor Widows, 168
Socioeconomic background, *see* Social status
Sociologists, 6, 56, 178
Sociology, 7, 49, 50, 178
Solmon, L. C., 36, 38, 48
Solomon, D., 17, 48
Spaeth, J. L., 7, 9
Spanish origin, people of, 30, 31, 32
Spatial ability, 18
Spaulding, R. L., 13, 15, 47
Special education, 5, 12, 14–15, 82, 108, 109
Speech problems, 12, 14, 50
Spelling, 17, 25
Sports, 4, 5, 39, 136, 148, 174, 186, 189, 190
Sprafkin, J., 69, 70, 77
Sproule, B. A., 185
SRA Achievement Series, 25
Stanford Achievement Test, 25
Stanford Early School Achievement Test, 25
Stanley, J. C., 43
Stanton, 148, 163
Stanton, Elizabeth C., 167
Starling, C., 188, 194
Starnes, T., 19, 46
Starsky, 71
Starsky and Hutch, 70, 71
State, 163
The Status of Title IX in Region IX, 147, 164
Statutes, 144, 145–146, 149
Stefflire, B., 24, 48
Steiger, J., 82, 97
Stein, A. H., 17, 48, 64, 67, 77
Stern, R., 101, 114

Sterner, R., 141
Sterotypes, 7, 174
  children's, 55
  and counseling, 156–157
  in curricular materials, 11, 24–26, 49, 69–71, 187
  and prejudice, 120
  in vocational education, 41
Stimulus response theory, 53
Stockard, J., 7, 9, 50, 52, 57, 59, 67, 72, 74, 77, 100, 107, 109, 110, 115, 135, 141, 191, 194
Strober, M., 84, 97
Stromberg, A., 114
Strong Vocational Interest Inventory, 26
Students for a Democratic Society, 171
Student's Nonviolent Coordinating Committee, 171
Superintendents
  attitudes regarding women, 107, 108, 134
  career paths, 105, 109, 138
  and school boards, 83–84
  women's representation as, 5, 88–91, 95, 107, 108, 109
Supreme Court, 145, 147, 148, 150, 159, 160, 187
Suter, L. E., 32, 48
Swanson, G., 140
Sweden, 21
Symbolic interaction, 57–59, 60, 69
Szanton, E., 82, 97

T

Tajfel, H., 125, 126, 127, 128, 134, 140, 141
Tanner, N., 192, 194
Tavris, C., 125, 135, 141
Taylor, S., 54, 77, 107, 108, 115
Teachers' unions, 177
Teachers
  career paths, 106–111, 138
  elementary, 3, 82, 85–87, 90, 101, 112
  historically, 112, 168, 169
  influences on students, 32, 62, 128
  interactions with students, 13, 15, 52, 55, 58, 62, 63
  junior high, 4, 82
  and math achievement, 23, 61
  prestige of, 92–93
  and reading achievement, 20–21, 73
  secondary, 4, 82, 87–88, 101, 112

and social change, 71
students' attitudes toward, 15–17
Teaching, 5, 32, 84, 99, 101, 105, 110, 112–113, 190
Technical education, 40
Teitelbaum, M., 43, 74, 76
Television, 55, 56, 70
Terman, L. M., 18, 48
Terrell, K., 7, 9, 33, 48
Testing, *see* Tests
Tests
administration of, 26
changes in, 186, 187, 188
stereotypes in, 11, 12, 25–26, 69
Textbooks, 11, 24–25, 69, 153–154, 187, 188
Theology, 42
Thompson, C. W., 18, 43
Thompson, G., 13, 15, 16, 46
Tiedeman, D. V., 65, 76
Timpano, D., 177, 183
Tinker, M. A., 20, 43
Tismer, W., 17, 47, 64, 76
Title VII, 150, 151, 157–158, 179
Title IX, 145–146, 147, 150, 151, 152–160
and social change, 134–135, 174, 179, 180, 186, 187, 189–192
and sports, 39, 136, 154–156
Tittle, C. K., 24, 25, 30, 47, 48
Tonick, I. J., 13, 15, 47, 62, 77
Total woman, 175
Touhey, J. C., 92, 97
Trades, 33, 40
Trask, A. E., 105, 114
Trecker, J. L., 25, 48
Treiman, D., 7, 9, 33, 48
Tresemer, D. W., 67, 77
Triandis, H. C., 122, 123, 126, 141
Troy female seminary, 27
Tuchman, G., 69, 77
Tucker, H., 83, 97
Turner, N. O., 22, 48
Twentieth century, 84, 166, 169–170, 177, 181
Tyack, D., 84, 97
Tyler, L. E., 18, 48

U

Uehling, B. S. 30, 45, 187, 194

Underachievement, 65
Underachievers, 13, 15, 19
United Methodist Church, 181
United States, 3, 21, 26, 27, 33, 69, 73, 82, 85, 146, 178, 186
United States Bureau of Education, *see* Bureau of Education
United States Constitution, 144–145, 155, 156, 186
United States Department of Commerce, Bureau of the Census, *see* Bureau of the Census
United States Department of Health, Education, and Welfare, *see* Health, Education and Welfare, Department of
United States Department of Labor, *see* Labor, Department of
United States Office of Education, *see* Office of Education
University of California at Berkeley, 23
University of Chicago, 38
University of Cincinnati, 178
University of Pennsylvania Law Review Editors, 156, 157, 164
Urbanization, 84
U'Ren, M., 24, 48

V

Values, 7, 8, 119, 121–123, 124–125, 130, 133–134, 170, 172–174
Vandenberg, S., 61
van der Sleen, J., 25, 47
Van Houten, D. R., 102, 113
Vassar, 27
Verbal achievement, 20–22, 61
Verbal skills, 11, 60, 192
Veroff, J., 66, 67, 77
Veterinary medicine, 42
Vietnam War, 38
Vijherizen, J., 25, 47
Vinovskis, M., 167, 168, 183
Violence, 70, 130–131, 132–133
Violent behavior, *see* Violence
Vision problems, 12, 14, 50
Visual–spatial ability, 22–23, 51, 61
Vocational education, 33, 40–41, 60, 71, 152, 153, 188
Vogel, S. R., 7, 8

W

Wage and Hour Division, 151
Wages, 107
  laws regarding, 161, 186, 189
  sex discrimination in, 4, 92, 93–95, 99,
    101, 111, 161, 186, 189, 192
  and teaching, 87
  and vocational training, 40
Waite, R. R., 24, 43
Walster, E., 34, 48
Warwick, E. B., 107, 108, 115
Washington, 177
Washington, D. C., 180
Washington Equal Rights Amendment, 156
Washington Interscholastic Athletic Association, 155
Washington State Supreme Court, 155–156
Wechsler Intelligence Scale for Children, 17
Wehren, A., 182
Weisskopf, S., 178, 183
Weisstein, N., 7, 9
Weitzman, L., 25, 48
Whitehead, T. N., 102, 115
Williams, 145, 163
Williams, J. P., 43
Williamson, J., 181
Wilson, W. C., 69, 76
Wisconsin, 32
Wishkah High School, 155
Wollstonecraft, Mary, 167
Women's Educational Equity Act, 153, 154,
  164, 174, 179, 180, 188

Women's Equity Action League, 179
Women's International League for Peace
  and Freedom, 171
Women's movement, 7, 113, 165–181, 193
Women Strike for Peace, 171
Women's Studies programs, 178
Wonder Woman, 56
Wood, J. W., 16, 48
Work force, *see* Occupations
Work pyramid, 138–140, 192
Working class compared to middle class, *see*
  Middle class compared to working class
World War II, 28, 84, 85, 93, 169
Writing, 20, 21

X

Xhonga, F. A., 187

Y

Yeakey, C. C., 108, 114
Yellow Springs, 155, 163
Yellow Springs High School, 155
Young, Ella Flagg, 84
YWCA, 178

Z

Ziegler, H., 83, 97
Zimet, S., 24, 43

EDUCATIONAL PSYCHOLOGY

continued from page ii

Victor M. Agruso, Jr. Learning in the Later Years: Principles of Educational Gerontology

Thomas R. Kratochwill (ed.). Single Subject Research: Strategies for Evaluating Change

Kay Pomerance Torshen. The Mastery Approach to Competency-Based Education

Harvey Lesser. Television and the Preschool Child: A Psychological Theory of Instruction and Curriculum Development

Donald J. Treffinger, J. Kent Davis, and Richard E. Ripple (eds.). Handbook on Teaching Educational Psychology

Harry L. Hom, Jr. and Paul A. Robinson (eds.). Psychological Processes in Early Education

J. Nina Lieberman. Playfulness: Its Relationship to Imagination and Creativity

Samuel Ball (ed.). Motivation in Education

Erness Bright Brody and Nathan Brody. Intelligence: Nature, Determinants, and Consequences

António Simões (ed.). The Bilingual Child: Research and Analysis of Existing Educational Themes

Gilbert R. Austin. Early Childhood Education: An International Perspective

Vernon L. Allen (ed.). Children as Teachers: Theory and Research on Tutoring

Joel R. Levin and Vernon L. Allen (eds.). Cognitive Learning in Children: Theories and Strategies

Donald E. P. Smith and others. A Technology of Reading and Writing (in four volumes).

> Vol. 1. *Learning to Read and Write: A Task Analysis (by Donald E. P. Smith)*
>
> Vol. 2. *Criterion-Referenced Tests for Reading and Writing (by Judith M. Smith, Donald E. P. Smith, and James R. Brink)*
>
> Vol. 3. *The Adaptive Classroom (by Donald E. P. Smith)*
>
> Vol. 4. *Designing Instructional Tasks (by Judith M. Smith)*

Phillip S. Strain, Thomas P. Cooke, and Tony Apolloni. Teaching Exceptional Children: Assessing and Modifying Social Behavior